Michigan Classics in Chinese Studies

美國孫念禮敬卿撰

曹大家文徵

江亢虎校閱并題簽

From Ku K'ai-chih. Courtesy of the British Museum.

THE COURT HISTORIAN FOR THE WOMEN OF THE HAN PERIOD

Pan Chao
Foremost Woman Scholar of China

Nancy Lee Swann

Center for Chinese Studies
The University of Michigan
Ann Arbor

Michigan Classics in Chinese Studies
No. 5

Published by Center for Chinese Studies
The University of Michigan
Ann Arbor, 48104-1608

Printed and made in the United States of America

ⓘThe paper used in this publication meets the requirements of the American National Standard for Information Sciences—Permanence for Publications and Documents in Libraries and Archives ANSI/NISO/Z39.48—1992.

Library of Congress Cataloging-in-Publication Data

Swann, Nancy Lee, 1881-1966
Pan Chao: foremost woman scholar of China / Nancy Lee Swann.
p. cm. — (Michigan classics in Chinese studies ; 5)
Originally published: New York : The Century Co, 1932.
Includes bibliographical references and index.
ISBN 0-89264-150-9 (alk. paper)
1. Ban, Zhao, ca. 49-ca. 120. 2. Historians—China—Biography. I. Title. II. Series.

DS748.16.B35 S93 2001
931'.04'092—dc21
[B]

2001028919

To the Memory of the Author's Mother

ALICIA EVANS SWANN

Tyler, Texas, U. S. A.

PREFACE

Pan Chao's *Lessons for Women* has slipped in and out of historical visibility since its appearance early in the second century (c. 106). This second reprinting of Nancy Lee Swann's study of Pan Chao, which includes a complete English-language translation of the *Lessons for Women*, marks a micro-cycle in the history of a text whose popularity has waxed and waned for centuries. So we may rightly ask: What explains the fate of Pan Chao's legacy in the past, and what has revived her appeal today?

Pan Chao's work virtually disappeared for centuries after the fall of the Han, during the Period of Disunion.[1] In fact, as Swann's careful historical research shows, most of what Pan Chao wrote did not survive at all, and her noteworthy contributions to the official history of the Former Han dynasty, the *Han shu*, were generally neglected by later scholars. The *Lessons for Women*, which became Pan Chao's signature piece, resurfaced during the T'ang dynasty, when it was admired as the model for a new genre of women's didactic books: the *Analects for Women* and the *Book of Filial Piety for Women*, both of which self-consciously invoked Pan Chao's authorial voice. Indeed, the former is written in the voice of the historical Pan Chao, and the latter was initially confused with Pan's own work when it first appeared.[2] During the Sung dynasty, Chu Hsi recommended *Lessons for Women*, made an effort to reprint it, and commended women who used it to instruct their daughters.[3] Still, Pan Chao's *Lessons* did not come into wide circulation until the print revolution of the late Ming period, when new interest in women's education brought instruction books of this kind greatly into vogue.[4] In 1580, *Lessons for Women* was republished by imperial command in a joint volume with a similar set of instructions titled *Nei hsün*, attributed to the Empress Jen-hsiao, accompanied by a laudatory preface composed by the emperor himself.[5] These became half of the so-called "Four Books for Women"—the female classical counterpart of the "Four Books" studied by men who were preparing for the civil service examinations.[6]

Thus canonized, Pan Chao's *Lessons* went through countless reprintings, finding its way into the homes of women throughout China. It was embraced by the rulers of the Korean Yi dynasty as the canonical foundation for reshaping gender relations in Korean families. In Korea, the *Lessons* received a strict classical interpretation, stressing obedience to mother-in-law, proper ritual preparations and performance, rigid separation of the sexes, and mastery of proper women's work, especially embroidery. These precepts became one foundation of what Martina Deuchler has termed a "Confucian transformation" that imposed profound constraints on Korean women's freedom of movement, inheritance rights, and privileges.[7] The Confucian government of Tokugawa Japan also promoted the original *Four Books for Women*, along with scores of similar didactic works designed to instruct elite women in proper behavior.[8] Thus by the eighteenth century, women throughout East Asia took inspiration from Pan Chao's original work.

The rest of her writing languished in obscurity until the classicists of the eighteenth and nineteenth centuries set about recovering and authenticating the surviving records of the Han dynasty, as Nancy Lee Swann shows. To their bibliographic diligence we owe the source of the translations provided here, which include—in addition to the *Lessons*—three poems and two memorials, together with details drawn from Pan's writings in history and from her official biography. To this day, little attention has been paid to these other fragments of Pan Chao's work. That Pan Chao was the world's first female historian is a detail that was appreciated only in passing by eighteenth- and nineteenth-century Chinese scholars, but then later celebrated by Chinese feminists, as we shall see below. In other words, the history of Pan Chao's *Lessons* maps for us the tastes of Chinese readers and publishers who ignored her historical writings and neglected her poems and memorials, but canonized her *Lessons for Women*.

Since the eighteenth century, Pan Chao's currency in China has risen and fallen. During the eighteenth-century classical revival, one of her most prominent admirers was the philosopher of history Chang Hsueh-ch'eng, who mentions Pan Chao four times in his important essay on the history of women's learning in China. Reflecting on Pan Chao's historical significance, Chang points approvingly to her life and writings as classical examples of pure women's learning in a golden age. Pan Chao, after all, was a learned woman in a world before civil service examination competition had corrupted the learning processes of men. In that world, where both men and women held responsibilities at the court, she was one of the first women to transmit the "learning of her family" when her male relatives were unable to continue to do so. Hence her completion of sections of the history of the Former Han dynasty, and thus her pivotal role as tutor to the great Han scholar Ma Jung. Chang Hsueh-ch'eng took a dim view of Pan Chao's later imitators, the alleged authors of the *Analects for Women* and the *Book of Filial Piety for Women*, whose works he judged "praiseworthy" but at best pale imitations of—more like fantasies based on—Pan Chao's classic work. Chang's idea was that all women should go back to study Pan's original work for strict instruction in women's virtue.[9]

A second point where Pan Chao catches the historian's eye comes in the late Ch'ing reform era, when China's first government-sponsored schools for girls opened. As envisioned by Liang Ch'i-ch'ao, one of their most articulate advocates, each of these schools would feature a shrine to Confucius where female pupils could pay homage as part of a daily school ritual. But female educators had other ideas. "No!" protested Hsueh Shao-wei, envisioning the environment where girls would learn best. Instead of honoring Confucius, she argued, a girls' school ought to install a shrine to Pan Chao, for "Confucius is as remote from young girls as the stars in the heavens, while Pan Chao speaks directly to their own experience and aspirations." Hsueh's contemporary, the female scholar Ch'iu Min-fang, even published an annotated edition of the *Lessons* which, on the face of it, may appear a conservative text in an age of reform for women. But Ch'iu had something quite different in mind. She saw Pan Chao as a courageous intellectual who stood up to resist men who insisted "only a woman without talent can be virtuous." If Pan Chao had not resisted, Ch'iu wrote, the Han dynasty history would never have been finished, the *Lessons* would never have been written, and no one in the late Ch'ing would know who Pan Chao was: "Pan Chao says to women of our time: 'To be a woman you must have an education!'"[10]

Among educated Chinese women in the early twentieth century, then, Pan Chao was rediscovered, admired for the quality of her mind and for the way she managed to make herself heard in a world dominated by men. From her earlier guise as the embodiment of genteel respectability, she had been transformed twice: honored in the eighteenth century as the founder of women's classical learning, by the twentieth century she had metamorphosed as the patron saint of women's modern education. Of course, not all twentieth-century reformers shared that view. Pan Chao's unintended role as the founding mother of Confucian didacticism for women made her a target of attack among revolutionary thinkers, who reviled books like the *Lessons* for promoting ideologies of female subservience. This may be why Nancy Lee Swann took pains personally to interview the great historian Ku Chieh-kang and the leading reform intellectual Liang Ch'i-ch'ao to ask them, pointblank, what they thought of Pan Chao. She wanted to reassure her readers that even these critics of the Confucian tradition respected Pan Chao as an intellectual in her own right.

Of course Pan Chao and her *Lessons* had a checkered career throughout the rest of the twentieth century. She and her work were vilified during the Maoist period, especially in the Cultural Revolution "Campaign to Criticize Lin Piao and Confucius," when the *Lessons* and its later sister texts, including the *Classic for Women*, or *Nü-erh ching*, were singled out as quintessential expressions of "feudal-patriarchal ideology."[11] Yet in the post-Mao era, with the resurgence of interest in histories of all kinds, women's history has come back into its own as a field of scholarly and popular interest in China. And with that Pan Chao and her *Lessons for Women* have once again returned to historical visibility, among Chinese as well as Euro-North American feminist historians eager to revisit China's classics and history, and Confucian ideologies, using gender as a category of analysis.[12] This makes Nancy Lee Swann's appreciation for Pan Chao the person—and her balanced attention to all of Pan Chao's writings, including her few surviving poems—an enduring contribution of Swann's own scholarship, and it makes us curious about Swann's own perspectives as a female sinologist in the context of her time.

Nancy Lee Swann was born in 1881 in Tyler, Texas, the fifth of the six children of Alicia Evans Swann, to whom she dedicated this book. Her interest in China began with her work there as a teacher for the YWCA following her graduation from the University of Texas.[13] After seven years in China, she returned home to complete a master's degree in 1919. She spent three more years in China before returning to the U.S. to enrolled in the doctoral program in the Department of Chinese at Columbia University, where she studied with Thomas F. Carter. She conducted her dissertation research on a fellowship to the North China Union Language School in Peking and completed her doctoral dissertation in classical Chinese in 1928, and shortly thereafter took up a position in what was then the Gest Chinese Research Library at McGill University. When the Gest moved to Princeton University after its purchase by the Institute for Advanced Study at Princeton in 1934,[14] Swann moved with it as curator, chief advocate and tireless nurturer. She retired after 1948 to her sister's home in Texas, where she died in 1966 at the age of 85.

Nancy Lee Swann's major publications number three: the present book (based on her doctoral dissertation), an annotated translation of chapters from the *Han shu* dealing with food and money (a work that was extensively reviewed in U.S. social science journals at the time of its publication in 1950, when Han dynasty economics was thought to hold clues to China's contemporary political economy),[15] and a detailed study of seven private classical libraries in the Hangchow region during the early Ch'ing period.[16] This latter article, in retrospect, is particularly interesting. In tracing the scholarly linkages that bound seven literati book collectors, Nancy Lee Swann pays special attention to personal relationships and networks established through female kin: mothers, daughters, and wives. Swann's appreciation for the crucial role of women in constructing "powerful relations" anticipates current research on that subject by feminist scholars.[17] And that in turn reminds us that among Swann's most important mentors was the distinguished scholar Tu Lien-che, whom she acknowledges in her preface. One suspects that it was under the influence of this learned mentor that Swann acquired her precocious grasp of the importance of female kin networks in late imperial China, and of the breadth and scope of women's learning in China's elite culture. In that respect, Nancy Lee Swann was, and her work remains, far ahead of the times. Its reprinting here is long overdue.

Susan Mann
May 2001

---

[1] Richard Mather notes a record of a third-century work that appears to follow PanChao's model. Titled *Nü hsün*, by Li Wan, it was composed as a guide for Li's daughters while she was exiled to present-day North Korea in consequence of her father's execution in a bitter factional dispute. See *Shih-shuo Hsin-yü: A New Account of Tales of the World, by Liu I-ch'ing with commentary by Liu Chün*, trans. Richard Mather (Minneapolis: University of Minnesota Press, 1976), 349, 548. Beatrice Spade's study of women's education during the Period of Disunion does not mention Pan Chao or the *Lessons for Women*. The learned Lady Sung, mother of Wei Ch'eng, who held a position as an instructor in a government academy during the fourth century, was employed to teach male scholars, not women. See Beatrice Spade, "The Education of Women under the Southern Dynasties,"*Journal of Asian History* 1.13 (1979): 28–29.

[2] See Heying Jenny Zhan and Roger Bradshaw, trans., "Book of Analects for Women," *Journal of Historical Sociology* 9.3 (September 1996): 261–89; and Patricia BuckleyEbrey, "*The Classic of Filial Piety for Girls* (excerpt), attributed to a woman née Cheng, c. 730," in *Under Confucian Eyes: Writings on Gender in Chinese History* ed. Susan Mann and Yu-Yin Cheng (Berkeley: University of California Press, 2001).

[3] Bettine Birge, "Chu Hsi and Women's Education," in *Neo-Confucian Education: The Formative Stage*, ed. William Theodore de Bary and John W. Chaffee (Berkeley: University of California Press, 1989), 349, esp. n. 109. On ChuHsi's interest in promoting Pan Chao's work, see also Wing-tsit Chan, *Chu Hsi: New Studies* (Honolulu: University of Hawaii Press, 1989), 541–42.

[4] Joanna F. Handlin, "Lü K'un's New Audience: The Influence of Women's Literacy on Sixteenth-Century Thought," in *Women in Chinese Society*, ed. Margery Wolf and Roxane Witke (Stanford: Stanford University Press, 1975), 13–38.

[5] The authenticity and authorship of this text are critically examined in Mayumi Yoshida, "Politics of Virtue: Political and Personal Facets of the *Neixun*" (Ph.D. diss., University of California, Berkeley, 1998).

[6] The standard history of the Four Books for Women is Yamazaki Jun'ichi, *Kyôiku kara mita Chûgoku joseishi shiryô no kenkyû* (A documentary study of Chinese women's history as seen from education) (Tokyo: Meiji shoin, 1986). See pages 75–80 on Pan Chao's *Lessons*.

[7] See Martina Deuchler, *The Confucian Transformation of Korea: A Study of Society and Ideology* (Cambridge: Harvard University Press, 1992), esp. 258. The *Four Books for Women* were translated into the Korean vernacular by Yi Tok-su (1673–1744).

[8] See Sugano Noriko, "Edo jidai ni okeru 'Jukyô' no Nihonteki tenkai (The Japanese evolution of Confucian teachings in the Edo period)," in *Ajia joseishi: hikakushi no kokoromi* (The history of women in Asia: Explorations in comparative history), ed. Hayashi Reiko and Yanagida Setsuko (Tokyo: Akashi shoten, 1997), 229–30. One of the Japanese counterparts, the *Onna daigaku* (Greater Learning for women), attributed to the Tokugawa Neo-Confucian scholar Kaibara Ekken (1629–1713), has been translated into English. See Shingoro Takaishi, *Women and Wisdom of Japan (Greater Learning for Women), translated from the Japanese of Ekiken Kaibara* (London: John Murray, 1905).

[9] Chang's essay on women's learning is translated in full in Susan Mann, "'Women's Learning,' by Zhang Xuecheng," in *Chinese Women Poets: An Anthology of Poetry and Criticism from Ancient Times to 1911*, ed. Kang-i Sun Chang and Haun Saussy (Stanford: Stanford University Press), 783–99; and excerpted in *Sources of Chinese Tradition*, ed. William Theodore deBary et al., revised edition, vol. 2 (New York: Columbia University Press, 2000), 57–60.

[10] See Hsia Hsiao-hung [Xia Xiaohong], "Ku-tien hsin-i: Wan Ch'ing jen tui ching-tien te chieh-shuo—i Pan Chao yü *Nü chieh* wei chung-hsin" (New meaning in ancient classics: Interpretations of the classics in the late Ch'ing era—The Case of Pan Chao and the *Nü chieh*), *Chung-kuo hsueh-shu* 1.2 (2000): 87–89.

[11] See Kay Ann Johnson, *Women, the Family and Peasant Revolution in China* (Chicago: University of Chicago Press, 1983), 196–97. Elisabeth Croll, reviewing the "Confucian heritage" of women in contemporary China, notes that it was often offset by an oral tradition quite "different from the homily and adage of Confucian rhetoric," and she observes that works like the *Lessons* were often reduced to one-line quotations glossing over their complexities and ignoring their historical context. See Elisabeth Croll, *Changing Identities of Chinese Women: Rhetoric, Experience and Self-Perception in Twentieth-Century China* (London: Zed Books, 1995), 12–17, quotation on page 14.

[12] For an example, see Cheng Pi-chün [Zheng Bijun], "Pan Chao yü *Nü chieh*," *Funü yen-chiu* 5 (1989), discussed in Tu Fang-ch'in [Du Fangqin], "Yen-chiu chu-t'i tui fu-nü-shih yen-chiu te ying-hsiang," in *Fa-hsien fu-nü te li-shih* (Tianjin: T'ien-chin she-hui k'e-hsueh yuan, 1996), 28. In the U.S., see publications celebrating the history of Chinese women that feature Pan Chao, including Esther S. Lee Yao, *Chinese Women: Past and Present* (Mesquite, Texas: Ide House, 1983), 65–66 et passim; and Lily Xiao Hong Lee, *The Virtue of Yin: Studies on Chinese Women* (Broadway NSW, Australia: Wild Peony Press, 1994), 11–24. The most important recent study of Pan Chao's *Lessons for Women* is Yu-shih Chen's "The Historical Template of Pan Chao's *Nü Chieh*," *T'oung Pao* 82. 4–5 (1996): 229–57. Chen's radical rereading of the Taoist language in Pan Chao's work brings the *Lessons for Women* into an utterly new perspective.

[13] I am indebted to members of the Swann family, particularly Frances Swann, and to Janet Fair of *Tyler Today* and the Smith County Historical Society for their help in recovering details of Nancy Lee Swann's life.

[14] See D. E. Perushek, "The Gest Chinese Research Library," *Princeton University Library Chronicle* 48.3 (1987): 239–52. I am indebted to Martin Heijdra, Chinese Bibliographer at the Gest Oriental Library and East Asian Collections at Princeton for bringing this article to my attention, and for his helpful response to my queries.

[15] Nancy Lee Swann, trans. and annot., *Food and Money in Ancient China* (Princeton: Princeton University Press, 1950). For the best scholarly review of this work, see Lien-sheng Yang, "Notes on Dr. Swann's *Food and Money in Ancient China*," *Studies in Chinese*

Institutional History (Cambridge: Harvard University Press, 1963), 85–118. The book was also reviewed in the *American Economic Review* (1952) and the *Journal of Political Economy* (1950), as well as in other, more sinological, venues.

[16] "Seven Intimate Library Owners," *Harvard Journal of Asiatic Studies* 1.3–4 (1936): 363–90.

[17] Beverly Bossler, *Powerful Relations: Kinship, Status, and the State in Sung China (960–1279)* (Cambridge: Harvard University Press, 1998). See also Bossler, "A Daughter Is a Daughter All Her Life: Affinal Relations and Women's Networks in Song and Late Imperial China," *Late Imperial China* 21.1 (June 2000): 77–106.

子曰學而時習之不亦說乎

"The Master said: 'Is it not pleasant to learn with a constant perseverance and application?'"

Analects I, I:1, *Classics,* I, p. 137.

INTRODUCTION

In the long history of Chinese literature from the days of the ancient odes down to modern times the place occupied by women has been small, and the rank attained by them has not for the most part equalled that of their far more numerous brothers in the Chinese world of letters. The one woman, however, who unquestionably belongs in the foremost rank of Chinese learning is Pan Chao,[1] Ts 'ao Ta-ku of the court of the Eastern Han emperor Ho (89–105 A. D.). Chosen by the emperor to occupy in fact, though not in title, the post of historian to the Imperial Court of China, she was the only woman who ever attained this distinction. On the invitation of the same emperor, she assumed the duties of instructress to the young empress and her ladies-in-waiting. She composed an essay of which S. Wells Williams [2] wrote in the year 1880 that, so far as he knew, it was the only treatise on the education of women which has come down to modern times in any language, east or west, from so early an era. From her numerous other writings there have survived also four narrative poems, one of considerable length, as well as two memorials to the throne. Whether she be regarded as a historian, or a moralist, or a writer of varied literary talent, Pan Chao stands forth even at this great distance in time, alike in her private life and in her literary accomplishments, as a remarkable representative of Chinese womanhood.

The field here selected for study, upon the suggestion of the late Thomas F. Carter, Professor in the Department of Chinese, Columbia University, is that of the life and writings of this remarkable woman. The material available for an account of her life is gathered into Chapter IV. Until Chinese scholarship has succeeded in determining the part played by each of the respective authors in the writing of the dynastic history of the Western Han, no more can be said of Pan Chao's share in the *Han Shu* [3] than is related in Chapter V. The translation of her extant writings (Chapters VI–IX) necessitated research in the history, the philosophy, and the ancient usages of her people, the results of which are incorporated so far as is feasible in explanatory notes. Chapters X–XII give a personal estimate of Pan Chao as a moralist, of her philosophy of life, and of the qualities of her literary style.

For an intelligent comprehension and proper appraisal of the life and writings of Pan Chao it was necessary to make a somewhat extended excursion into the field of history, both as regards the world in which she lived and the family to which she belonged. The discoveries of ancient relics in north China have assumed an enhanced importance since they began to be used for the purpose of shedding light on the genuineness and authenticity of Chinese records. The Han remains from the refuse heaps of Central Asia corroborate by their archaeological evidence the statements in the Han annals indicating that China in the first century A. D. was the eastern equivalent of Rome in the hegemony of that part of the world which was known to their rulers. In the light of these discoveries, Chinese and western scholars have produced scientific studies on the history of the Han period, and the brief survey in Chapters I and II of Pan Chao's world and of the history, literature, and learning of the age in which she lived is based upon such material.

The considerable amount of space devoted to the Pan family is due to the belief that a better picture can thus be presented of the life and time of Pan Chao herself. The primary sources for this part of the work (Chapter III) are included in the "List of Translations and their Chinese Sources" (pages 156–158). Chief among these primary sources are the biographical chapters of the *Han Shu* and the *Hou Han Shu;* and although these chapters have been resorted to by others for information on specific subjects, the examination and translation of the relevant chapters and the investigation necessary for their elucidation by means of explanatory notes has constituted a work of research in a substantially virgin field. This study of the family background and the account of Pan Chao's life (Chapter IV) form a major part (Part II) of the whole study and are intended to provide the historical setting which is requisite for a proper appreciation of the attainments of Pan Chao in literature, and in private and public life.

Of the problems raised in the course of this study, several have necessarily been left unsolved, among which are four questions of considerable importance: (1) the genuineness of the primary sources; (2) the exact sense, or the original text, of an epitaph preserved only in an eighteenth-century translation; (3) the nature of those writings of Pan Chao, and of those events and periods of her life, about which the surviving records give little or no information; and (4) the trustworthiness of a modern historical narrative of the Han periods for the dates of her birth and death. It is unlikely that all of these problems will ever be completely solved, but they are listed here in the hope that students of Chinese history and literature may furnish additional material bearing upon them.

The records in which the sources for this study are preserved are usually considered trustworthy. Yet Pelliot [4] in a review of Chavannes' "Les Pays d'occident d'après le *Wei lio*" [5] notes that in a T'ang manuscript found in Japan, containing the treatise on "Economics" [6] of the *Han Shu* with the commentary of Yen Shih-ku (581–645 A. D.), there are in this single chapter a hundred characters which differ from the usual text. This work is a portion of one of the three canonical histories which have never ceased to be objects of respect and have accordingly been transmitted with the greatest care; and analogy seems to suggest that all those portions of early works used in this study may have suffered alteration to something like the same extent.

The Chinese text for the epitaph used in this study has not yet been found. The translators were resident in Peking when they sent back to France the sketches of the lives of fifty-two famous Chinese scholars which were published under royal patronage in Paris in 1778. Hidden away in some collection or compilation not yet systematically examined, this epitaph may be preserved in the form in which it came into the hands of these early French missionaries.

It is also possible that further biographical information concerning Pan Chao may exist in the form of quotations or annotations embedded in works which have not been consulted for the purposes of this study. A vast number of texts have been amassed by the Chinese people in the eighteen centuries since her death, and the frequency of the allusions to her in the Chinese literature known to students gives ground for the hope that fresh information about her may be found among the contents of the many texts which remain to be explored.

The only source which purports to give exact dates for her birth and death is a modern historical narrative of the Han period, the trustworthiness of which has not as yet been established, but which merits more credence than if it were a western writing because of the peculiar Chinese practice of literal reproduction of older texts even in works which are supposed to be original.

For the guidance of the western reader, it is necessary to note a few arbitrary decisions made by the author regarding the form of presentation. The transliteration of the Chinese characters is that of

Wade, which despite its defects is generally accepted; the exceptions, very few in number, are noted in each case. The names Yao, Shun, Yü, Ch'in Shih Huang-ti, Han Wu Ti, Wang Mang, Pan Piao, Pan Ku, Pan Ch'ao, and Pan Chao are printed in transliteration only. Other Chinese names and words are printed in transliteration in the text, and at their first appearance are accompanied by notes with the Chinese characters. Titles of works referred to in the notes are given in full, with place and date of publication, at their first appearance, and afterwards in abbreviated form. Chinese titles occurring in the notes are given first in transliteration followed by Chinese type, and later in transliteration only; in a few cases a translation of the title into English is added at the first mention of the work and replaces the transliteration in subsequent references. The transliterations *Han Shu* and *Hou Han Shu* are used throughout instead of the translations of the titles of the two dynastic histories of the Han period. The spelling in English of the names of places and peoples of Central Asia is that of M. Aurel Stein's *Serindia.*

Reference to particular editions of the works cited is in some cases due to the fact that this study was largely prepared in Peking (Peiping), China, where these were the only editions available; it reached its final form in America at a much later date. For the use of the works consulted in China the author is indebted to the various libraries of Peiping, but she found the most of them in the library of the North China Union Language School, and in the two libraries now united to become the National Library of Peiping. This study was accepted in February, 1928, in partial fulfillment of the requirements for the degree of Doctor of Philosophy, Columbia University, New York City. Before publication in all cases where the works used were available, they have been reconsulted either in the libraries at Columbia University, Harvard University, and the Library of Congress, or in The Gest Chinese Research Library, McGill University. Grateful acknowledgment is made of the contribution of $500.00 by the Publication Committee of the Harvard-Yenching Institute to finance the final revision of the manuscript and the deposit of seventy-five copies of its printed form in the Columbia University Library. The circumstances under which the study has been written and revised must be the author's excuse if any mistakes have occurred in references owing to the impossibility of reconsulting some of the works used in Peiping.

A Bibliography is attached to each of the first five chapters, giving complete information as to works consulted on specific points. They are listed in order of their importance for the subject matter of the chapter. The "List of Translations and their Chinese Sources" at the end of the book enumerates and describes the Chinese texts in which are preserved any portions of the writings of Pan Chao, and any information concerning her and her family. A much more extended bibliography of the works consulted for more general purposes, both in Chinese and in other languages, has been omitted from the present volume for consideration of space. Some of these works are referred to in notes although their contribution to the study does not give them a place in the bibliographies at the end of the chapters.

The acceptance of this study for publication by The American Historical Association through its Revolving Fund, contributed by the Carnegie Corporation of New York, makes it possible for the author to send it forth into the world of Chinese studies. She desires to express her gratitude to the Committee on Award and Publication of the Association, to all those who have afforded help in the course of this study, both in China and in America, and in particular to the faculty and staff of the North China Union Language School (with which was associated in 1925–1927 the Yenching School of Chinese Studies), Miss Tu Lien-chê, Dr. Fung Yu-lan, Professor Lewis Hodous, Professor W. E. Soothill, Dr. J. J. L. Duyvendak, Dr. Kiang Kang-hu, Charles S. Gardner, L. C. Goodrich, and B. K. Sandwell.

NANCY LEE SWANN
(Tyler, Texas, U. S. A.)

September 1, 1931,
The Gest Chinese Research Library,
McGill University,
Montreal, Canada.

NOTES

[1] 班昭，曹大家. 漢和帝.

[2] *The Chinese Recorder,* XI (1880), 51.

[3] Or *Ch'ien Han Shu,* 前漢書. See A. Wylie: *Notes on Chinese Literature* (reprint, 1922), pp. 16-17.

[4] *Bulletin de l'École française d'Extrême-Orient,* VI (1906), 361-400, 366. notes; cf. II (1902), 335.

[5] *T'oung Pao,* VI (1905), 519-571.

[6] 食貨志. 顏師古.

[7] *Mémoires concernant l'histoire, les sciences, les arts, les moeurs, les usages, etc., des Chïnois* (15 vols.), III.

CONTENTS

ILLUSTRATIONS

PART I

PAN CHAO'S WORLD

CHAPTER I

The Age in Which She Lived

The age in which Pan Chao gained the distinction, which was hers in her own generation and has remained so for eighteen succeeding centuries, of ranking as the foremost woman scholar of China, was remarkable for the premium which it placed upon literature and learning. In western chronology it was the first century after the birth of Christ, the age during which the Roman Empire dominated the Mediterranean; in the annals of China it was the period of the great dynasty under which the Far East enjoyed a Han Peace rivalling the Pax Romana of the West.[1] This Han dynasty lasted, except for a very brief interlude of usurpation,[2] for more than four hundred years.[3] It was in the second half of the period of Han power, called the Eastern or Later Han,[4] that there lived the woman historian and writer, Pan Chao.

For about a thousand years before the rise of the Han dynasty the ancient feudal states in what is now the territory of northern China had been cultured and civilized communities settled in the midst of peoples of lower civilization. The origin of the Chinese people has not as yet been traced farther back than the early settlements along the Yellow River in what are now southern Shensi and Shansi.[5] About 1200 B. C. the Chou clans moved in from a northwesterly direction, and in time these semi-Chinese people conquered the Shang[6] tribes who, according to the identification (1910) by Lo Chên-yü, had their capital, Yin Hsü, in a bend of the small Yüan River at the modern village of Hsiao-tun Ts'un,[7] northwest of An-yang, in the extreme north of Honan. These ancestors of the Chou rulers adopted the Chinese name *Chu-hsia*[8] only after they had established themselves in the great central plain of Honan. The Chou clans owed much of their influence and prestige in their new situation to the dexterous use of feudal methods of organization, including the establishment of members of their own clans in positions of authority in neighboring states. The Chou clans themselves were still in a state of mobility,[9] and gradually forced their way, or were pushed by the pressure of tribes behind them, down the Yellow River. Their position was not unlike that of the Greek states in the early days of the Hellenic civilization, and like the Greek states they imparted a varying measure of culture to the different barbaric tribes among whom they found themselves. They thus extended their power both by peaceful penetration and by aggressive warfare; and in this process, as was natural, the outer ring of Chou states found opportunities for expansion that were not available to those of the inner group. As the centuries went by, these civilized communities fought among themselves for increase of territory and of influence (722–221 B. C.), until the border state of Ch'in, under Ch'in Shih Huang-ti and his prime minister Li Ssû,[10] had swallowed up the rest. At a slightly later stage, between 140–87 B. C., the powerful Han Wu Ti carried yet further the process of unification and of expansion by conquest,[11] until the Middle Kingdom included much of modern China and held the hegemony of the Far East.

By the time of the Eastern Han dynasty the feudal organization of the Chou clans had given place to the highly centralized empire of the Han family. The problem of governing the empire which had been thus consolidated had become a cultural and moral rather than a political one, and the search for its solution carried the thinkers of the age back to the ideals of the Classical writers, the philosophers and moralists who had formed the thought of China during the Classical Age (circa 600–200 B. C.). These intellectual tendencies of the period of the Eastern Han may be exemplified by the advice given by Pan Chao's father [12] when still in his twenties to an aspirant for the imperial throne under whose protection he had placed himself; the advice was given in the time of Wang Mang the Usurper, after ten years of political disorder and social confusion:

"There is a great difference between the rise and fall of the House of Chou and those of the House of Han. In the olden days under the Chou dynasty the nobility consisted of five ranks.[13] The feudal lords administered government in their own territory. Although the root (the central government) was feeble, the branches and leaves (the feudal lords) were strong and large.[14] In the end the struggles between the feudal states led to political alliances.[15] This was the natural consequence of the conditions of the time.

"But the House of Han followed the Ch'in method of government, under which the feudal system was replaced by an organization of prefectures and counties.[16] The emperor had autocratic power; his ministers were without the right of succession.[17] It then happened that the emperor Ch'êng (32–7 B. C.) became subservient to certain families with which the imperial House had allied itself by marriage, and that the emperors Ai and P'ing both reigned for short periods only. The dynastic succession underwent three breaks.[18] It was because the Wang family secured power in the affairs of the empire that the imperial title was stolen. The danger arose from the sovereign, but the impairment (of authority) did not reach down to the common people. . . . All over the empire there is not a person but stretches his neck and sighs, looking for (the return of the House of Han). For the past ten years perplexing disturbances have been breaking out in capital and provinces, both far and near. Those who have taken the name of Liu [19] have gathered like clouds; all claim membership in the family of Liu. . . . Just now the brave heroes occupying a certain territory (in the attempt to found a dynasty) are all devoid of such qualifications as existed in the Seven States (of the Contending States period, 481–221 B. C.) in which were established families which continued through generations. Furthermore the people, in their ballads and in their murmurings, make it plain that they are thinking of and longing for the Han virtue. These facts can already be ascertained."

The idea of unification by means of virtue rather than of subjugation by means of force [20] was the orthodox view of the Han Confucianists. The "Analects," which contain the bulk [21] of the teachings of Confucius himself, inculcate this doctrine. Mencius was especially fervent in its advocacy. It was through the emphasis laid on this teaching that the legendary characters Yao, Shun, and Yü [22] became the standard examples of virtue and good judgment. The Confucian theorists in their desire to obtain the sanction of antiquity for their teachings maintained that Yao and Shun had long ago attained to these lofty ideals; and it was by this means that the universal belief of the Chinese people in a unified China existing in a Golden Age in a far distant past was first brought into being. "Formerly," said Ku Chieh-kang,[23] who may be regarded as spokesman for contemporary Chinese thinking of the more radical type in the historical field, in a lecture in Peking (July, 1926), "when the northern Chinese noted how the people of the Wu kingdom tattooed their bodies, and how the people of Ch'u chattered like birds, they were ashamed to associate with them. But with the rise of the theory of a unified China in a Golden Age of the past, they came to believe that after all the ancestors of all the various tribes were members of one family, linked up to a common primordial ancestor, and they all called themselves sons and grandsons of Huang-ti." This historical error was perhaps one of the greatest factors in effecting the cultural and ethical unification of the various racial elements which make up the people of China proper.

The Han philosophers inherited the doctrines of several important schools of thought which had been rivals in the cultural life of the Classical Age of ancient China. It is recorded in the biography of Pan Chao's elder brother Ku that he "completely investigated" not only the utterances of "the scholars of the Nine Schools" [24] but also those of many others. In the field of philosophy, which in Chinese thought includes that of religion, the three most significant divisions in the Classical Age were [25] the Tao or Lao-Chuang school, the Ru or the Confucius-Mencius school, and the Mo or Mo Ti school and the Neo-Mohists. By the time of the Eastern Han dynasty the distinctive features of the doctrines of these three and several other schools of thought had been reinterpreted by the philosophers and writers of the Western or Earlier Han [26] dynasty, and had been intermingled and woven into a new Confucianism. The Han thinkers and writers had revised, edited, and when they thought necessary, rewritten the books of the Classical Age, and especially those of the Ru school of thought. In the light of the twentieth century criticism, much of this Han editing seems to have been done in a pedantic and often superstitious spirit, and all of it apparently with the underlying purpose of providing propaganda for the Confucian theory of subjugation by virtue rather than by force.

This revolt of the literati of Pan Chao's period against the imperialistic doctrines of Ch'in Shih Huang-ti and Han Wu Ti involved a complete revaluation of the literary heritage handed down from an age in which the Chinese people were politically but not yet culturally united. The syncretistic tendencies of the Confucian students working on the classical literature were paralleled by the change which went on at the same time in the religion of the people. By the middle of the Eastern Han period the theistic monism of the Mohists, intermixed with a thousand superstitious features of the popular religion, had, as Hu Shih [27] has suggested, established itself under many Buddhist [28] forms of organization. In both fields the leaders of the synthetic movement went back to the authority of the writers and philosophers of ancient ages for support for their doctrine of unification by virtue.

Imbued with this ideal the Confucian theorists unconsciously set about the establishment of what Ku Chieh-kang calls the four delusions [29] in the Chinese traditional account of their ancient history. These four delusions he enumerates as follows:

(1) That the Chinese people came originally from one place.
(2) That they are descended from a common ancestor.
(3) That they were civilized from the beginning.
(4) That the time of the inception of their life was the Golden Age of Chinese civilization.

These delusions, he thinks, explain [30] in part the rise of the doctrine of the virtue or holiness of the emperor as the Son of Heaven, and of the related doctrine of his obligation to abdicate in favor of a more virtuous successor [31] should such a one be manifested by the Will of Heaven.

These tendencies of the Confucian school of thought were already in evidence as far back as the period of the Contending States, and they developed in spite of persecution under the Ch'in dynasty. As was to be expected, much of the Classical literature was lost or at least mutilated in the hundreds of years of civil strife which occurred during the Classical Age itself, as well as through the violent hostility of Ch'in Shih Huang-ti. But soon after the foundation of the Han dynasty the Confucian school received a great accretion of influence from the fact that its early emperors made the Confucian doctrines the basis of the state religion, and imposed upon the leaders of the school the task of searching out, revising, and publishing the writings of the Classical Age. The Confucianist triumph in the official establishment of their cult was accompanied by an equally pronounced advancement in the political sphere. "As early as the second century B. C. the classical language," wrote Hu Shih [32] in 1924, "had already become unintelligible to the people. . . . In order to meet this most serious difficulty the government hit upon a system under which public offices were conferred upon those who had studied the classic writings." Thus by the end of the reign of the powerful Han Wu Ti, under whom the concept of unity in the political field had been made a fact by military force, the Han Confucianists were already dominant in the empire. But in the words of Hu Shih [33] in another connection, the Confucianism thus established as the state religion in the second century B. C. was really theistic monism in a Confucian guise.

"The Confucianism of Han was chiefly ethical and political; the Confucianists exalted the conception of a teleological Heaven as a higher authority which would watch over and reward or punish the acts of the rulers on earth, . . . a politico-religious conception of Heaven."

Being thus in a position to sway the central government of a unified country, the Han Confucianists could set themselves the more diligently to the task of cultural and moral unification. Their strenuous efforts towards this end gave to China a period of very remarkable culture and refinement. It was an age when customs and usages were being solidified into national codes of etiquette and into imperial laws for the better ordering of society. It was an age of comparative freedom of intercourse with distant countries, both by land through Central Asia over the passes of the Pamirs and by sea through the adventures of navigators as far as the coast of India; so that while Chinese traders were finding new markets for their wares the philosophy, learning, religion, and art of the West and of India were making their entrance into China. It was an age in which a small force of soldiers, under the leadership of brilliant generals, was able to reimpose the supremacy of Han upon the petty tribal states of Central Asia.

In an age thus characterized by great literary productiveness, by the extension of international contacts, by rapid religious development, and by national unification along lines of peaceful growth, Pan Chao is to be found making for herself, in the field of literature and learning, a place as the foremost woman scholar of China.

NOTES

[1] Grousset added "Scythian Peace in Central Asia." See René Grousset: *L'Histoire de l'Asie,* I, 65-67.

[2] Of Wang Mang, 9-22 A. D.

[3] 206 B. C.—220 A. D.

[4] Hereafter styled Eastern Han.

[5] For a discussion of the origin of the Chinese, and the birthplace of their civilization, see Henri Maspero: *La Chine antique,* pp. 17, 21.

[6] 商. Maspero (same, pp. 36-37) places the fall of the Shang dynasty at the end of the eleventh or the beginning of the tenth century B. C.; cf. also same, p. 48, note 3, and p. 55.

[7] 小屯村, the village identified by 羅振玉 in his book, *Yin Hsü Shu-ch'i K'ao-shih,* 般虛書契考釋 (1914), p. 1, as the capital captured by 周武王, is just north of the small 洹水（安陽河） and northwest of 安陽; cf. Maspero (same).

[8] *Chu-hsia,* 諸夏. Hereafter, whenever the transliteration of a Chinese text occurs in the body of the book, the text itself, if it has not already been in-

cluded in a previous note, will be given in the note nearest to the transliteration

[9] 中國. Cf. Mencius, III, I, 4: 7, 12, III, II, 9: 3, VI, II, 10: 5; James Legge: *The Chinese Classics* (Oxford, 1895), II, 250, 253, 279, 442; cf. *Classics,* I, 378-429.

[10] Ch'in Shih Huang-ti (221-210 B.C.), see Edouard Chavannes: *Les Mémoires historiques de Se-Ma Ts'ien,* II, 100-195; Han Wu Ti, 漢武帝 (140-87 B.C.), same, I, pp. LXII-CVIII.

李斯. See Chavannes: same, I, pp. CX-CXIII; II, 169-173; *Shih Chi,* 史記, *chüan* 87; Charles Piton, "The Chancellor of the First Emperor," *The China Review,* XIV (1885-1886), 1-12; Legge: *Classics,* I, Prolegomena, 6-9; Herbert A. Giles: *A Chinese Biographical Dictionary,* no. 1203.

[11] For wild tribes fought by Chinized Tartars, see de Mailla: *L'Histoire générale de la Chine* (Paris, 1777-1785), II, Des Han, 55-56.

[12] Biography of Pan Piao, *Hou Han Shu* (王先謙 edition relegates the 志 to the end, see Appendix, p. 160), *chüan* 40a. Pan Piao "sickened by the words of Wei Hsiao, 隗囂, (died 33 A.D., see Giles: *Biog.,* pp. 572, 861.), given in answer to this advice, and also distressed that the time was just then difficult, wrote an essay entitled, 'The Mandate of Rulers,'" preserved in the *Han Shu,* *chüan* 100, 敍傳.

[13] Maspero (same, p. 99, note) says that "La hiérarchie ne comptait que trois degrés à l'époque des (Chou), et non cinq, comme l'ont dit les écrivains du temps des Han, et comme on l'a toujours répété depuis:——. A l'époque moderne où la hiérarchie a vraiment cinq degrés, la traduction ordinaire sera reprise."

[14] The image of a weak root and strong branches is of course absurd.

[15] 從横, also written 縱衡, is a technical term, used for the alliances from north to south, and east to west, in the period of the Contending States (481-221 B.C.), see F. Hirth: *The Ancient History of China,* pp. 308 ff; Maspero: same, pp. 407, 588-589.

[16] 郡縣. For the exact translation of these terms see J. J. L. Duyvendak: *The Book of Lord Shang* (London, 1928), p. 18, note; Chavannes: same, II, 530-531.

[17] 臣無百年之柄. "His ministers had not the 100 years' handle."

[18] The emperor Ch'êng, 成帝, had no son of his own to succeed himself; the emperor Ai, 哀帝, reigned only six years (6-1 B.C.), and the emperor P'ing, 平帝, only five (1-5 A.D.).

[19] 劉, the family name of Han Kao Tsu, 漢高祖, the founder of the Western Han dynasty.

[20] See Mencius, II, I, 3: Legge: *Classics,* II, 196-197.

[21] Contemporary scholarship recognizes that without doubt the "Analects" contains written and spoken sayings of Confucius' followers reporting the words of their Master. Yet into the record of these sayings have crept additions and explanations: according to Ts'ui Shu's, 崔述, (1740-1816) critical study, the greater part of the last five sections, Books 16-20, as well as certain phrases and passages in other sections, should be discarded, see Liang Ch'i-ch'ao's *Yao Chi Chieh-t'i Chi Ch'i Tu-fa,* 梁啓超要籍解題及其讀法, pp. 2-5; cf. Maspero: same, p. 546, note.

[22] On the historicity of Yao, Shun, and Yü, see Maspero: same, pp. 31-32.

[23] 顧頡剛. Translation by A. W. Hummel. Chinese: Ch'u, Wu, 楚, 吳, p. 5.

[24] *Han Shu, chüan* 30, I-wên Chih, 藝文志, summarized by Chavannes: same, I, pp. XIII-XV.

[25] 道老莊儒墨翟. Ru Giles would write "Ju."

[26] Hereafter styled Western Han.

[27] 胡適, "Buddhistic Influence on Chinese Religious Life," *The Chinese Social and Political Science Review,* IX (January, 1925), 143.

[28] On the Han bas-relief is pictured the first Chinese Buddhist, see Chavannes: *La Sculpture sur pierre en Chine au temps des deux dynasties Han* (Paris, 1893), p. 81. For introduction of Buddhism into China, see the dynastic history of Wei, 魏書, *chüan* 114, 釋老.

[29] Ku Chieh-kang: *Ku Shih Pien,* 古史辨, I, 99-101, 153.

[30] Same, pp. 129-130, 132.

[31] Ku Chieh-kang wrote that 禪讓之說是儒家本了尊賢的主義鼓吹出來的, see *Ku Shih T'ao-lun Chi,* 古史討論集, p. 10.

On the virtue of "le roi" of pre-Ch'in period, see Maspero: same, pp. 144-147.

[32] "The Chinese Renaissance," *The China Year Book,* 1924, pp. 644-645.

[33] "Buddhistic Influence on Chinese Religious Life," *Chinese Soc. and Polit. Science Review,* same.

BIBLIOGRAPHY

Lecture: 秦漢統一的由來 by 顧頡剛, "The Origin of the Ch'in and Han Unification of China" by Ku Chieh-kang, translated by A. W. Hummel, Yenching School of Chinese Studies, Peking, July, 1926. Published in the second volume of *Ku Shih Pien* (see below). (Peiping, 1930.)

Ku Shih T'ao-lun Chi, 古史討論集. A selection of nine articles first published in 1924-1925 in 努力, a short-lived Peking periodical. In these articles a group of Chinese critical historians discussed the sources of Chinese traditional history. (Shanghai, 1925.)

Ku Chieh-kang: *Ku Shih Pien,* vol. I, 古史辨. The entire collection of articles first published in 努力, together with articles written and letters exchanged which were not published in the periodical. This is the most complete discussion of the sources of Chinese traditional history yet made by Chinese historians of whom the compiler and editor is the most outspoken representative. (Peking, 1926).

Liang Ch'i-ch'ao: *Yao Chi Chieh-t'i Chi Ch'i Tu-fa,* 梁啓超：要籍解題及其讀法. Lectures on the authorship, authenticity, and methods for study of eleven sources for Chinese history previous to the Christian era. While this study is brief, it is as yet the most finished statement made by Chinese scholarship. (Peking, 1925).

Harada, Yoshito: *Lo-Lang,* 樂浪. A report on the excavations (by order of The Faculty of Letters, Tokyo Imperial University) of Wang Hsü's, 五官掾王旴, tomb in an ancient Chinese colony in Korea. Japanese text, with English résumé, appendices with German résumé, and 126 plates depicting objects found, etc. This is the most recent study of the archaeological discoveries relating to the Han period which has revealed both manners and customs as well as objects of the period, and the cultural intercourse between the East and West, first century A. D. (Tokyo, 1930).

Hu Shih: *Outlines of History of Chinese Philosophy* in the pre-Ch'in period, beginning with the earliest written records to circa 221 B.C., 中國哲學史大綱, vol. I. Having been a student of western philosophy, the writer seems to have read into Chinese records ideas upon which to build a philosophy which is a syncretism of those of the Far East and the West. (Shanghai, 1926).

Hu Shih: *The Development of the Logical Method in Ancient China.* This is an English abridgment of one department of *Outlines of History of Chinese Philosophy,* although published some four years earlier than the latter. The conclusions of the work with reference to Mo Ti have been disputed by Henri Maspero in *T'oung Pao,* XXV (1927), 1-64. (Shanghai, 1922).

Giles, Herbert A.: *A History of Chinese Literature,* Books I and II. Although this is an all too brief account, it is the best available (Shanghai, 1923).

Cordier, Henri: *L'Histoire générale de la Chine,* vol. I. An attempt at a general history, too condensed for consecutive reading. 4 vols. (Paris, 1920).

Chavannes, Edouard: *Les Mémoires historiques de Se-Ma Ts'ien,* vols. I and II. By far the most scholarly investigation yet made of the sources of Chinese history previous to the Christian era. (Paris, 1895-1897).

Maspero, Henri: *La Chine antique.* A history of ancient China (621 pages) from the Shang dynasty to the triumph of Ch'in Shih Huang-ti, 221 B.C., with a comprehensive survey of the society, religion, literature, and philosophy of the pre-Ch'in period. (Paris, 1927).

Grousset, René: *L'Histoire de l'Asie,* II, 60-61, 65-67, 86-87, 175-196. An excellent short history of China treated as an important part of the history of Asia. The pages listed here and elsewhere are good secondary sources for more detailed accounts than are attempted in this study. (Paris, 1922).

Hirth, Friedrich: *The Ancient History of China.* A review of the ancient history of China up to the end of the Chou dynasty (221 B.C.), prepared from lectures (1904-1907) at Columbia University, New York, for such "students as did not intend to become specialists in the language and literature of China." (New York, 1923).

CHAPTER II

The Literature of the Age in Which Pan Chao Lived

The literature and learning of the age in which Pan Chao lived were based largely upon intensive study of the Classic writings. Before the end of the Western Han dynasty the surviving writings of the Classical Age had been gathered from every part of the empire. Under the patronage of emperors who were themselves lovers of literature and art, the great literary achievements of the past had been reëdited and reissued in terms more suitable to the new age. The inspiring motive in this work of reformulation was the idealism of the Confucian theorists who sought to obtain from the literature of former times an authority for the new doctrines of their own generation. Such was the force of this idealism that the great thinkers who directed the movement made no effort either to record their own names and personalities or even to indicate their own contributions to the contents of the new editions, with the result that Chinese scholars of the present day have the utmost difficulty in detecting the accretions and alterations made by these Han Confucianists. But it was the work of these Han editors which preserved for future generations the great standard editions of the Classic writings, containing both original text and commentaries, which later on became the foundation not only of China's great creative period of literature under the T'ang dynasty but also of the Era of Han Learning,[1] in the recent Ch'ing period, the scholarship of which has paved the way for the twentieth century renaissance in China.

It was under the Han dynasty that the Confucianists succeeded in having the writings of Confucius and his followers officially adopted by the government as the National Classics. In the latter [2] half (722–221 B.C.) of the Chou period the student was as familiar with the teachings of the Lao-Chuang and Mohist schools as with the doctrines of Confucius, of Mencius, and of their followers.[3] The selection of the Confucian writings as possessing a higher authority than the rest, and their elevation to a canonical position, were the results of the acquiescence of the Han emperors in the teachings of the Confucian theorists concerning imperial policies for the control of society. In the *Han Shu*[4] there is a chapter on "The History of Literature" which Legge translated[5] in part. The following is an excerpt from Legge's translation:

"After the death of Confucius, there was an end of his exquisite words; and when his seventy disciples had passed away, violence began to be done to their meaning. . . . Amid the disorder and collisions of the warring states (481–221 B. C.), truth and falsehood were still more in a state of warfare, and sad confusion marked the words of the various scholars. Then came the calamity inflicted under the Ch'in dynasty (221–205 B. C.), when the literary monuments were destroyed by fire, in order to keep the people in ignorance. But, by and by, there arose the Han dynasty, which set itself to remedy the evil wrought by the Ch'in. Great efforts were made to collect slips and tablets, and the way was thrown wide open for the bringing in of Books. . . . The emperor Hsiao-wu[6] (140–87 B. C.) . . . formed the plan of Repositories, in which the Books might be stored, and appointed officers to transcribe Books on an extensive scale, embracing the works of the various scholars, that they might all be placed in the Repositories."

The emperors Ch'êng and Ai (32–7 B. C.) continued this work, and

"whenever any book was done with, (Liu) Hsiang[7] (80–9 B. C.) forthwith arranged it, . . . and made a digest of it, which was presented to the emperor. While this work was in progress, Hsiang died, and the emperor Ai appointed his son Hsin[8] . . . to complete his father's work. On this, Hsin collected all the Books, and presented a report of them under seven divisions."

"The above important document is sufficient," continued Legge, who wrote in 1892, "to show how the emperors of the Han dynasty . . . turned their attention to recover the ancient literature of the nation. . . . The collections reported on by Liu Hsin suffered damage in the troubles which began A. D. 8 and continued till the rise of the second or eastern Han dynasty in the year 25. The founder of it (Kuang-wu, 25–57 A. D.) zealously promoted the undertaking of his predecessors, and additional repositories were required for the Books which were collected. His successors, the emperors Hsiao-ming (58–75 A. D.), Hsiao-chang (76–88 A. D.), and Hsiao-ho (89–105 A. D.),[9] took part themselves in the studies and discussions of the literary tribunal. . . ."

The work of the Han scholars seems thus to have been an effort to draw upon many sources for a genuine edition of the writings and utterances of their Holy Men, and to produce commentaries on this edition which should show that the doctrines of the Holy Men constituted an adequate authority for the idealism of the Han age. "The idea of forgery by them on a large scale," wrote Legge in his *Prolegomena,*[10] "is out of the question. The catalogues of Liu Hsin enumerated more than 13,000 volumes of a larger or smaller size, the productions of nearly 600 different writers, and arranged in thirty-eight subdivisions of subjects." Besides the orthodox works of the Confucianists, there were included the works of the Taoist school, amounting to 993 sections, from thirty-seven different authors, and the works of Mohist writers to the number of six, with their productions in eighty-six sections.[11] Out of these classical books the group, the compilation of which is loosely attributed to Confucius, was called by the Han writers *Ching.*[12] Between the years 175–183 A. D. the text of the five *Ching,* as it had been fixed, was cut in slabs of stone, and set up [13] outside the gate of the National Academy [14] in Lo-yang.

It is now frankly admitted by contemporary Chinese scholars that the *Ching* as such was the creation of the Han Confucianists. While in pre-Ch'in times there had existed a *Shih* or "Book of Poetry," an *I* or "Book of Changes," a *Shu* or "Book of History," a *Li* or "Book of Rites," and a *Ch'un-ch'iu* or "Annals," these were merely books on different subjects with no relationship one with the other. As for the *Yüeh* or "Book of Music," which was classed with the above five as the sixth *Ching,* it did not exist at all. From the time of the Han dynasty all through the long centuries of the history of Chinese literature, there have been critics who did not hesitate to question the authenticity of the *Ching* as a work or compilation of Confucius himself, but it was not until the Era of Han Learning (c. 1600–1800) that a few Chinese scholars began to make a scientific examination of these and other Classic writings in something approaching to a modern spirit; and though the work of these scholars of the seventeenth and eighteenth [15] centuries was able and stimulating, it seems to have been still inspired very largely by the desire to support the theory of the virtue or holiness of the ancient Holy Men. It was not until the beginning of the literary revolution in 1917 [16] that Chinese scholarship really began to face this fact, but at the present time there are among the younger students of Chinese literature a number who recognize that the traditional history therein recorded is far from identical with the real history of the Chinese people, and these are hard at work upon the problem of separating fact from idealization.[17] As a result of this process, many of the writings of the Han Confucianists will inevitably have to be discarded as records of historical fact, but they must forever hold a prominent place in the literature of the nation which they did so much to unify in respect of culture and of morality.

Han philosophy did not derive its conceptions from any single tradition. It was rather a synthesis of the three noble streams of pre-Ch'in thought which flowed respectively from the teachings of three almost contemporary philosophers, Lao, Mo, and K'ung,[18] and were each enriched by the contributions of large schools of disciples. The earlier years of the Han dynasty witnessed a marked development in the thought of Taoism. The popularity of Mohism, which developed after the death of Mo Ti himself, had by this time waned considerably. His doctrine of universal brotherly love—more nearly parallel to Christian social ideas than any other Chinese conception—suffered too much misunderstanding and misrepresentation to be able to compete for long with the doctrines of the Confucianists and Taoists, both of whom were quietly assimilating his theistic monism while loudly condemning his social teachings. Confucianists were busy fixing the ceremonies of their cult for use at court; and the Lao-Chuang school of Taoism was drifting away from philosophical meditation into superstitious practices, and thus preparing the way for its own decline.

Meanwhile Huai-nan Tzû (d. 122 B. C.), classed by the Chinese as a Taoist, attempted on a grand scale [19] the synthesis of all good from the opposing systems of philosophy. He reinterpreted the non-activity [20] of the Taoists to mean positive adaptation, so that to him man appeared rather as making an almost conscious use of natural materials in harmony with Nature than as simply doing nothing at all; and he even appealed to the legendary Yao, Shun, and Yü as illustrations of this conception. His admirable efforts were however neutralized by the activities at the imperial court of a large group of soothsayers and charlatans who by their gross quackery brought Taoism into thorough disrepute as a philosophy. By the end of the first century A. D.[21] the reasonable parts of the Taoist philosophy had been absorbed into Confucianism, while the religion of Taoism had begun to arise out of a combination of these superstitions with the theistic monism of the Mohists under Buddhist forms of organization.

Hardly less catholic in his eclecticism than his contemporary Huai-nan Tzû was Tung Chung-shu,[22] at one time teacher of the celebrated Ssû-ma Ch'ien [23] and the leader of the Ru or Confucian philosophers of his period. His work at the court of Han Wu Ti completed the preparation for the establishment of Confucianism as the orthodox philosophy of the Han emperors in spite of the prevalence of superstitious Taoist practices in private life. He was a pioneer in the field of intimate philosophical discussion of the relation of man to Heaven. The latter he conceived as having a Will, revealed to man through reprimands of Nature, which must be interpreted to the people by their ruler. The life of man was one of rewards and punishments, and it was Heaven which both favored and punished. Man should not consciously seek either wealth or position. In the valuation of human actions, emphasis must be placed on motives and purposes; but activity there must be. Human nature was potentially good, it had a tendency towards goodness. With due attention to the teachings of the past, to education, and to temperance, this human nature would become what it was meant by Heaven to be—loving, righteous, courteous, intelligent.[24]

Fifty years and more after Tung Chung-shu, in the days of the erudite editor of the Classics, Liu Hsin, a new view of human nature was put forth by the philosopher Yang Hsiung [25] (53 B. C.–18 A. D.). This writer maintained that human nature is a mixture of good and evil, and that its development depends upon environment. He had considerable influence for a time, but in the days of the Sung dynasty Chu Hsi [26] (1130–1200) stigmatized him as a traitor on account of his services as minister to the usurper Wang Mang, whom he joined apparently for the purpose of saving his own life, and his reputation suffered a decline.

The next commanding figure in the line of original thinkers is Wang Ch'ung [27] (27–97 A. D.), whose critical philosophy reveals the pressure of orthodoxy upon a personality unable to find complete freedom either in thought or in expression. He was fearless and frankly mechanistic, but apparently accepted the Confucian ethics in their entirety. By the time of his philosophic activity the most reasonable parts of the Taoist philosophy had been absorbed by Han Confucianism and the rise of Taoism as a religion had already begun, so his attacks were directed against the metaphysical beliefs of Confucianism and the superstitious practices of the Taoist religion. With characteristic independence of spirit, devotion to truth, and anxiety for clearness of presentation, he criticized the views of his age with regard to Heaven, fate, reward and punishment, ghosts and sacrifices, and the belief in a Golden Age in the past, and he even questioned the authority of Confucius.

Of the Chinese historical works of the Han dynasty an early European writer [28] has aptly said that "Chinese genius was not then extinct; it produced works which have been the wonder of all succeeding ages. There is a surprising number which narrate the events of the times with more minuteness than the best Grecian historians do the transactions of their country." Ssû-ma Ch'ien, who lived in the reign of Han Wu Ti (140–87 B.C.), has been repeatedly called the Herodotus of Chinese history,[29] and even though the "Historical Record" attributed to him be a compilation, Chavannes came to the conclusion[30] that "le nom de Se-Ma Ts'ien est devenu inséparable de celui du peuple chinois; aussi longtemps que vivra la mémoire de cette nation quarante fois séculaire, aussi longtemps durera la gloire de Se-Ma Ts'ien." According to Fan Yeh[31] there were several authors who wrote in continuation of the historical work of Ssû-ma Ch'ien, and in a list of such authors suggested by a commentator on this statement may be found the names of the philosopher Yang Hsiung and of the celebrated editor of the Classics, Liu Hsin, whose list of works, divided into seven divisions, is the genesis of Chinese cataloguing and bibliography.[32] Another historical work of this period which deserves mention is the famous biographies of eminent women[33] compiled by Liu Hsiang a little before the time of the literary activities of the Pan family to which the following chapters are devoted.

To this brief summary of philosophers and historians there might well be added a whole group of men of learning. Contemporaries of Pan Chao herself include, besides her brother Ku, the distinguished writers Ts'ui Yüan[34] and Fu I; Chang Hêng the scientist and poet; Hsü Shên the lexicographer; Ma Rung, himself a pupil of Pan Chao, famous for his own erudition and as an educator; and his brother Ma Hsü, also her pupil, and continuator of her work. Not quite so heterodox as her father's more widely known pupil Wang Ch'ung, himself an associate of the Ma Rung, was the independent thinker Wang Fu, popularly known as The Hermit. Among the pupils of Ma Rung was the scholarly Chêng Hsüan, eminent authority on the Classics, whose commentaries became standard for future generations. Contemporary with the latter, and thus a few years younger than Pan Chao, were Ying Shao,[35] who wrote upon the customs and usages of his time; Li Ying, political thinker and leader; Kuo T'ai, the scholar and teacher associated with the National Academy; and Wang Su, the famous commentator and reputed author of the "Family Sayings of Confucius."

The encouragement given to literature by the House of Han provided these and many other scholars of the time with their opportunity for study. At the same time the century-long efforts of the Confucian theorists had been rewarded by the official establishment of their cult at the court of a united empire. A union of Chinese wisdom and Chinese military strength established Han Confucianism as the strongest support of the imperial throne, itself the symbol of political unity. China, brought to a state of order and possessing a lettered class, now devoted herself to the cultivation of that love of literature which was in time to be regarded as one of the chief of the national characteristics. The labors of the learned men and women at the court of Han were extensive and important enough, as Wylie wrote in his *Notes on Chinese Literature,*[36] "to stamp the character of the Chinese as a literary people." And for three generations, from the beginning of the reign of the emperor Ch'êng (32–7 B. C.) into that of the emperor An[37] (107–125 A. D.), there was always a member of the Pan family among the scholars at court.

NOTES

[1] 漢學, circa 1600-1800. A time of investigation of Han writings.

[2] In Chinese records two periods: (a) Ch'un-ch'iu, 春秋 (722-481 B. C.), and (b) Chan-kuo, 戰國 (481-221 B. C.).

[3] For the place of Hsün Tzû, 荀子, in Chinese thinking, see H. H. Dubs: *Hsüntze, The Moulder of Ancient Confucianism* (London, 1927).

[4] *Han Shu, chüan* 30, I-wên Chih.

[5] *Classics,* I, Prolegomena, pp. 3-5. For the part relating to Liu Hsiang, 劉向, and Liu Hsin, 劉歆, see J. Eitel, *China Review,* XV (1886-1887), 90-95; XVII (1888-1889), 330 ff.

[6] Mentioned elsewhere as Han Wu Ti.

[7] Giles: *Biog.,* no. 1300.

[8] Same, no. 1304; *Han Shu, chüan* 36, 劉歆傳, for the translation of parts of which by Otto Franke, *Ostasiatische Neubildungen* (1911), and by Bernhard Karlgren, see same, "On the Authenticity and Nature of the *Tso Chuan,*" *Göteborgs Högskolas Arsskrift,* XXXII (1926). Liu Hsin (same, p. 18) committed suicide, 22 A. D.

[9] Mentioned elsewhere as the emperors Kuang-wu, Ming, Chang, and Ho, 光武帝, 明帝, 章帝, 和帝.

[10] P. 10.

[11] *Han Shu, chüan* 30, I-wên Chih. Legge in his translation erroneously used "collections" for *p'ien,* 篇.

[12] 經:詩易書禮春秋樂, Ku Chieh-kang; *Ku Shih Pien,* I, 75-78.

[13] See "Water Classic" by Li Tao-yüan, *chüan* 16, 酈道元 : 王氏合校水經注 (1892); Chu I-tsun: *Ching I Kao, chüan* 287, 朱彝尊 (1629-1709); 經義考 (1756); Paul Pelliot, *T'oung Pao,* XXIII (1924), 1.

[14] 太學. It was re-established by Kuang-wu, 29 A. D., see *Hou Han Shu, chüan* 1, fifth year, tenth moon; Cordier: *Histoire générale,* p. 256.

15 Ts'ui Shu (1740-1816) and a few others of the critical school lived into the early years of the nineteenth century.

16 This literary revolution arose under the leadership of Hu Shih, at that time a professor in the National University at Peking, see Hu Shih, "The Chinese Renaissance," *China Year Book*, 1924, pp. 633-651.

17 The discussion concerning the historicity and authenticity of the earlier writings has really only begun. Among the recognized leaders was the brilliant scholar and celebrated publicist, Liang Ch'i-ch'ao (died Jan., 1929) who, having belonged to the latter days of the Ch'ing scholarship, became one of the chief contributors to the renaissance of the twentieth century.

18 老子墨子孔子, Lao Tzû, Mo Ti, Confucius, the conventional forms.

19 With the aid of eight editors and many thousand scribes. 淮南子. By name Liu An, 劉安, Prince of Huai-nan, of the imperial family of the House of Han, see Giles: *Biog.*, no. 1269.

20 無爲

21 Chang Tao-ling, 張道陵, (34-156 A. D.) is said to have been the first Taoist "pope," 天師, Giles: same, no. 112.

22 Giles: same, no. 2092. See the opinion of Dubs on Tung Chung-shu, 董仲舒, in *Hsüntze*, pp. 32 ff. 136.

23 司馬遷

24 仁義禮智

25 揚雄, Giles: same, no. 2379; A. Wylie: *Notes on Chinese Literature*, p. 82; Arthur Waley: *The Temple and Other Poems* (New York, 1923), pp. 47-50.

26 朱熹

27 王充, Alfred Forke: *Lun-Hêng*. Selected essays of the Philosopher Wang Ch'ung (Berlin, 1907, 1911); Wylie: *Notes*, p. 82; Giles: *Biog.*, no. 2166; same: *Hist. Lit.*, p. 93.

28 *The Chinese Repository*, III (1834-1835), 58-60.

29 Wylie: same, p. 15.

30 *Mémoires*, I, p. CCXXV.

31 范曄, *Hou Han Shu, chüan* 40a.

32 七略, *Han Shu, chüan* 30.

33 列女傳, *Lieh Nü Chuan*.

34 崔瑗傅毅, see *Chung-kuo Jên-ming Ta Tz'û-tien*, 中國人名大辭典, (referred to hereafter as *Chinese Biog.*), pp. 911 and 1135.

張衡, Giles: *Biog.*, no. 55; Waley: *The Temple*, p. 50; *Hou Han Shu, chüan* 59.

許愼, Giles: same, no. 787; *Hou Han Shu, chüan* 79b.

馬融, 馬續, Giles: same, no. 1475. Giles would write Ma Jung or Ma Yung.

王符, Giles: same, no. 2168.

鄭玄, same, no. 274; Legge: *Li Ki, Classics, The Sacred Books of the East*, XXVII, 8.

35 應劭, Giles: *Biog.*, no. 2498; 李膺, no. 1233; 郭太, no. 1073; 王肅, no. 2227. 孔子家語, see *San Ting Kuo-hsüeh Yung Shu Chuan Yao*, a bibliography by Li Li, 李笠：三訂國學用書撰要 (1927), p. 42; Maspero: same, p. 543, note 2 (faux du IIIe s. p. C.).

36 P. 243.

37 安帝

BIBLIOGRAPHY

Lecture by Ku Chieh-kang (Peking, 1926).

Ku Chieh-kang: *Ku Shih Pien.*

Liang Ch'i-ch'ao: *Yao Chi Chieh-t'i Chi Ch'i Tu-fa.*

Legge, James: *The Chinese Classics,* I, Prolegomena, 1-11. In this introduction he discussed the genuineness and authenticity of the texts of the Classics which he translated. Oxford edition (1893-1895) used in this study, except vol. III. (Hongkong, 1865, edition).

Legge: The Book of Changes (*Yi King*) and The Book of Rites (*Li Ki*), in *The Sacred Books of the East* (vols. XVI, XXVII, XXVIII), edited by F. Max Müller, Oxford, 1882, 1885. This series unfortunately not only does not have the Chinese text, but also uses a transliteration of the Chinese peculiar to itself.

Han Shu, chüan 30, I-wên Chih. In this *chüan* is preserved the most complete list of the ancient literature of the Chinese, the commentaries upon which were written in part by the Pan family (credited to Pan Ku).

Hou Han Shu, chüan 40, biographies of Pan Piao and Pan Ku. With the exception of long poetic writings incorporated in the biography of Pan Ku, this *chüan* is one of the primary sources of this study.

Wylie, A.: *Notes on Chinese Literature.* This comprehensive introduction to the whole of Chinese literature is largely a translation in a very much abridged form of the encyclopedic catalogue of the great thesaurus *Ssû K'u Ch'üan Shu,* 四庫全書 (1775-1790), prepared under the patronage of Ch'ien-lung of the recent Ch'ing dynasty, 清乾隆. As the only work of its kind in English, it is indispensable to the student. New edition (Shanghai, 1922).

Giles: *History of Chinese Literature.*

Maspero: *La Chine antique.*

Giles, H. A.: *A Chinese Biographical Dictionary.* Frequent reference is made to this convenient handbook which is generally reliable for the main outlines of the lives which it contains. Cf. Pelliot in *T'oung Pao,* XXV (1927), 65-81, for a discussion of the Chinese sources for biographical dating. Ancient Chinese famous men often have had dates assigned to them by calculation rather than from authentic records (cf. Maspero: *La Chine antique,* p. 615, note 1). Unless their use were judged to be of vital importance, traditional dates have been kept in this study. (London and Shanghai, 1898.)

Chung-kuo Jên-ming Ta Tz'û-tien, 中國人名大辭典. The best general biographical dictionary in Chinese. It may be used to advantage in connection with Giles. Exact dates are usually lacking. (Shanghai, 1921.)

I Nien-lu Hui-pien, 疑年錄彙編. A compilation which gives age and dates of birth and death for over 3700 Chinese notables. Cf. Pelliot's review, *T'oung Pao,* XXV (1927), 65-81. (1925.)

Tz'û Yüan, 辭源. An encyclopedic dictionary which is invaluable for information upon general topics as well as in the field of biography. (Ten editions. Shanghai, 1915-1927.)

Mayer, W. F.: *The Chinese Reader's Manual.* An older and less complete handbook (reprint, Shanghai, 1910).

Couling, S.: *The Encyclopedia Sinica.* A handbook rather than an encyclopedia (London, 1917).

Bretschneider, E.: Botanicon Sinicum, "Notes on Works Consulted," *Journal of the Royal Asiatic Society, North China Branch,* XXV (1890-1891), 4-16. A very short bibliography of the Chinese Classics.

Hu Shih, "The Chinese Renaissance," *The China Year Book,* 1924, pp. 633-651. This is an excellent survey of the historical background of the literary revolution by the leader of the movement.

Grousset: *L'Histoire générale de l'Asie,* II, 60-87, 175-196.

PART II

PAN CHAO'S FAMILY

A GENEALOGICAL TABLE OF THE PAN FAMILY

KU WU-T'U

穀 於 檡 鬬
(烏 菟) 子
文

(Ancestor in the Ch'un-ch'iu, 春秋, period, 722-481 B. C.)

|

壹, I

(Ancestor at the end of the Ch'in dynasty, 221-207 B. C.)

|

孺, Ju

|

長, Ch'ang

|

回, Hui

|

況, K'uang

|

- 女 (A daughter)
  班捷伃 Pan Chieh-yü (Concubine to the emperor Ch'êng, 成)
- 伯, Po (1st son)
- 斿, Yu (2nd son)
  To him the emperor Ch'êng, 成, (32-7 B. C.) gave valuable books.
  - 嗣, Ssü (A student of the Lao-Chuang thought.)
- 穉, Chih (3rd son)
  - 彪, Pan Piao 3-54 A. D.
    - 固 Pan Ku 32-92 A. D.
    - 超 Pan Ch'ao 32-102 A. D.
    - 昭 Pan Chao b. 45-51 A. D. d. 114-120 A. D.

Outlined by

Tu Lien-chê, 杜聯喆
M. A., Yenching University, Peiping

CHAPTER III

Her Ancestry, Her Father, and Her Two Elder Brothers

The Pan family traced their ancestry back to one Ku-wu-t'u [1] of the State of Ch'u in the Ch'un-ch'iu (722–481 B. C.) period of the Chou dynasty. Ku-wu-t'u was born out of wedlock in 604 B. C., into a branch of the royal family of the State of Ch'u, whose surname is given by Ssû-ma Ch'ien in his "Historical Record" as Mi.[2] According to accounts in the *Tso Chuan* and the *Han Shu*,[3] this ancestor was abandoned in a swamp, where a tigress nourished him with her milk. When reclaimed by his grandparents he not unnaturally received, in addition to the style Tzû-wên, the designation Ku-wu-t'u, for the people of Ch'u, one of whose names for tiger was *pan*,[4] also called tiger *wu-t'u* and milk *ku*.

When the State of Ch'u was conquered by that of Ch'in (223 B. C.), the descendants of Ku-wu-t'u moved north into the region now included in the modern province of Shansi. From this time onward the family bore the name of Pan. At the end of the reign of Ch'in Shih Huang-ti (210 B. C.) a son, I, fled farther north to the region outside the Great Wall. There he settled, became very rich in cattle and sheep, and lived, it is said, to be more than a hundred years old. His descendants to the fifth generation attained both fame and prosperity, and because of their merits were promoted in official rank.

Their progress was not limited to the spheres of wealth and of official position. They excelled in scholarship also. Pan Hui of the fourth generation gained the degree of *mao-ts'ai*,[5] which corresponds to that of *hsiu-ts'ai* of both earlier and later dynasties; and Pan K'uang of the next generation was made *hsiao-lien*, which corresponds to the *chü-jên* of later dynasties. The literary standing of Pan K'uang, together with his talents and industry, attracted the attention of high court officials, one of whom recommended him to the throne for promotion in office. He and his family having thus become known in palace circles, his children received the favor of being ordered to court; and he thereupon resigned his provincial post and removed with his family, first to the city of the imperial tombs, where lived all the great officials and notable families, and later to the capital Chang-an itself.

His daughter was taken into the women's apartments of the court of the emperor Ch'êng (32–7 B. C.). She entered the palace with the rank of *shao-shih,*[6] but soon by favor of the emperor was given the title of *chieh-yü*. Of all the imperial concubines of the time she was the most distinguished in respect of literary abilities.[7] She is best known, however, for her refusal to ride with the emperor Ch'êng in his litter, "lest she should distract his thoughts from affairs of state."[8] This incident is related in the chapter of the *Han Shu*[9] dealing with the relatives of the emperors, and it is there recorded that this action won for Pan Chieh-yü the lifelong friendship of the empress dowager, to whose palace she retired when the emperor all too soon turned from her to other favorites. This incident and her literary abilities[10] gained for Pan Chieh-yü a place in "Biographies of Eminent Women"[11] in the sections which were added to the original edition of Liu Hsiang, and which tradition assigns in part to the brush of Pan Chao.

Pan Chieh-yü had three brothers, all of whom proved to be students, and held official positions at court. The second brother Yu, who collaborated with Liu Hsiang in the editing of rare old books, was selected to read from these volumes before the emperor,[12] who valued so highly the capacity and attainments of the young scholar that he gave him from the imperial archives duplicate copies of old manuscripts which had until then been inaccessible to scholars. Unfortunately Yu, like his elder brother Po, died young. He left one son Ssû, who was a very brilliant personage in the literary circles of his generation. By the time the third brother, Pan Chih, came to manhood, Wang Mang, who in former days had been very friendly with the Pan brothers, was rising to power. Since Pan Chih was unwilling to identify himself with Wang Mang's plans for the usurpation of the imperial throne, he retired on his own initiative, before the coup d'état, to a small official post; and consequently the Pan family was not prominent in official life during the Wang Mang period.

This third brother Chih was the father of Pan Piao, and the grandfather of Pan Chao. Pan Piao travelled and studied with his cousin Ssû, who loved the philosophy and esteemed the learning of the Lao-Chuang school;[13] but unlike this cousin Pan Piao was a strict Confucianist, and confined his studies to the Confucian doctrines. Their possession of the rare and precious books given to Ssû's father by the emperor Ch'êng brought to the family many visitors from great dis-

From Ku K'ai-chih. Courtesy of the British Museum.

THE REFUSAL OF PAN CHIEH-YÜ TO RIDE IN THE LITTER WITH THE EMPEROR CH'ÊNG (32-7 B. C.)

(SEE P. 26)

tances. Pan Piao was only twenty years old when the rule of Wang Mang the Usurper came to an end and the whole country was plunged for a time into chaos; but as if to confirm his faith [14] in the destiny of the House of Han, a descendant of the imperial family fought his way to the throne, and received after death the significant title of Kuang-wu [15] (25–57 A. D.). As adviser to a military leader fighting on behalf of the man who subsequently became emperor, Pan Piao showed such ability that he was summoned to court. Besides scholarly rank he was there several times offered both civil offices and advisory posts, some of which he accepted; but he did not care for official position, and resigned after a short time in each office. He preferred to devote himself to studies, and especially to history. He died in the thirtieth year (54 A. D.) of the Chien-wu period,[16] at the age of fifty-two,[17] by which time he had written, according to his biographer, "narrative poems, expositions, treatises, historical records, memorials, in all enough to fill nine books." [18]

Besides his daughter Chao,[19] Pan Piao was the father of twin sons, Ku and Ch'ao. In accordance with Chinese practice [20] Ku, the first born, was recognized as the elder, and is always referred to as such. Like his father, he loved learning. His biographer wrote:

"When Pan Ku was nine years old he was able to write in the literary style, and to recite both the 'Book of Poetry' and the 'Book of History.' It followed that when grown he knew widely both records and books, and of the writings of the Nine Schools [21] as well as of the many independent thinkers there was none which he had not completely investigated. In what he studied he did not have a fixed pattern (by which he measured everything).[22] He did not make divisions into paragraphs and sentences [23] (while reading), but he got the general sense, and no more. Because he lived in harmony with everybody, and was tolerant of others, all the scholars loved him."

At the court of the emperor Chang (76–88 A. D.) Pan Ku wrote his *Liang Tu Fu* or "The Two Capitals," [24] in which famous *fu* this particular form of Chinese narrative poetry of imagination perhaps reached its greatest height. Besides this narrative poem his biographer recalls that "every time the emperor went out to travel or to hunt, Pan Ku offered poems and essays of praise. And whenever the court had a big conference the emperor ordered him to propound questions for debate by the officials." Although the emperor gave him gifts and showed him especial kindness, Pan Ku, being at that time still only a minor official, thought that his official rank should be elevated, "his family having been talented and learned for two generations." He therefore followed the precedent set by Tung-fang So [25] and by Yang Hsiung, and composed a satire, which he entitled *Pin Hsi,* and was accordingly raised in rank. This was the time, moreover, when the emperor Chang, who loved literature, gathered the savants of the period around him for the discussion of the Five Classics, and ordered Pan Ku to edit these discussions, which he did under the title of *Po-hu T'ung Tê Lun* [26] (79 A. D.). Among other compositions Pan Ku wrote an essay called *Tien Yin* in which he lauded the virtue of the House of Han. Of this essay he stated [27] that Hsiang-ju [28] in a treatise on the great sacrifice to Heaven and Earth wrote fluently but not classically, and that in an essay of praise of the Hsin [29] dynasty Yang Hsiung was classical in style but not true to facts, while as for himself he thought that he had reached his goal, the combination of a classical style with fidelity to truth. Although Pan Ku, who with his brother was born in 32 A. D., was primarily a man of letters, he became involved in a military enterprise which led to his untimely death in prison in 92 A. D. at the age of sixty-one.[30]

The younger brother, Pan Ch'ao, on the other hand, was decidedly a man of action. "He held great hopes," wrote his biographer,[31] "and he did not observe small conventionalities. Nevertheless, in his family life he was filial and thoughtful. Not being ashamed of hard work, and fearing no disgrace thereby, he worked diligently and laboriously at home." In 62 A. D.[32] he followed his elder brother Ku and their mother to Lo-yang. The family was poor, and in order to provide for their living expenses he secured a permanent position as copyist in a government office. It was while thus engaged that he gave utterance, according to his biographer, to the hope which no doubt sent him forth at a later date to the distant Pamirs in Central Asia.

"One day after a long period of hard labor, he stopped his task, threw down his brush, sighed, and said; 'If a great man be without any other purpose, at least he ought to imitate Fu Chieh-tzû [33] and Chang Ch'ien,[34] and accomplish an exploit in foreign parts to win the investiture of a marquis.[35] How can one live long between the brush and the ink slab?' When those around laughed at him, Pan Ch'ao said; 'You, little people, how can you know the purpose of a strong man?' "

And true enough, Pan Ch'ao was sent out in 73 A. D.[36] as military officer with a civilian named Kuo Hsün on a mission to East Turke-

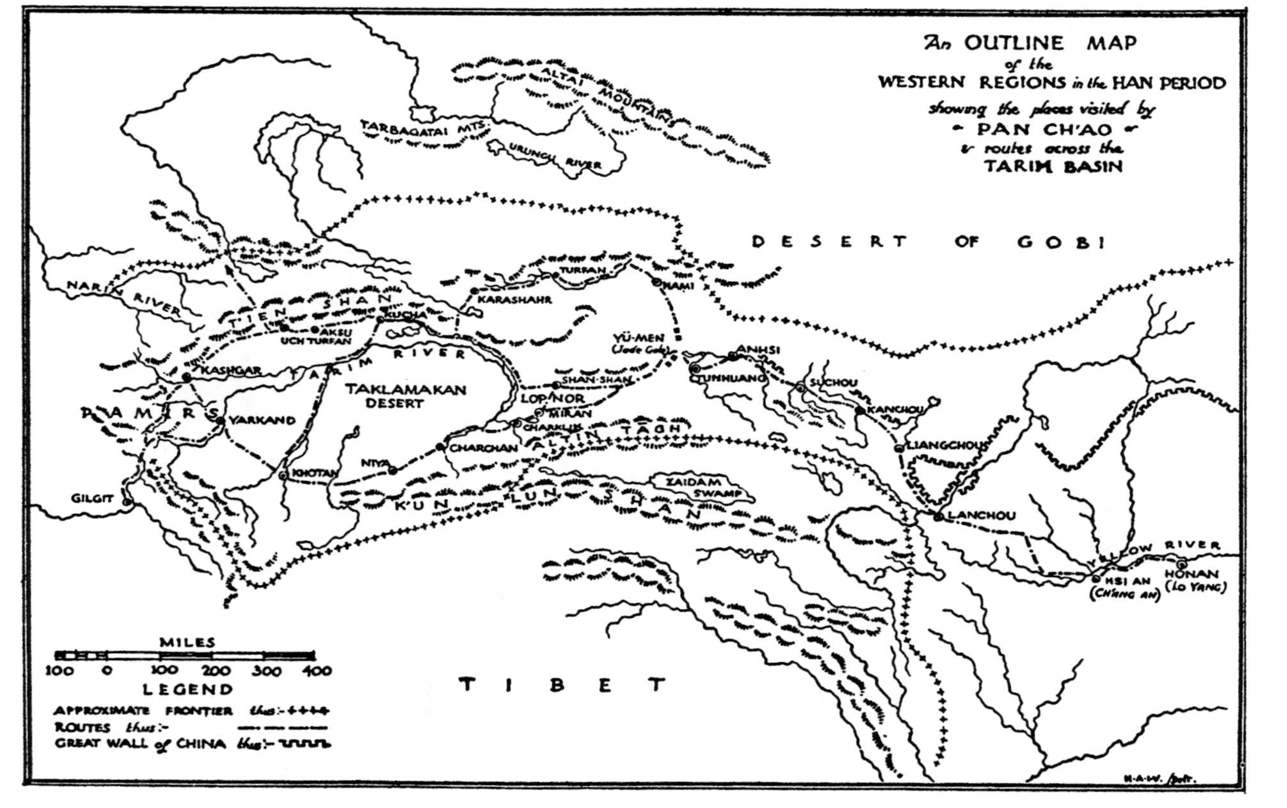
An OUTLINE MAP
of the
WESTERN REGIONS in the HAN PERIOD
showing the places visited by
PAN CH'AO
& routes across the
TARIM BASIN
DESERT OF GOBI
ALTAI MOUNTAINS
TARBAGATAI MTS.
URUNGU RIVER
NARIN RIVER
T'IEN SHAN
TURFAN
HAMI
KARASHAHR
KUCHA
AKSU
UCH TURFAN
TARIM RIVER
KASHGAR
TAKLAMAKAN DESERT
PAMIRS
YARKAND
YÜ-MEN
(Jade Gate)
ANHSI
TUNHUANG
SUCHOU
KANCHOU
LIANGCHOU
SHAN-SHAN
LOP NOR
MIRAN
CHARKLIK
ALTIN TAGH
CHARCHAN
NIYA
KHOTAN
GILGIT
ZAIDAM SWAMP
KUN LUN SHAN
LANCHOU
YELLOW RIVER
HSI AN
(CH'ANG AN)
HONAN
(LO YANG)
TIBET
MILES
100 0 100 200 300 400
LEGEND
APPROXIMATE FRONTIER thus:-
ROUTES thus:-
GREAT WALL of CHINA thus:-
H.A.W. fecit.

stan. After five years among the tribes along the South Road [37] west of Shan-shan, with whom the Chinese had been more or less constantly friendly since the mission of Fu Chieh-tzû in 77 B.C., Pan Ch'ao came to realize that the opposition to the control of these nations by the Chinese was really to be found in the great Tokharan or Indo-Scythian centers on the North Road. These centers were at the time under the influence of the great Yüeh-chih, who had but recently left their imprint there in the course of their long trek across Asia from the distant borders of China to the northwest lands of India (175 B.C.–10 A.D.). They had, moreover, the opportunity at all times for alliance with the various warlike tribes of the then powerful Hsiung-nu [38] against the Han encroachments. Hence they held themselves aloof from the mission of Pan Ch'ao, and even sought to dissuade the neighboring peoples to the south from permitting the advance of the Han emissaries in their penetration into the Tarim Basin.

In 78 A.D. Pan Ch'ao asked for reinforcements for the purpose of bringing these centers under Chinese control. If the highway for the silk commerce across East Turkestan to the distant western world [39] were to be kept open, then Han militarism must conquer these peoples of the North Road, and Han Peace must replace Scythian Peace east of the Pamirs. The conquest of the stronger and more strategically located of these centers would establish Han supremacy in East Turkestan. This supremacy was actually secured, in circumstances which permitted the military officer of the mission to give ample proof of his skill and bravery; he was elevated (91 A.D.) to the post of Governor-general of East Turkestan, the previous occupant of which had been slain in 76 A.D.; and in 95 A.D. an imperial mandate raised him to the rank of marquis, with a remuneration amounting to the proceeds from the taxes of a thousand families. The peace which he established was durable, because, while keeping open the great trade routes across the deserts, it left the control of local affairs to local authority. Pan Ch'ao's chief concern was to keep warfare away from the borders of China, and to protect the highways of trade to the western world; and recent discoveries in the sands of these deserts show that under the control of China in Han times the tribes enjoyed a large measure of local autonomy.

Although a man of action, and one who had no fear of using force or strategy to accomplish his purposes, as his life in the west sufficiently shows, Pan Ch'ao also embodied the cultural ideals of the Han Confucianists. His rapid success in East Turkestan was not entirely due to the policy expressed in his two most famous utterances. He certainly did not fear to enter the tiger's cave; [40] he decidedly did succeed in fighting barbarian with barbarian.[41] Yet the reputation which he acquired as a brilliant general [42] is still further enhanced by the statesmanship of his policy as a colonial official. His advice to his successor in Central Asia reveals the broad principles of his conduct.

"On the frontier the officials themselves are not filial sons and obedient grandsons. Most of them out there are criminals,[43] deported to fill up the military colonies of the border lands. Furthermore, the barbarians possess hearts of birds and wild beasts, and so it is difficult to hold their allegiance; it is easy to fail with them. . . . A detailed policy of government will not do; it will lose you the sympathy of your inferiors in rank. You ought to be broad and lax in your dealings; pass over small mistakes; hold only to main principles. That is all."

In 100 A. D.[44] Pan Ch'ao sent up a petition asking that he might be relieved from his post on account of old age. This petition was seconded by another sent to the throne by his sister, Chao, who gave in greater detail the story of her brother's long service in the far west.

"The emperor Ho (89–105 A. D.), moved by her [45] words then ordered Pan Ch'ao's return. After thirty-one [46] years in the Western Regions (in Yung-yüan), the fourteenth year (102 A. D.), the eighth moon, he arrived in Lo-yang. . . . For years he had had a disease in the breast and ribs; and when he reached the capital the illness grew worse. The emperor dispatched a eunuch of the palace [47] to enquire about his health, and to take him healing medicine, but in the ninth moon he died at the age of seventy-one [48] years. The court sympathized with and pitied him, and sent messengers to mourn and to sacrifice. Both the posthumous honors and the funeral gifts were exceedingly large."

Since in his later years Pan Ch'ao lived in comparative peace as governor and commanding general of Chinese forces in East Turkestan, he must certainly have heard many accounts of the lands farther west. Although the mandate of ennoblement says that he crossed the Pamirs and entered into the Valley of Gilgit,[49] Chavannes suggested that this language may be a figure of speech rather than a record of historical fact. But even if Pan Ch'ao himself did not go over the divide, he had numerous opportunities for intercourse with persons from beyond the pass. In the chapter of the *Hou Han Shu* on the Western Regions [50] there is preserved a very brief record of an expedition sent by him into that far western world (97 A.D.) under the leadership of a subordinate officer, Kan Ying. In the paragraph on Parthia occurs the now familiar story of how Kan Ying was turned back by his fear of travel by sea.[51] In Pan Ch'ao's petition begging for the appointment of a substitute so that he might return home before he died or was killed, he spoke of sending home his son Yung [52] along with a tribute-bearing train en route to China. The commentator on this passage quotes a statement from the *Tung Kuan Han Chi* [53] that it was an embassy from Parthia with which this son travelled. The biographer notes that, with the exception of a few years around 90 A.D.,[54] "every year the Yüeh-chih paid tribute and homage, sending gifts of precious things, of *fu-pa* [55] and of lions." Now the Yüeh-chih had intercourse with the Roman Empire as well as with the Chinese,[56] and the mutual relationship of these and other peoples must have brought to Pan Ch'ao many stories and many products of the far western culture.

The ruler of the Yüeh-chih Empire at the time of Pan Ch'ao's western career (73–102 A.D.) was probably the predecessor of the celebrated Kaniska whose people accepted Indian nationality but possessed a Hellenic culture.[57] This people, called Yüeh-chih [58] by the Chinese, and Tokhāra or Indo-Scythians [59] by the Greeks, possessed great military power, but its chief interest was its religious policy. By the cross-fertilization of Buddhism and Hellenism a new religion was then arising on the northwest border of India in the shape of the Mahāyāna form of Buddhism. Under Kaniska's patronage, if not under that of his predecessor, the missionaries of this new religion were also harbingers of a new culture, and introducers of many products of a foreign civilization.

Thus during the latter part of the first century of the Christian era and the early years of the second the high plateau lands of Central Asia were the meeting-place of the cultures of the world; and China's representative at these crossroads was Pan Ch'ao, a brilliant general, an extraordinary colonial statesman, and an outstanding exponent of Han Peace.

NOTES

[1] *Chinese Biog.*, 鬭穀於釋字子文, p. 1807; his father was Tou Po-pi, 鬭伯比, p. 1807, son of a Duke of Ch'u (789-763 B.C.), 若敖, p. 703. See *Classics*, V, *Tso Chuan*, Duke Hsüan, 宣公, fourth year, p. 295, translation, p. 297. His mother's parents caused his abandonment and subsequent reclama-

tion. See Maspero: same, p. 129; cf. S. F. Couvreur: *Tch'ouen Ts'iou et Tso Tchouan* (1914), pp. 586-587.

[2] 芈(音彌) *Chüan* 40, 楚世家; Chavannes: *Mémoires*, II, 77, note.

[3] *Chüan* 100, 敍傳. Such honorific legends are not uncommonly associated by Chinese prominent families with their earliest ancestors. As years and virtue go together, a later descendant, I, 壹, is reported to have been more than one hundred years old.

[4] Generally it is 斑, not 班, which is used for the stripes and spots of a tiger, but the *K'ang-hsi Dictionary* quotes one reference illustrating the use of 班 as meaning "variegated or mixed colors." The *Chinese Biog.* (Supplement on surnames, p. 42) states that the surname should have been written 斑 in the histories.

[5] See *Êrh-shih-êrh Shih Cha-chi, chüan* 2, 廿二史劄記; 賢良方正茂材直言多舉現任官.

As the emperor Kuang-wu (25-57 A. D.) had in his personal name the character *hsiu*, 秀, the scholarly rank was changed to *mao-ts'ai*, see *Tz'û Yüan*, 申, p. 22.

In Han Wu Ti's reign each *chün*, 郡, named a scholar for its *hsiao-lien*, 孝廉, and a *chou*, 州, a *hsiu-ts'ai*. This custom lapsed under the Sui and T'ang dynasties, but was revived at intervals later, see *Tz'û Yüan*, 寅, p. 11. For an exact meaning of the terms *chün* and *chou*, see the references above, Chapter I, note 16.

[6] 少使, a low rank among the ladies of honorable rank in the palace (see *Tz'û Yüan*, 寅, p. 109).

[7] 倢伃. The writer has been unable to find a source for the statement by Giles that "*chieh-yü* was a title conferred upon the concubine most distinguished for literary ability" (*Gems of Chinese Literature, Verse*, p. 26; *Biog.*, no. 1599). Upon request for information concerning his source from the author of this study Professor Giles in a personal letter (dated March 1, 1931), without stating the source for his assertion in earlier writings, noted that "*Kang Hsi* gives 婦官 as a definition of the term under 婕, and 女官 under 妤." *Chieh-yü* is apparently written either with the 女 or the 人 radical without conveying a difference in meaning.

According to *San T'ung K'ao Chi Yao* (1899), *chüan* 19, 三通考輯要, 后妃及後宮皇太子妃, with the rise of the house of Han the ranks of the women of the palace were readjusted by various emperors. Among them was that of *shao-shih*, 少使, into which Pan Chieh-yü was placed upon her entrance into the palace. *Chieh-yü*, which corresponded to the ranks of *shang-ch'ing*, 上卿, and of *lieh-hou*, 列侯, among the men at the court, was one of the ranks established by Han Wu Ti (140-87 B. C.) (See *Tz'û Yüan*, 子, p. 214).

[8] This quotation is an interpretation, not a translation of her words. The incident forms the subject for Plate IV of the Ku K'ai-chih, 顧愷之, scroll in the British Museum, which scroll illustrates a tract written in the third century A. D., "Admonitions of the Instructress to the Court Ladies," 女史箴, by Chang Hua 張華 (232-300 A. D.), Giles: *Biog.*, no. 65; *Adversaria Sinica*, II, no. 1; Ferguson, *JRAS, NCB*, XLIX (1918), 101-110; for an English

translation of the incident, see Arthur Waley: *The Introduction to the Study of Chinese Painting,* p. 50; Giles: *Hist. Lit.,* p. 101.

[9] *Chüan* 97, 外戚傳; also in *Lieh Nü Chuan, chüan* 8, 列女傳, 班婕妤.

[10] A collection of her writings is listed in the "Bibliography" section of the Sui (590-617 A. D.) dynastic history, *Sui Shu, chüan* 35, 隋書經籍志四集. Chinese sources for her extant writings, and sources for translations of her charming lyric poem are listed in the bibliography of this chapter.

[11] *Sui Shu, chüan* 33, 隋書經籍志：列女傳注；劉向撰曹大家注.

[12] *Han Shu, chüan* 100; cf. p. 16.

[13] 嗣雖修儒學然貴老嚴之術. (*Han Shu, chüan* 100).

[14] See above, Chapter I, note 12.

[15] 光武, "Glorious in War." (For a study of the character *wu,* see L. C. Hopkins, "Pictographic Reconnaissance," *Journal Royal Asiatic Society,* October, 1927, pp. 769-770.) His name was Liu Hsiu, 劉秀 (4 B. C.—57 A. D.), Giles: *Biog.,* no. 1305.

[16] The names of the reign periods of the Han emperors were changed at irregular intervals when some marked fortune, good or bad, seemed imminent or had descended upon the land. The names chosen usually suggested the characteristics desired by the court for a new period. (See Chavannes: *Mémoires,* I, p. C.)

[17] The age of a Chinese is reckoned by the number of calendar years in which he has lived. Thus, if born on the last day of one year, he is calculated to be two years old on the first day of the next. Pan Piao therefore was born in 3 A. D.

[18] *P'ien,* 篇.

[19] There was a daughter (older than the twin sons), who married into the Chou, 周, family, mentioned in a work now lost, but of which fragments have been gathered from later works by different scholars, see *San Fu Chüeh Lu* by Chao Ch'i, 趙岐:三輔決錄摯虞注, (*Êrh-yu T'ang Ts'ung Shu,* 1821, 二酉堂叢書), *chüan* 1, p. 22, quoted in an annotation in the biography of Pan Chao, *Hou Han Shu, chüan* 84.

[20] Chavannes was evidently unacquainted with this custom, see *T'oung Pao,* VII (1906), 216, note 4.

[21] *Han Shu, chüan* 30, I-wên Chih, see Chapter I, note 24.

[22] That is: he was free from bias.

[23] He did not stop to punctuate his text.

[24] 兩都賦, *Hou Han Shu, chüan* 40a; Waley: *The Temple,* p. 17; Georges Margouliès: *Le "Fou" dans le Wên-siuan* (Paris, 1926), Intro., and pp. 30-74.

[25] 東方朔, biography in *Han Shu, chüan* 65; see Giles: *Biog.,* no. 2093; same: *Hist. Lit.,* p. 97.

揚雄, biography in *Han Shu, chüan* 87; see pp. 16, 17.

Tung-fang So (born 160 B.C.) came into favor through a cleverly written recommendation of himself in answer to the call of the throne for men of talent. Yang Hsiung (53 B. C.—18 A. D.) kept himself in imperial favor by his brush, even writing an essay of praise of the usurper Wang Mang. Pan Ku in a dialogue between a host and his guest wrote a satire upon his period, which called attention to himself. Although the sentence following this entry in the *Hou Han Shu* (*chüan* 40b), 後遷玄武司馬, makes no positive statement that his satire was the reason for his promotion, it seems to have been the occasion for it. The text of *Pin Hsi,* 賓戲, is included in *Han Shu, chüan* 100. The texts of the three essays may be seen together in the *Wên Hsüan, chüan* 45.

[26] 白虎通德論, known usually as *Po-hu T'ung,* see Wylie: *Notes,* p. 159. 典引, preserved in *Hou Han Shu, chüan* 40b.

[27] Opinion of his biographer, same.

[28] Ssû-ma Hsiang-ju, 司馬相如, (died 117 B.C.), see Giles: *Biog.,* no. 1753; Waley: *The Temple,* pp. 38-46. The theory of these sacrifices to Heaven and Earth arose toward the end of the Chou dynasty, see Chavannes: same, III, 413-519; Maspero: same, p. 277.

[29] 新朝, the name of the dynasty which Wang Mang attempted to establish.

[30] Or sixty western reckoning. His service was with Tou Hsien, 竇憲 (Giles: *Biog.,* no. 1956), and upon the fall of the latter, as a follower Pan Ku was thrown into prison by a local magistrate in revenge for ill treatment at the hands of sons of Pan Ku.

[31] *Hou Han Shu, chüan* 47.

[32] Yung-p'ing, 永平, period, fifth year.

[33] 傅介子. In 77 B.C. he was sent to Lou-lan, 樓蘭, on a mission which was so successful that he was given the title of a marquis. After this exploit Lou-lan was known in Chinese records as Shan-shan, 鄯善, see *Han Shu, chüan* 70 and 96 (Trans., see Wylie: *Journal of the Anthropological Institute,* XI, 1881.); M. Aurel Stein: *Serindia,* I, 318-325.

[34] 張騫. After his mission to the west (139-126 B.C.) he was given the title of marquis, see *Han Shu, chüan* 61 (Trans., see Wylie: same, X (Aug., 1880.); 63-73); Chavannes: *Mémoires,* I, pp. LXXI-LXXV; F. Hirth: The Story of Chang K'ien," *The Journal of the American Oriental Society,* XXXVII, 89-152.

[35] Chang Ch'ien (126 B.C.), 博望侯.

Fu Chieh-tzû (77 B.C.), 義陽侯.

Pan Ch'ao (95 A.D.), 定遠侯.

[36] Yung-p'ing period, sixteenth year.

His military rank was first 軍假司馬, then 軍司馬. According to the commentator (*Hou Han Shu, chüan* 47, 通鑑胡注百官志, Wylie: *Notes,* p. 25) the great general's, 大將軍, headquarters had five departments to each of which departments were attached two officers with *ssû-ma* rank, (a) 軍假司馬; (b) 軍司馬. On *ssû-ma* in the Western Chou period, see Maspero: same, p. 74.

[37] Beyond the "Jade Gate" the highway from China proper to the west divides into two great roads: (1) South Road, which runs along the southern rim of the Tarim Basin through Khotan, Yarkand, and Kashgar; (2) North Road, which follows the northern rim of the Basin at the eastern extremity of which it joins the South Road in the way over the Pamirs. During Han times a "Road of the Center" left the South Road not far out from the Jade Gate, crossed to Shan-shan and the river bed beyond, turned northward and joined the North Road just west of Karashahr.

[38] 匈奴. The Chinese term for the peoples of the north and northwest lands (the Huns), whose inroads upon Chinese territory presented the greatest external menace to the peace of the empire during both the Western and the Eastern Han periods. (See *Serindia,* p. 331, note 11; Grousset: same, II, 177.)

[39] See a discussion of the trade by Hirth in *China and the Roman Orient,* pp. 225 ff; Stein, "Central-Asian Relics of China's Ancient Silk Trade," *Hirth Anniversary Volume* (London, 1923), pp. 366-374.

[40] The *Tz'û Yüan,* 申, p. 109, in conformity with the usual acceptation, credits Pan Ch'ao with having originated this aphorism, 不入虎穴,不得虎子.

[41] 以夷狄攻夷狄,計之善者也. See *Han Shu, chüan* 49, in a petition an official of Han Wên Ti, Ch'ao Ts'o, 鼂錯, (died 155 B.C., Giles: *Biog.,* no. 204; same: *Hist. Lit.,* pp. 80-81), said: 以蠻夷攻蠻夷中國之形也. This policy outlined by Ch'ao Ts'o, and carried out with marked success by Pan Ch'ao was also adopted by T'ang T'ai-tsung (627-649 A.D.) in his campaigns in Central Asia (see Grousset: same, II, 221), and has in fact always been the Chinese policy, even in modern times.

[42] For a brief résumé of his successive operations which are related in detail by his biographer, see *Serindia,* I, 330-331.

[43] See same, pp. 751, 761; Chavannes: *Documents chinois découverts par Aurel Stein,* no. 263.

[44] Yung-yüan, 永元, period, twelfth year.

[45] 其 may be her or their.

[46] Or thirty western reckoning.

[47] *Chung-huang-mên,* 中黃門, see Chavannes, "Trois généraux chinois," *T'oung Pao,* VII (1906), 243. Cf. *Hou Han Shu, chüan* 78, 黃門注.

[48] Or seventy western reckoning.

[49] 超遂踰葱領,迄縣度, *Hou Han Shu, chüan* 47.
T'oung Pao, VII (1906), 237, note 4.

[50] *Hou Han Shu, chüan* 88. 班超遣掾甘英窮臨西海而還.

[51] Although this "Great" or "West Sea,"大海, 西海, has been identified (see J. MacGowan: *The Imperial History of China,* [Shanghai, 1906], p. 119, note; Vincent A. Smith: *Oxford History of India,* ed. 1923, p. 129) with the Caspian Sea, it is most likely the Persian Gulf, see Chavannes, *T'oung Pao,* VII (1906), 210, VIII (1907), 178, note; Hirth: *China and the Roman Orient,* pp. VI, 39, 151, 166; Cordier: *Histoire générale,* I, 270.

[52] 勇. Pan Ch'ao had three sons. The eldest died young in official life. Of the second the biographer recorded nothing. The third son Yung was born in East Turkestan, and doubtless was only half-Chinese. In relating how a subordinate officer criticised Pan Ch'ao for "carrying his beloved son in his arms," the biographer has revealed the father's love for the boy as a baby. His dispatch of this son years later to the capital before his own death shows his desire to have his half-Chinese son recognized at court. In after years it was Yung who became his father's successor in service in the Western Regions, see *Hou Han Shu, chüan* 47; Chavannes, *T'oung Pao,* VII (1906), 245-255.

[53] 東觀漢記, *chüan* 16, 班超; see Chavannes, same, p. 213, p. 239, note 4.
安息國; see *Hou Han Shu, chüan* 88; translated by Chavannes, *T'oung Pao,* VIII (1907), 177; *Hou Han Shu, chüan* 4, 永元, thirteenth year, eleventh moon (101 A.D.).

[54] In this year a great expedition against the Chinese forces in East Turkestan was sent out by the Yüeh-chih ruler, see biography of Pan Ch'ao, *Hou Han Shu, chüan* 47.

[55] 符拔. This has been identified as "antelope," see Chavannes, *T'oung Pao,*

VII (1906), 232, VIII (1907), 177, note. Hirth (*China and Roman Orient,* pp. 7-8) noted that "the lions" in the 1167 A. D. edition of *Hou Han Shu* was written 師 whereas modern editions have 獅, but both the Ch'ien-lung (1739 A. D.) and the Wang Hsien-ch'ien (1915 A. D.) editions retain the 師 in the biography of Pan Ch'ao, and in the records of the Western Regions (條支國 and 安息國), except in one of the three places in the Wang Hsien-ch'ien edition (*Hou Han Shu, chüan* 88, 安息國, 101 A. D.) 獅 is found. (See reprint of the Chinese text of the Ch'ien-lung edition in *T'oung Pao,* VIII (1907), 234.)

[56] See Chavannes, *T'oung Pao,* VIII (1907), 151-152; Grousset: *Histoire,* II, 61 ff.

[57] See Grousset: same, pp. 56-69. Compare *Scrindia,* p. 243, note 10; I. Kennedy, "The Secret of Kanishka," *JRAS* (1912), pp. 666-688 ff; H. Oldenberg, "On the Era of Kaniska," *The Journal of the Pali Text Society* (1912), pp. 1-18; Vincent A. Smith: *Oxford History of India* (ed. 1923), pp. 126-131, 146.

[58] The Chinese text has *Yüeh-shih,* 月氏, which in Han times was read 月支. (See *Han Shu, chüan* 96a, p. 1 注.)

[59] Chavannes; *Documents,* p. 178, note on no. 846.

BIBLIOGRAPHY

Han Shu, chüan 100, biographical account of the Pan family. This biography as well as the one below is the product of members of the Pan family, so that the more honorific statements made therein should be accepted with due caution.

Han Shu, chüan 97, biographical sketch of Pan Chieh-yü.

Hou Han Shu, chüan 40 and 47, biographies of Pan Piao, Pan Ku, and Pan Ch'ao. The author, Fan Yeh, had no reason for flattering the Pan family pride, although, as indicated in the Appendix of this study, much of the material for his book must have been collected under the supervision of Pan Ku and Pan Chao while they were in charge of the historical section of the imperial repositories. Yet he was such an admirer of their work that on the whole he adopted for his own history the plan of their *Han Shu,* which plan, however, was derived originally from the "Historical Record" of Ssû-ma Ch'ien. *Chüan* 47 contains also the biography of Pan Yung following that of his father; and a memorial by Pan Chao, which is translated with notes in Chapter VI of this study.

Hou Han Shu, chüan 88, 西域傳, a record of the relation of the Chinese Empire with neighboring peoples in the Western Regions.

Wên Hsüan, chüan 27, 詩樂府怨歌行,班婕妤. This, the earliest and best specimen of "General Collections," 總集, has been preserved in two editions. About 658 A. D. Li Shan wrote a commentary on the work under the title *Wên Hsüan Chu,* 李善文選註. This was followed during the next century by five other commentaries which were collated and combined into a single work in circa 718 A. D. In the Sung dynasty this edition was published, with Li Shan's commentary also embodied in the work, entitled *Liu Ch'ên Chu Wên Hsüan,* 六臣註文選. Modern editions of the *Wên Hsüan* are numerous.

Ku Wên Yüan, chüan 3, 古文苑,賦, has preserved the long narrative poem

Tao-su Fu, 擣素賦, of Pan Chieh-yü. This valuable literary collection in 21 *chüan*, even in modern editions, after several rearrangements, comprises 260 pieces of verse, narrative poems, and various classes of literature which are supposed to supplement those preserved in the *Wên Hsüan* (see Wylie: *Notes*, pp. 239-240). Additions to the collection have been gathered into a continuation work, *Hsü Ku Wên Yüan*, 續古文苑.

Kung-kuei Wên Hsüan, *chüan* 1, 6, 7, 11, 宮閨文選. This collection of the writings in chronological order of the women of the palace, beginning with those of Pan Chieh-yü, contains under arrangement according to composition the most complete collection of her extant works, a total of five selections (6 vols., 1846).

Chung-kuo Fu-nü Wên-hsüeh Shih, 中國婦女文學史, 班婕妤, 班昭. A collection of the literature produced by Chinese women, not a history of the literature produced by Chinese women. Western style of binding (third edition, Peking, 1916-1918).

Tsu-kuo Nü-chieh Wên-hao P'u-hsü, 祖國女界文豪譜序, 曹昭, 丁氏, 曹豐生, 班婕妤. Another, but earlier, collection which also contains selections from previous works. The material here listed is taken practically verbatim from the *Han Shu*, *Hou Han Shu*, and *Wên Hsüan* (1906).

Liang Ch'i-ch'ao: *Yao Chi Chieh-t'i Chi Ch'i Tu-fa.*

Ku Chieh-kang: *Ku Shih Pien.*

Chavannes: *Mémoires*, I.

Chavannes, "Trois généraux chinois," *T'oung Pao*, VII (1906), 210-245. Pages 210-215, a study of the composition of the *Hou Han Shu;* pages 216-245, translation with notes of the biography of Pan Ch'ao (pp. 245-255, of Pan Yung; pp. 255-262, other biographies), and at end of the whole article an index. These accurate translations and excellent notes are invaluable to this study.

Chavannes, "Le pays d'occident d'après le *Heou Han Chou*," same, VIII (1907), 149-234. A translation with notes of the *chüan* on the relation of the Chinese with the peoples of the Western Regions (*Hou Han Shu*, *chüan* 88), pp. 151-152, bibliographies of the Yüeh-chih, and of China and the Roman Orient in the first two centuries of the Christian era.

Hirth, Friedrich: *China and the Roman Orient.* Translation of Chinese records with an Introduction by the translator, the early date (1885) of which preceded the discoveries in Central Asia of relics of Han times. (Shanghai, 1885.)

Hirth: *The Story of Chang K'ien.* China's pioneer in Western Asia. Text and translation of *chüan* 123 of Ssû-ma Ch'ien's "Historical Record." Reprint from the *Journal of the American Oriental Society*, XXXVII, 89-152.

Stein, M. Aurel: *Serindia.* The story of Pan Ch'ao's exploits in the far west runs like a scarlet thread through volume I, and the finds in Niya Site, the desert of Lopnor, and the Han limes are the dry bones of Han life in the Western Regions. Places mentioned in the Han text can be found in the Maps, vol. V. (5 vols., London, 1921.)

Stein, "Central-Asian Relics of China's Ancient Silk Trade," *Hirth Anniversary Volume*, pp. 366-374 (London, 1923).

Conrady, August: *Die Chinesischen Handschriften und Sonstigen Kleinfunde Sven Hedin in Lou-lan.* Hedin's discoveries preceded those of Stein, and this work is a detailed account of the finds in the desert of Lopnor, or Lou-lan, or Shan-shan. (Stockholm, 1920.)

Grousset: *Histoire,* II, 1-90, 165-196, 221. This includes a very good brief account of the ancient people known in Chinese records as Yüeh-chih. On pp. 188-191 is an interesting short summary of Pan Ch'ao's career in the west.

Cordier: *Histoire générale,* I, 267-276.

Chavannes: *Les Documents chinois découverts par Aurel Stein.* This study of the relics may be used with advantage by the reader of *Serindia.* (Oxford, 1913.)

Giles: *A Chinese Biographical Dictionary.*

Giles: *A History of Chinese Literature,* p. 101.

Giles: *Gems of Chinese Literature, Verse,* p. 26 (London, 1923).

Martin, W. A. P.: *Chinese Legends and Lyrics,* p. 49 (Shanghai, 1912).

Imbert, Henri: *Pan Tsié-yu et Tschao-Kuin,* pp. 1-9. A short sketch of the lives of two celebrated concubines of two emperors. The one of Pan Chieh-yü contains a translation of her famous lyric poem and those of other poems about her by four later poets. (Peking, 1921.)

Ayscough, Florence, and Lowell, Amy: *Fir-Flower Tablets,* p. 142 (Boston and New York, 1921).

Waley, Arthur: *An Introduction to the Study of Chinese Painting,* p. 50 (London, 1923).

Chao I: *Êrh-shih-êrh Shih Cha-chi,* 趙翼:廿二史劄記, "Notes on the Twenty-two Histories," *chüan* 2. The author lived 1727-1814, so his remarks, although often of little value in their contribution of new material, do reflect somewhat the spirit of constructive criticism which characterized the scholarship of his day. They are not so stimulating nor scientific as some of the work of his younger contemporary, Ts'ui Shu, 崔述 (1740-1816).

CHAPTER IV

The Life of Pan Chao

The most considerable as well as the most reliable source of direct information concerning the life and writings of Pan Chao is found in her biography in the *Hou Han Shu* compiled by Fan Yeh early in the fifth century A. D. This biography can claim the authority of a contemporary record, for, as is indicated in detail in the appendix to this study, its main outlines if not its actual text were almost certainly prepared three centuries earlier. The work is composed in a dry, compactly informative style which is characteristic of early Chinese chronicles. It is noteworthy that the author of its final form, whether it be Liu Chên, Li Ch'ung, or Fan Yeh,[1] has permitted no single word of criticism, either in praise or blame, to tincture the laconic sobriety of the record. Chavannes observed the same impersonality in the narrative style of Ssû-ma Ch'ien, and it may also be noticed in the *Han Shu*. The phraseology is so simple and straightforward as to render re-statement superfluous.

The Biography of Pan Chao by Fan Yeh

"Pan Chao, the wife of Ts'ao Shih-shu[2] of Fu-fêng (in Shensi), was the daughter of Pan Piao of the same district. Her personal name was Chao, and her style Hui-chi.[3] She displayed profound erudition and talent of a high order. After the early death of her husband, Pan Chao observed the canons of widowhood.[4]

"Her elder brother Ku wrote the *Han Shu* in which the 'Eight Tables' and the 'Treatise on Astronomy' were not finished at the time of his death. Thereupon the emperor Ho commanded Pan Chao to come to the Tung Kuan Library[5] in order to continue and complete the work.

"The emperor many times summoned Pan Chao to the palace, where he ordered the empress and the ladies of honorable rank to treat her as a teacher.[6] They addressed her accordingly in terms of respect.[7] Every time there was a presentation of tribute or of unusual gifts the emperor commanded her to compose commemorative verses for the occasion.[8]

"When the empress Têng became regent (106 A. D.) she conferred with Pan Chao concerning affairs of state. As a result of his mother's diligence both at court and in outside activities, Pan Chao's son Ch'êng [9] was by imperial grant created a marquis, and appointed minister to the prince of Ch'i.

"At the time when the *Han Shu* first appeared, most of the scholars could not comprehend it. Ma Rung, a native of the same district as Pan Chao, was allowed as a special favor to go to the library, where he studied under her. Later Ma Rung's elder brother Hsü [10] was ordered to continue and complete Pan Chao's work.

"In the middle of the Yung-ch'u [11] period (107–113 A. D.), the empress's elder brother, General Têng Chih, grieved on account of his mother's (death), sent up a petition to the throne begging to be retired from office.[12] Now the empress was reluctant to allow this, and therefore asked (Pan) Chao her opinion. (Pan) Chao then presented a memorial,[13] . . . in accordance with which the empress permitted the general to retire. Whereupon (Têng) Chih and other (members of his family) each in proper order returned to his own place of residence.[14]

"(Pan Chao also) wrote 'Lessons for Women' in seven chapters, (a treatise which) affords assistance in the education of women . . . .[15] Ma Rung was so pleased with the treatise that he ordered the wives and daughters [16] (of his family) to practice its precepts. (Pan) Chao's younger sister-in-law, Ts'ao Fêng-shêng, likewise talented and cultured, wrote essays which are worth reading, in which she took issue [17] with Pan Chao.

"When (Pan) Chao was seventy and more years old, she died. The empress wore half-mourning for her, and appointed a mourning period. She also sent messengers to superintend, and to represent her in, the funeral arrangements.

"The literary works (of Pan Chao) included Narrative Poems, Commemorative Writings, Inscriptions, Eulogies,[18] Argumentations, Commentaries, Elegies, Essays, Treatises, Expositions, Memorials, and Final Instructions, in all (enough to fill) sixteen books. Her daughter-in-law, of the Ting family, collected and edited her works, and appended thereto an appreciation [19] of Pan Chao."

A small amount of supplementary information concerning the life of Pan Chao may be gleaned from her "Lessons for Women" and her two extant memorials—all of which are translated in two following chapters—as well as the biographies of her family in the two Han histories. As late as the middle of the seventh century, the time of the compilation of the chapters on literature in the Sui dynastic history, her "Lessons" existed as a separate work. When Fan Yeh compiled the *Hou Han Shu* her collected writings were also extant, so that it is probable that he had these works at hand to collate with the annals and biographies composed by Liu Chên and Li Ch'ung. It may be taken as certain that the text of her works preserved in the *Hou Han Shu* is a reasonably correct one.

Statements from these sources enforce Fan Yeh's terse assertion that Pan Chao was deeply learned and highly talented. According to her own account in the preface to her "Lessons," she owed much of her exceptional education to her parents. She acknowledges her indebtedness to her scholarly father, and speaks of a cultured mother upon whom she relied for literary instruction as well as training in good manners. Of the women of her connection, her younger sister-in-law, her son's wife, and the "daughters" for whom she wrote her "Lessons for Women," were all educated. Her father and elder brother were recognized scholars, and her home was a resort of the learned of the time. While it was not a wealthy one, its possessions included the rare and precious books given to her great-uncle by the emperor Ch'êng. Since these books were duplicates of certain inaccessible manuscripts in the palace, they doubtless furnished the Pan family with valuable material for historical composition. As her father was an ardent Confucianist, while the cousin Ssû with whom he studied was one who "reverenced the Lao-Chuang school of thought," [20] Pan Chao had unusual opportunities for acquainting herself with the tenets of both schools of philosophy. The literary achievements of her great-aunt, Pan Chieh-yü, no doubt set a precedent for her own scholarly training. In the biography [21] of the empress Têng are enumerated "Classical writings and history as well as astronomy and mathematics" as the subjects which Pan Chao taught her royal pupil. The "Eight Tables" and the "Treatise on Astronomy" were the sections of the Han history which were left unfinished by her brother Ku, and which she was chosen to complete. It is inconceivable that any but a very highly trained scholar could have been selected to be in fact, if not in name, the historiographer of the China of Han times.

It is a phenomenon which may be noted at almost all times in Chinese history that, in spite of the manifold restraints and limitations which the orthodox moralists placed upon the activity of woman, individual women of spirit and energy have been able to dominate men, and not infrequently even to seize upon the supreme imperial power. The tyranny of the mother-in-law in private life has been the theme of so many writers that it needs no special emphasis here. At the death of the emperor Ho (105 A. D.) the reins of government came into the hands of his twenty-five-year-old empress (Têng T'ai-hou) as regent for the infant heir apparent. A year later the baby emperor died, and was succeeded by his cousin, the emperor An, a boy of thirteen years,[22] but the empress kept her power at court until her death in 121 A. D.[23] Fan Yeh records that "When the empress Têng became regent (106 A. D.) she conferred with Pan Chao concerning affairs of state." And at the close of the empress's biography he writes [24] that "at one word from Mother Pan the whole family resigned," an incident which the annotation explains as referring to Pan Chao's memorial concerning the retirement of the empress's elder brother, General Têng. This fleeting glimpse of the political activity of the Pan Chao of later years clearly shows that she was one of those numerous women of strong mind who have played a striking part on the stage of Chinese history; and it indicates also that although primarily a woman of letters she could also play a leading part in the politics of the court.

The compilers of the *Mémoires concernant les Chinois* have preserved in translated form an epitaph on Pan Chao which they credited to her daughter-in-law. Unfortunately they failed to state the source either of the epitaph itself or of the long sketch of the life of Pan Chao in which they included not only the epitaph but also what they called a translation of her "Lessons for Women." These compilers were living [25] in Peking when they sent back home their sketches of the lives of fifty-two famous Chinese scholars which were published in 1778 at Paris, under royal patronage, as the third volume of the *Mémoires.*

The Chinese text of this epitaph is now unknown, though it may be still in existence,[26] hidden away somewhere among the vast mass of records contained in the local gazetteers and other collections which abound in Chinese literature. Beside the dynastic histories, Wylie [27] listed fourteen classes of historical writings, and these do not include the local series of topographical publications. Every province has its gazetteer, which in addition to a detailed description of cities, educational institutions, hills and rivers, antiquities, passes, defenses, bridges, tombs, temples, and productions of the soil, includes also chapters on literature and biographies of men and women of note. Besides these general provincial compilations there exist accounts, of a more or less historical, geographical, and topographical nature, for nearly all the administrative and natural divisions of China. There is also the individual collection, a form of compilation which since its rise in the first century A. D. has been "one of the most prolific branches of Chinese literature," [28] although large numbers of such collections have disappeared with the lapse of time. Somewhere in the collected works of some essayist or historical critic, or in one of the multitudinous historical or literary compilations, this epitaph may yet be preserved in the original form in which it somehow fell into the hands of these early French missionaries. In their translation its style is laudatory, such a style as a daughter-in-law should adopt when writing of a gifted mother-in-law. Its phraseology, almost everywhere compact, suggests a direct translation from the concise forms of Chinese classical writing.

Epitaph of Pan Chao

"Pan-hoei-pan, *surnommée* Tsao *la grande-Dame, femme de* Tsao, *fille de* Pan-che, *sœur de* Pan-Kou, *a mis la derniere main aux ouvrages de son pere et de son frere, qu'elle a expliqués et embellis.*

Elle a été maîtresse de l'Impératrice et des Dames du Palais. En donnant à ses illustres Eleves des leçons sur la poésie, l'éloquence et l'histoire, elle leur apprit à parer l'érudition des ornemens de la littérature, et à enrichir la littérature des trésors de l'érudition.

"Par un bienfait, dont aucune femme n'avoit encore joui, l'Empereur lui donna la Surintendance de celle de ses bibliotheques qui renfermoit le dépôt précieux des Manuscrits anciens et modernes, non encore débrouillés.

"A la tête d'un nombre de Savants (sic) *choisis, elle travailla dans cette bibliotheque avec un succès qui fit l'admiration de tous les Lettrés, et qui surpassa ses propres espérances. Elle tira du profond oubli, dans lequel elles etoient ensévelies, quelques productions utiles des Savans des siecles passés; elle expliqua avec une clarté qui ne laissa rien à desirer, quelques bons ouvrages des Savans modernes, qu'une trop grande obscurité et un goût tout-à-fait bizarre rendoient presque inintelligibles.*

"Elle s'eleva, sans y prétendre, au rang des plus sublimes Auteurs, parmi lesquels la finesse de son goût, la beauté de son style, la profondeur de son erudition, et la justesse de sa critique lui firent décerner une place distinguée. Elle s'abaissa, le voulant bien, jusqu'au niveau des femmes les plus ordinaires, auxquelles, par la simplicité de ses mœurs, par son assiduité à vaquer aux affaires domestiques, et par son attention scrupuleuse à ne négliger aucun des menus détails du ménage, elle ne dédaigna

pas de se rendre semblable, pour leur apprendre que, dans quelque poste qu'elles puissent se trouver, quel que soit le rang qu'elles occupent, les devoirs particuliers du sexe doivent toujours être remplis par préférence, et être regardés comme les plus essentiels et les premiers de leurs devoirs.

"Jouissant de tous les honneurs qu'on accorde aux talens et au vrai mérite, quand ils sont reconnus; estimée des gens de Lettres, dont elle etoit regardée comme l'oracle; respectée des personnes de son sexe, auxquelles néanmoins elle n'avoit pas craint de dire les plus humiliantes vérités, elle vécut jusqu'à une extrême vieillesse, dans le sein du travail et de la vertu, toujours en paix avec elle-même et avec les autres.

"Puisse le précieux souvenir de ses vertus et de son mérite le faire vivre dans les siecles à venir, jusque chez les plus reculés de nos descendans!"

Composed by Ting Shih,
daughter-in-law to Pan Chao.

This epitaph contains important biographical information not found in the *Hou Han Shu*. From it we learn that Pan Chao "explained" and "embellished" the work of her father and brother. In the absence of the Chinese text, these words are susceptible of two interpretations. They may refer to a commentary on the original text; and such a commentary may quite possibly have been prepared by her, for Fan Yeh mentions this kind of literary work as being included among her writings collected and edited by her daughter-in-law. (It was not until Pan Chao's pupil Ma Rung invented the device of a double line of small characters for textual comment and explanatory notes that the respective contributions of author and commentator were clearly differentiated in Chinese books.) On the other hand the words may point to just such a revision of the text itself as is suggested by Liu Chih-chi (661–721 A. D.) of the T'ang dynasty in his *Shih T'ung,*[29] which ascribes to Pan Chao's work on the *Han Shu* a greater importance than is accorded to it by most other Chinese scholars.

The second significant addition to the available biographical knowledge is that which concerns the editing of books in the imperial library. Ever since the days of great literary activity at court following the establishment of the repositories by Han Wu Ti (140–87 B. C.), the imperial libraries had been centers for editorial labor. This account of Pan Chao's work at the head of a number of selected scholars also substantiates Liu Chih-chi's delineation of her as working in the library with ten pupils, one of whom was Ma Rung, and another probably his elder brother, Ma Hsü,[30] and may explain the inclusion of "commentaries" among her literary compositions. The statement of the epitaph likewise corroborates in some degree the tradition which declares that Pan Chao rearranged, edited, and supplemented the "Biographies of Eminent Women" by Liu Hsiang (80–9 B. C.), and gave it the form in which it is listed in the bibliographical chapters of the Sui dynastic history. It also fortifies the conclusions of the Sung scholar, Tsêng Kung,[31] who accepted as genuine the traditional accounts of Pan Chao's share in the work in so far as it included biographies of women prior to her generation.

Pan Chao lived in an era of transition in regard to writing materials. "Writing on bamboo slips was still currently practised in China itself until about 200 A. D.," [32] but silk had come into general use under the Western Han dynasty, and the official announcement of the invention of paper [33] was made by Ts'ai Lun in 105 A. D. at the court of the emperor Ho. Pan Chao's work as director of editorial operations in the library may have included the supervision of the copying of old books upon the newly invented substance.[34] Her own collected works may well have been among the earliest books to be written upon paper.

The epitaph furnishes information upon still another point. In Fan Yeh's biography of her it is recorded that Pan Chao was "treated like a teacher" and "addressed in terms of respect," but no mention is made of any subjects taught by her. The epitaph mentions "poetry, eloquence, and history," which certainly cannot be a translation of the "Classical writings, history, astronomy, and mathematics" listed in the biography of the empress Têng as being the subjects taught by Pan Chao to her imperial pupil after the death of the emperor Ho (105 A. D.).

Unlike the epitaph, the long biographical sketch which also appears in the *Mémoires* must be used with caution. The style is totally different from that of a genuine Chinese historical work, and it is possible that the whole article, including the professed translation of the "Lessons for Women" which forms part of it, may have been based upon an oral traditional version.[34] The mode of expression is that of a tract written with the motive of exalting the repute of Pan Chao rather than a clear and simple statement about her life and works. This motive is particularly evident in the "translation" of the "Lessons," but there is much to suggest that the entire biography may have been similarly inspired.

Several minor statements which occur in the *Mémoires* but not in the laconic biography by Fan Yeh must be discarded as well-intentioned but historically unsound attempts to invest the dry bones of the *Hou Han Shu* record with the breath of life. The inexactitude of one of the most interesting of these additions is proved by the testimony of Pan Chao herself. The French biography portrays her as making her first steps in education by listening to her brothers at their books while she sat and sewed in the adjoining room; when her father discovered what the child was doing, he provided her with an instructress. But the child was at least thirteen years younger than her twin brothers, and was not more than nine years old at the death of her father, so that this statement can hardly be viewed as anything but a romantic detail. The fact, definitely asserted in the *Mémoires,* that after the premature death of her husband Pan Chao returned to her parental home is perhaps implied in the Chinese texts now available, but there is not even a suggestion by Fan Yeh that the husband was eligible for early official employment. The statement that Pan Ku was accustomed to give credit to his sister for her part in their historical investigations by announcing her name when reading at court any of her compositions; the description of the balcony-study of Pan Chao in the library; and the description of her as the final literary authority in a court where competition in poetry and eloquence was particularly keen, and where the emperor and his young empress were the center of a contending group of literary rivals—all these charming additions to the picture given by Fan Yeh cannot be regarded as anything else than apocryphal.

No further biographical material has been found in any later writers. Liu Chih-chi and his commentator [35] P'u Ch'i-lung (b. 1679) added nothing except a few statements about the editing of the *Han Shu.* These were practically repeated by the Sung scholar Chao Kung-wu in his essays [36] (1151 A.D.). Somewhat earlier in the same dynasty (c. 1056–1063 A.D.) Tsêng Kung [37] made his study of Liu Hsiang's "Biographies of Eminent Women," in which he outlined Pan Chao's share in the editing of the celebrated work listed in the bibliographical chapters of the *Sui Shu.* In literary collections of the following centuries the biography from the *Hou Han Shu* is usually reproduced verbatim in whole or in part. Hsieh Wu-liang in his "History of the Literature of Chinese Women" [38] (1916–18) cites the judgment of Tsêng Kung on Pan Chao's share in a later edition of Liu Hsiang's "Biographies of Eminent Women"; notes the use of quotations from added biographies in various later literary collections but not in earlier books; points out the fact that Pan Chao annotated her brother's rhythmic prose work *Yu T'ung* preserved in the *Wên Hsüan;* and finally suggests that on internal evidence the prefaces to the "Eight Tables" and the chapters on Wang Mang in the *Han Shu* are in the style of Pan Chao rather than of Pan Ku.

Western sources offer even less information. S. Wells Williams,[39] writing in 1880, apparently accepted without question the sketch of Pan Chao by the French missionaries of a century earlier, and drew upon it freely for information. It must have been from the French version that he translated the concluding sentence of the epitaph, although he did not cite his authority, for he made a mistake [40] which reveals his use of the secondary source. Other western writers [41] have usually done no more than abstract Williams' brief statement, or give the few known facts of her life from a hasty study of her biography in the *Hou Han Shu.* Favier, who wrote in 1897, acknowledged his indebtedness to the *Mémoires concernant les Chinois.* Of the works examined for the present study, only three make any mention of Pan Chao's plea for the education of girls, and Giles in *Adversaria Sinica* is the only one to perceive its full importance. Williams stated that her "Lessons" are "the only treatise on the education of women in any language, east or west, which has come down to modern times from that early era." [42]

The biography of Pan Chao is characteristically Chinese in its almost total lack of what westerners consider vital dating; reliable dates even for her birth and death are conspicuously absent.[43] It is possible, however, to supplement, and in one case to correct, such dates as are given in western works, by references to known events of ascertained date, both in her biography itself and in her various writings. Fortunately there are no myths to be excised from these sources, and this absence of legendary complications compensates for the paucity of facts.

It can be established that she was born between 45 and 51 A. D. The former extreme date is derived from her own statement in her introduction to "Lessons for Women," which was composed not earlier than 106 A. D., that more than forty years had elapsed since her marriage at fourteen years of age. The latter date is arrived at by subtracting her age at death, which was at least seventy, from 120 A. D., the last year in which she could have died. Inasmuch as Pan Chao also wrote in this introduction that she was "fortunate to have received not a little favor from (her) scholarly father" [44] who died in

54 A. D., she must have been born fairly early within this seven-year period in order to have gained any deep impression from his instruction.

Her poem "Travelling Eastward" was composed in 95 A. D. According to modern texts it is dated "the seventh year of Yung-ch'u" (113 A. D.), but the Ch'ing scholar Yüan Yüan [45] showed the error in this date. The *Wên Hsüan* commentary [46] quotes the mistaken statement of the *Tung Kuan Han Chi* that Yung-ch'u was a period in the reign of the emperor Ho. With the exception of the last one, the years of this emperor's reign are known as Yung-yüan (89–104 A. D.). The change of *yüan* 元 to *ch'u* 初, in the text of the poem could very easily have been made by some copyist who substituted the one character for the other when writing from an indistinct manuscript. The preface of the poem informs the reader that it was written while Pan Chao was en route to the post of her son who had an appointment as a district official in Ch'ang-yüan. But it is quite incredible that Ts'ao Ch'êng in 113 A. D., after he had been ennobled and made minister to the Prince of Ch'i, and at a time when Pan Chao herself was influential at court, could have received a small appointment to a district magistracy. The conclusion of Yüan Yüan that the date of the poem is the seventh year of Yung-yüan (95 A. D.) instead of *Yung-ch'u* (113 A. D.) is clearly the correct one.

The fact that Pan Chao in 95 A. D. was travelling away from the capital which she loved suggests that her appointment to the imperial library did not occur immediately after the death of her brother Ku in 92 A. D. Her absence may explain the scattering of his manuscript, which was alleged by Liu Chih-chi of the T'ang dynasty. A handwritten cyclopedia of 1677 A. D. is the authority for the statement that Pan Chao herself memorialized the throne asserting that "only your handmaiden and her two elder brothers could continue and complete the history of Han," whereupon the emperor called her to the task.[47] Her absence, in any case, could not have been very prolonged, for in the biography of the empress Têng it is stated that "from the time when the empress entered the quarters of the honorable ladies of the palace (i. e. 96 A. D.) she studied . . . under Ts'ao Ta-ku." [48]

After Pan Chao had taken up the work of historiographer at court she composed at least four of her extant works. Both the poem "The Bird from the Far West" and her memorial in behalf of her brother Ch'ao were written about 101 A. D. The occasion for the poem was the presentation to His Majesty of a large strange bird. Yüan Hung (328–376 A. D.) of the Chin dynasty said [49] that Pan Ch'ao's son Yung brought the gift "the tenth moon of the thirteenth year of the emperor Ho" (101 A. D.), but the *T'ung Chien* [50] dates the incident 102 A. D. In her memorial Pan Chao gave the age of her brother as seventy years, which according to Chinese reckoning, since he was born in 32 A. D., would date the memorial 101 A. D. Upon the presentation of her memorial the emperor ordered her brother's return,and Pan Ch'ao arrived in Lo-yang the eighth moon of 102 A. D. Her "Lessons for Women" cannot have been completed earlier than 106 A. D., for in the preface she speaks of the honor conferred upon her son; this honor, which consisted in his elevation to the rank of marquis with the privilege of wearing the Gold and Purple, was accorded him by the empress Têng, who did not assume the imperial power until 106 A. D. Pan Chao's memorial to the empress Têng was presented in the middle of the Yung-ch'u period, (107–113 A. D.). Since the retirement of General Têng is represented as having been the result of the favorable reception of this memorial, and is recorded in the imperial annals as the last entry for the year 110 A. D., the composition must have been written not later than that year.[51]

Pan Chao died between 114 and 120 A. D. The former extreme date is arrived at by adding the lowest statement of her age, namely, seventy years, to 45 A. D., the earliest possible year of her birth. The latter limit is fixed by the fact that the empress Têng, who mourned her, herself died the third moon of 121 A. D.

The semi-historical narrative (*Hui-hsiang*) *Tung Han Yen-i* states [52] that Pan Chao died at seventy years of age in the spring of 117 A. D. This would place her birth in 48 A. D. These dates come precisely midway in the periods which can be established on outside evidence, and they may quite possibly be based upon exact knowledge. The narrative is worthy of some credence because of the peculiar Chinese practice of literal reproduction of previous writings in a way which would expose a westerner to charges of plagiarism. The edition of the narrative which has been used for this study is undated, but it is certainly a late Ch'ing reprint of an earlier work which if trustworthy must have been quoting a statement of some even earlier composition now lost or unknown. The margin of error in any event is not more than three years in either direction, but until the exact statement is confirmed from some other source the vaguer estimate based on outside evidence must stand.

For a long time after the dissolution of the Han dynasty, Pan Chao was remembered by her countrymen chiefly as a moralist. Her unimpeachable behavior during the long life of widowhood which followed her husband's early death was so aptly described by Fan Yeh that his phraseology became established as the classical description of a model young widow. No one seems to have appreciated her scholarly work, with the exception of a single historical critic of the T'ang dynasty and another of the Sung.[53] The traditional accounts agree in attributing to Pan Ku the sole authorship of the *Han Shu*. The greater portion of her other writings having disappeared in the turmoil [54] of the fourth, fifth, and sixth centuries, her work was not conspicuous among the products of Han scholarship which exercised so great an influence in the creative periods of the T'ang and Sung dynasties as well as in the conventionalism which paralyzed Chinese thought under the Ming emperors. During these many centuries it was Pan Chao's moral teachings alone which made any contribution to the life of her people. The moral platitudes of her successors,[55] absurd as they are in the light of modern thought, nevertheless contain many indications of the influence of Pan Chao's "Lessons," and they doubtless met a need of their own times.

With the rise of the Era of Han Learning under the last dynasty, when critical study created a new appreciation of scholarship, Pan Chao once again began to be known for her historical researches and other literary labors as well as for her "Lessons for Women," and her name became a synonym for all that is wisest and best in the sex. Her extant writings were incorporated in various collections, and her short biography in the *Hou Han Shu* was quoted in full or in part by many compilers. Her life and works, together with those of other members of her family, were frequently suggested as subjects for the essays required in the examination system of the Ch'ing dynasty.[56] With the awakening of interest in her writings and personality, imaginative portraits of her began to appear in art. The most famous of these is found in both of the celebrated collections; the *Wu-shuang P'u* of the early part of the K'ang-hsi period (1662–1722 A. D.), and the *Chieh-tzû Yüan Hua Chuan* (1679) by Wang An-chieh. This imaginative portrait by an unknown artist became the model or the inspiration for many others in various later collections.[57] None of these portrayals rank high in comparison with the great paintings of figures in the T'ang and Sung periods, but they give evidence of a widespread interest in Pan Chao as a representative Chinese woman.

NOTES

[1] See Appendix, pp. 158-160.

[2] 曹世叔, Ts'ao's only claim for fame now rests upon his relationship to Pan Chao. See Mayers, no. 535; Giles: *Biog.*, no. 1597.

扶風, southwest of modern Si-an-fu, Shensi.

[3] The reading of the text is that she had the two personal names, Chao, 昭, and Chi, 姬, and the style of Hui-pan, 惠班. The translation is that of the comment by the Ch'ing scholar, Wang Hsien-ch'ien, 王先謙 (1842-1918), who thought that the three characters, 班一名, had crept into the text. He followed the reading of the *Hsiao Ming Lu*, 小名錄, by Lu Kuei-mêng, 陸龜蒙 (died 881-885 A.D., Giles: *Biog.*, no. 1420) of the T'ang dynasty, and of an annotation in the *Wên Hsüan*, 文選李善註, which quoting Fan Yeh's *Hou Han Shu* omitted the three characters. See also *Wên Hsüan P'ang-chêng, chüan* 12, 文選旁證, 東征賦 (c. 1800).

In an encyclopedia in manuscript, which has not been found listed in Chinese catalogues, and which was written and compiled by Lü Hsi, 呂錫 (A.D. 1677), under the title, *Mo-yüan Shêng-hsi Nang-chi*, 墨園勝奚囊集 (110 *chüan*. Gest Chinese Research Library copy, *chüan* 75), the *tzû*, 字, of Pan Chao is given as Hui-chi, and according to this same authority it was bestowed upon her by the emperor Ho.

姬 was the family surname of the Chou dynasty. See Mayers, no. 225. As suggested to the writer, it was applied to both Huang-ti and Yao, as well as to the founder of the Chou. It was given later to ladies of honorable rank, then also to beautiful women, 美人, and still later to concubines, 姬妾. See the annotation on the name of Han Wên Ti's mother, *Han Shu, chüan* 4, 文帝紀注.

[4] 有節行法度. This became a well-known classical phrase in the description of an ideal widow. Later writers credit it to this biography of Pan Chao.

[5] 東觀藏書閣. An imperial repository for books, where under imperial patronage scholars were allowed to study, cf. p. 13. While Pan Chao never enjoyed the title of court historiographer, such, in fact, was her position in the library.

[6] Astronomy and mathematics, together with the classical writings and history, were the subjects which Pan Chao taught the empress, according to the biography of the latter in *Hou Han Shu, chüan* 10, 和熹鄧皇后. Poetry, eloquence, and history are mentioned instead in the Epitaph of Pan Chao written by her daughter-in-law of which a translation is given below. Possibly all these subjects were taught.

[7] The text reads literally: "They called her *'Ta Ku'*, 大家." This was an old form for the modern *Ta Ku*, 大姑, which is an address of respect in family circles today. It corresponds in usage to "aunt" as applied to women by children of friends. In China children and adults alike would use this mode of address for an aunt who is the younger sister of the father of the children. In Han times it was a polite address for honored ladies in the palace, see *Wên Hsüan P'ang-chêng, chüan* 12, and *T'ung Chien*, 資治通鑑, *chüan* 48. Note the similar use of "uncle," pp. 77, 81.

[8] For an account of the *fu*, 賦, see Maspero: same, pp. 598-606; Margouliès:

Le Fou, pp. 1-20; Waley: *The Temple*, Intro., pp. 12-18; same, Appendix I, 137-138. Pan Chao's "The Bird from the Far West" illustrates just such an occasion. The *T'ai-p'ing Yü-lan*, 太平御覽, 雀 section, names this poem as follows: 曹大家集作大雀頌.

[9] 成. Pan Chao comments on this favor in "Lessons" (pp. 82, 91), where this son is called *Ku*, 穀, or *Tzû-ku*, 子穀.

The Han emperors appointed princes of the blood to the former feudal divisions of the country, but retained the right of the appointment of their chief ministers. So Ts'ao Ch'êng, 曹成, was appointed minister to the prince of Ch'i, 齊相. See *Han Shu*, *chüan* 19, 百官公卿表; also 廿二史劄記, *chüan* 2, 漢初諸侯王自置官屬.

[10] See p. 17; also *Hou Han Shu*, *chüan* 60a, 馬融傳, and *chüan* 24, 馬援傳 (Ma Yüan, Giles: *Biog.*, no. 1490), for 馬續. Ma Hsü's father worked with Pan Ku (see Appendix, p. 158) in the reign of Ming Ti, cf. Chapter V, note 23.

[11] 永初. In the second year of this period, *i.e.*, in 108 A. D., 鄧騭, was made 大將軍; and the last record of the fourth year, *i.e.*, 110 A. D., says that he retired, see *Hou Han Shu*, *chüan* 5, 安帝紀; also *Hou Han Shu*, *chüan* 16, 鄧禹傳 (Giles: *Biog.*, no. 1908).

On account of the death of a parent an official retired from office for a period of twenty-seven months. See the *Li Chi*, 禮記, *SBE*. Legge, XXVII, 49, 130, 160; XXVIII, 391.

Mo Ti (*chüan* 25, 節葬, A. Forke: *Mê Ti*, des Sozialethikers und seiner Schüler philosophische Werke (Berlin, 1922), chap. 25, p. 302) included the mourning period for parents in his list of mourning usages that caused poverty among the people, and so to him this was a social evil which deserved censure.

For an account of the disapproval of such mourning customs by modern young Chinese, see the translation with comments of an article by Hu Shih, by E. T. C. Werner, "Reform in Chinese Mourning Rites," *New China Review*, II, 1920, 223-247; for Chinese text, see 胡適文存, *chüan* 4, pp. 127-146, 我對於喪禮的改革.

[12] "I beg my body," 乞身.

[13] This memorial is translated in full, Chapter VI.

[14] There were four brothers of whom the general was the eldest, *Hou Han Shu*, *chüan* 10, biography of the empress Têng.

[15] The title in Chinese is 女誡七篇, *Nü Chieh Ch'i P'ien* or "Women's Lessons in Seven Sections." Translation in full, Chapter VII.

[16] 妻女. But not necessarily relatives in the first degree.

[17] 曹豐生. The Ch'ing commentator, Wang Hsien-ch'ien, thought that this statement had crept into the text by mistake, but he adduces insufficient evidence to justify discarding it. Cf. Reference given in Chapter III, note 19.

[18] Eight of these categories have been translated otherwise by Wylie (*Notes*, p. 238). The first four he denominated 賦, "Anomalous verse"; 頌 "Eulogium"; 銘, "Monumental Legends"; 誄 "Obituaries." Those here called Elegies, Essays, Treatises, and Expositions, he translated 哀, "Laments"; 辭, "Farewells"; 書, "Epistles," and 論, "Discourses." Legge (Classics, I, 206,

note) wrote that "*Lei,* 誄, is a special form of composition corresponding to the French éloge, specimens of which are to be found in the *Wên Hsüan.*"

Ting Shih, 丁氏.

[19] Wylie (*Notes,* p. 238) translated 讚, "Commendations." A collection of works, 班昭集, is mentioned in the history of the Sui dynasty, 隋書經籍志, which history was written during the T'ang dynasty. See 祖國女界文豪譜序, 漢秦, 丁氏.

Wylie: same, pp. 225-227: "The largest division of Chinese literature, termed 集, *chi,* may be not inaptly designated Belles-lettres, including the various classes of polite literature, poetry, and analytical works.——The second subdivision in this class is designated 别集, or 'Individual Collections,' consisting of the miscellaneous original productions of individual authors. Such works began to appear soon after the commencement of the Christian era, the earliest examples being published in that form after the death of the authors. Subsequent writers adopted the model——, down to the present day, this has formed one of the most prolific branches of Chinese literature.——The vast majority of such productions scarcely survive the age that gives them birth."

[20] In the biographical sketch of the Pan family in *Han Shu* (*chüan* 100, 敍傳) is preserved a short survey of the teachings of Chuang Tzû by Pan Ssû.

[21] *Hou Han Shu, chüan* 10, 和熹鄧皇后：經書兼天文算數.

[22] 安帝, Chinese reckoning.

[23] *Hou Han Shu,* same.

[24] *Hou Han Shu,* same, concluding personal comment, 論, contains the statement that 班母一說, 闔門辭事, "At one word from Mother Pan the whole family resigned." The commentator then referred to the memorial of Pan Chao (Chapter VI), the setting for which is given above.

[25] Cordier: *Bibliotheca Sinica* (Paris, 1904-1908), I, col. 56: "On lit à la page 316 de la Table générale publiée dans le deuxième tome, que les auteurs de ces Mémoires sont MM. Amiot, Cibot, Ko et Poirot. La liste des articles du P. Amiot occupe 14 colonnes—de cette Table."

Same: col. 666: "Portraits des chinois célèbres (par le Père Amiot). Tome III. 52 Biographies arrangées chronologiquement."

[26] The Ch'ing scholar Yüan Yüan, 阮元 (1764-1849), listed 175 works not catalogued in the Ch'ien-lung collection in his *Ssû K'u Wei-shou Shu-mu T'i-yao,* 四庫未收書目提要 (1822, 5 *chüan*), cf. Pelliot, *BEFEO,* II, 1902, 331.

[27] *Notes,* pp. 15-81.

[28] Same, p. 227.

[29] 劉知幾：史通 (710 A.D.). See also the bibliographical essays of the Sung scholar, Chao Kung-wu: *Chün Chai Tu Shu Chih* (1151 A.D.), *chüan* 5, 晁公武：郡齋讀書志, 前漢書.

[30] See above, p. 41.

[31] 曾鞏列女傳目錄序 (c. 1056-1063).

[32] Chavannes, "Les livres chinois," *Journal asiatique* (1905), p. 43 ff.

[33] *Hou Han Shu, chüan* 108, 蔡倫傳; Wylie: *Notes,* p. XIV, note; T. F. Carter: *The Invention of Printing in China and Its Spread Westward* (New York, 1925), pp. 3-6.

[34] In the British Museum (King's Library) besides the documents on wood

from the refuse heaps of the Han "limes" are a fragment of a Chinese silk envelope of Han times (Chavannes: *Doc.*, no 503, p. 110) and two scraps of paper, with Chinese writing, of the Eastern Han period (Chavannes: *Doc.*, nos. 707-708, p. 151).

The French missionaries may well have used a free translation of passages from the biography of the empress Têng, whose court in 109 A.D. is pictured there as a center for literary achievements, see *Hou Han Shu, chüan* 10a.

[35] 浦起龍. He made the mistake of identifying one Ts'ao Shou, 曹壽, who was collaborator in the composition of 114 *chüan* of historical writings of the Yüan-chia, 元嘉, period, first year (151 A.D.), of the emperor Huan, 桓帝, with the husband of Pan Chao, who died long before this time, see *Shih T'ung, chüan* 12, 史通通釋,古今正史注.

[36] *Chün Chai Tu Shu Chih.*

[37] *Lieh Nü Chuan Mu-lu Hsü* (see note 31).

[38] 謝无量：中國婦女文學史, pp. 27-28, cf. pp. 47-48.

Yu T'ung, 幽通賦,文選, *chüan* 14.

[39] *The Middle Kingdom,* edition 1848, I, 454, has a bare mention of Pan Chao. A fuller treatment is made in "Education of Women in China" (*Chinese Recorder,* XI [1880], 50-53) which in an abridged form appears in later editions of *The Middle Kingdom* (1883-1901), I, 573-574.

[40] He incorrectly translated the French word "le souvenir" by its English cognate "this souvenir," *Chinese Recorder,* p. 52.

[41] Mayers, no. 535; Giles: *Biog.*, no. 1597; Couling: *Encyclo. Sinica,* p. 421; *Chinese Repository,* II (1833-1834), 313-316, IX (1840), 546-547; Giles: *Hist. Lit.*, p. 108; Giles: *Adversaria Sinica,* pp. 364-365; A. Favier: *Péking. Histoire et description* (Peking, 1897), pp. 44-45; J. MacGowan: *Imperial History,* note, p. 120; Margaret Burton: *The Education of Women in China* (New York, 1911), pp. 12-17; Ida Belle Lewis: *The Education of Girls in China* (New York, 1919), p. 13; Mrs. S. L. Baldwin: *The Chinese Book of Etiquette and Conduct for Women and Girls entitled Instruction for Chinese Women and Girls, by Lady Tsao* (New York, 1900); A. C. Safford: *Typical Women of China* (Shanghai, 1899), pp. 181-183. The last two of these works claim to be translations; the first of "Lessons for Women" (see Chapter VII), and the second of a Ming edition of "Biographies of Eminent Women" (see p. 17, Chapter X, note 8). Both "translations" seem to the author of this study to be free interpretations of the Chinese texts (see also Chapter VII, note 70).

[42] *Chinese Recorder,* XI (1880), 40-53.

[43] As indicated in the appendix of this study the records make no mention of an early composition of biographies of notables of the last years of the reign of the emperor An (*i.e.*, 114-125 A.D.), during which time occurred Pan Chao's death.This may account for the omission of date by Fan Yeh.

[44] 蒙先君之餘寵.

[45] (1764-1849) Giles: *Hist. Lit.*, pp. 417-418; same: *Biog.*, no. 2573. He is quoted by his pupil Liang Chang-chü in *Wên Hsüan P'ang-chêng, chüan* 12, 梁章鉅 (1775-1849): 文選旁證, wherein Yüan dated Pan Chao's memorial to the empress Têng 107 A.D. instead of 110 A.D.

[46] 文選李善註：永初，永元.

[47] Cf. Note 3 above. *Mo-yüan Shêng-hsi Nang-chi, chüan* 75.

[48] Cf. Note 7 above.

[49] This is a quotation from Yüan Hung, 袁宏, by the Ch'ing scholar Hui

Tung, 惠棟 (c. 1750) in Wang Hsien-ch'ien's commentary on the *Hou Han Shu*. Yüan Hung wrote *Hou Han Chi*, 後漢紀 (c. 376 A.D.), from which this quotation probably was taken; see Appendix, p. 159.

[50] 通鑑, *chüan* 48.

[51] The mother of the empress became ill in the ninth moon (*T'ung Chien, chüan* 49), and died in the tenth moon, 110 A.D., see *Hou Han Shu, chüan* 5, next to the last entry in the year, 110 A.D.

[52] (繪像) 東漢演義, *chüan* 2: 四年春月 (117 A.D.). 昭卒,年七十.

[53] Liu Chih-chi and Chao Kung-wu respectively.

[54] The Imperial or Royal Libraries were burned or scattered more than once during this period, see Wylie: *Notes*, Intro., pp. XV-XVII.

[55] For example: 鄭氏女子經;宋若華女論語;女史;女訓;閨範;女範. With the exception of his inclusions of parts of the 列女傳, and the whole of the "Lessons for Women," Lan Lu-chou's *Nü Hsüeh*, 女學, belongs in this same class despite his emphasis on the need of educating girls; cf. pp. 136, 139.

[56] See *Shih-yün Ta Ch'üan*, 詩韻大全,詩腋部詠史門,曹昭.

[57] 無雙譜; 芥子園畫傳; 王安節 (see *Tz'û Yüan*, 巳, p. 194; 申, p. 5). Two such are reproduced in the *Mémoires conc. les Chinois* and in Favier's *Péking*.

BIBLIOGRAPHY

Hou Han Shu, chüan 84, biography of Pan Chao; *chüan* 40 and 47, biographies of her father and elder brothers; and *chüan* 10, biography of the empress Têng. Edition of Wang Hsien-Ch'ien, 王先謙 (長沙, 1915).

Han Shu, chüan 100, biographical sketch of the Pan family. Edition of Wang Hsien-ch'ien (Ch'ang-sha, 1900).

Writings of Pan Chao, see "List of Translations and Their Chinese Sources," Appendix, pp. 156-158.

Les Mémoires concernant les Chinois, III, 361-384, "Portrait" of Pan Chao, which comprises the translation of an epitaph that appears to be genuine, together with a highly unreliable biography and an extremely free "translation" of the "Lessons for Women." (Paris, 1778-1785).

Sui Shu, chüan 33-35, 隋書經籍志, bibliographical chapters. This very important work is discussed in Chapter XII.

Yüan Yüan, 阮元, as quoted by his pupil Liang Chang-chü, 梁章鉅 (1775-1849), in *Wên Hsüan P'ang-chêng, chüan* 12, 文選旁證. This is an excellent short paragraph on dating the poem "Travelling Eastward" from external evidence.

Liu Chih-chi: *Shih T'ung*, 史通, *chüan* 1, 8, 9, 12. Treatises on the histories written previous to his generation (661-721), which bear such marks of critical and scientific research that he may be considered an early forerunner of contemporary Chinese historical study now based largely on the work of Ts'ui Shu (1740-1816). Annotated by P'u Ch'i-lung, 浦起龍 (born 1679), and published under the title *Shih T'ung T'ung Shih*, 史通通釋 (reprint, 1885).

T'ung Chien, chüan 48, 資治通鑑. This great historical compendium by Ssû-ma

Kuang, 司馬光 (1019-1086), in the Sung period, comprising 294 *chüan*, covering a period from 403 B.C. down to the end of the "Five Dynasties" (907-960). The celebrated Sung philosopher Chu Hsi (1130-1200) and his pupils reconstructed and condensed the work of Ssû-ma Kuang, reducing it to 59 *chüan*. This latter work, entitled *T'ung Chien Kang Mu*, 通鑑綱目, was translated, without critical comment, however, by the French missionary de Mailla (13 vols. in 4, 1777-1785), and was the first great work of translation done by westerners on Chinese historical writings. According to Hirth (*Ancient China*, p. 265), and to Erich Hauer ("Why the Sinologue should study Manchu," *JRAS, NCB*, LXI [1930], 156), this great task of translation was lightened a little by the use also of the Manchu version of the *Kang Mu*.

Tsêng Kung's Lieh Nü Chuan "Preface" (c. 1056-1063; see note 31). After study of the text of the *Lieh Nü Chuan* this Sung scholar accepted the traditional account (also recorded in *Sui Shu* bibliographical chapters) that Pan Chao wrote comments on and added to the text of the "Biographies of Eminent Women" by Liu Hsiang.

Chao Kung-wu: *Chün Chai Tu Shu Chih* (1151 A.D.), *chüan* 5. (See above, note 29.) A bibliographical work of a Sung scholar.

Hsieh Wu-liang: *Chung-kuo Fu-nü Wên-hsüeh Shih*, pp. 27-28.

Tsu-kuo Nü-chieh Wên-hao P'u-hsü, selections concerning Pan Chao.

Lan Lu-chou: *Nü Hsüeh*, 藍鹿州:女學(1738). 2 vols. Extracts from classical, literary, and historical writings, divided into four parts for illustration of the virtues, sayings, conduct, and works of renowned women in former times. Without following her arrangement, he quoted entirely Pan Chao's "Lessons," and in his preface advised education of girls as fundamental for training in morals.

Li Ju-chên: *Ching Hua Yüan*, 李汝珍: 鏡花緣 (c. 1825). Hu Shih's edition, "Flowers in the Mirror," Preface, vol. II, *chüan* 42. Although this work is valueless as a novel, it contains a unique and daring "declaration of the rights of women." Cf. Hu Shih, "A Chinese Declaration of the Rights of Women," *Chinese Soc. and Polit. Science Review*, VIII (1924), 100-109.

Shih-yün Ta Ch'üan, 詩韻大全:詩腋部詠史門,曹昭. A small booklet containing suggestions for subjects for essays required in the examination system of the recent Ch'ing dynasty.

Wu-shuang P'u, 無雙譜. An art collection of which one volume is devoted to imaginative portraits of famous people. K'ang-hsi period edition.

Chieh-tzû Yüan Hua Chuan by Wang An-chieh, 王安節:芥子園畫傳. A well-known encyclopedia of painting. It contains portraits of Pan Chieh-yü, Pan Ku, Pan Ch'ao as well as of Pan Chao (1679).

Williams, S. Wells, "Education of Women in China," *The Chinese Recorder*, XI (1880), 50-53. An article based upon the observations of one long resident in China, whose opinions reflect the current ideas of the day. He used the *Mémoires conc. les Chinois* without acknowledgment.

Williams: *The Middle Kingdom*, I, 572-577. A short summary of material in the article above, which is not found in the first edition, 1848 (1883-1900).

Favier, A.: *Péking. Histoire et déscription*, pp. 44-45. A short survey of Pan Chao's life as a historian and moralist, with reference to the *Mémoires conc. les Chinois* for further information (Peking, 1897).

Giles, H. A., "Childbirth, Childhood, and the Position of Women," *Adversaria*

Sinica, p. 365. This article shows that a study of the text itself of the biography of Pan Chao was made by the writer, who is the one westerner to refer in detail to Pan Chao's plea for education of girls (Shanghai, 1914).

The Chinese Repository, II (1833-1834), 314. Not a translation of the text; probably a reflection of current ideas. This periodical is of inestimable value for the study of the years during which it appeared.

MacGowan, J.: *The Imperial History of China,* p. 120, note. A statement rather more complete than the other such brief accounts of this gifted woman listed above, notes 39-41 (Shanghai, 1906).

PART III

PAN CHAO'S LITERARY LABORS

CHAPTER V

HER SHARE IN THE *HAN SHU*

Among the historical books which contain the record of Chinese civilization, the famous *Han Shu* of the Pan family, father, son, and daughter, stands second only to the great "Historical Record" of Ssû-ma Ch'ien. The general attribution of this compilation to the son Ku is probably due to tradition based on the incomplete accounts of various later writers who ascribe to him the sole authorship. As yet no modern Chinese scholar has made a scientific study of this, the first real dynastic history, for the specific purpose of investigating the part played in its authorship by the different members of the family.

It is true that the need for such research is less urgent in the case of this Han record than with many other similar writings. It is clearly the work of the Pan family. While the son alone is generally named as the author, the father and still more the sister share as fully in its renown as they are understood to have shared in its creation. Are they not of one family, of one name, and of one blood? The modern Chinese scholar, strongly imbued with the feeling of family unity, and faced with much more vital problems concerning the historicity of yet earlier records, has been inclined to regard the task of distinguishing the respective contributions of the different members of the Pan family as one of great difficulty and comparatively little importance.

Of Pan Piao as a historian his biographer wrote that he showed great ability; a lover of books, he devoted himself whole-heartedly to study, and especially to history. Fan Yeh preserved his valuable survey of the historical records of the Chinese people up to the time of the Eastern Han, in which survey Pan Piao wrote: [1] "Of Yao, Shun, and the San-tai period the 'Book of Poetry' and the 'Book of History' give accounts.[2] Each generation had its historical board in order to take charge of its archives and its books. In its time each feudal state also had its historian. Therefore Mencius said: [3] 'The *T'ao-wu* of Ch'u, the *Ch'êng* of Chin, and the *Ch'un-ch'iu* of Lu, all are the same.' In the age of Ting Kung (509–495 B. C.) and Ai Kung [4] (494–468 B. C.) of Lu, a scholar of Lu, Tso Ch'iu-ming, discussed and arranged these writings, and composed the *Tso Shih Chuan* in thirty sections. In twenty sections he noted differences and likenesses in records, which he called the *Kuo-yü*.[5] In this way histories like the *Ch'êng* and the *T'ao-wu* were outshone and so lost; while only the *Tso Chuan* and the *Kuo-yü* were preserved. Tso also made records in fifteen sections, extending from the time of Huang-ti to the period of the Ch'un-ch'iu (722–481 B. C.), of emperors, of feudal lords, and of nobles, which he named *Shih-pên*.[6] After the period of the Ch'un-ch'iu the seven states fought among themselves, and Ch'in conquered the feudal lords. At that time there was the *Chan-kuo Ts'ê* ('Treatises of the Contending States') in thirty-three sections.

"When the House of Han rose and stabilized the empire, the *T'ai-chung Ta-fu,* Lu Chia,[7] recorded the achievements of that time; he wrote the 'Annals' of Ch'u and of Han in nine sections. In the generation of Han Wu Ti (140–87 B. C.) the *T'ai-shih-ling,*[8] Ssû-ma Ch'ien, made selections from the *Tso Chuan* and the *Kuo-yü,* and an abridgment[9] of the *Shih-pên* and *Chan-kuo Ts'ê,* and basing events on the chronology of Ch'u, Han, and other states, composed his work. This history, beginning with Huang-ti and ending with the capture of the *Lin*[10] (122 B. C.), included annals of the emperors, biographies of the hereditary nobles and of eminent men, special treatises, and tables,[11] altogether one hundred and thirty sections, of which ten have been lost."

About a hundred years later, near the end of the Western and the beginning of the Eastern Han, although several writers[12] had attempted to compose a history which should continue the "Historical Record," Fan Yeh stigmatized their products as being "so poorly written that they were unworthy to follow and continue the work of Ssû-ma Ch'ien." But he called the effort of Pan Piao, who wrote in a large number of sections (literally "several tens"),[13] a success. Liu Chih-chi,[14] the historical critic of the T'ang dynasty, stated in his *Shih T'ung* that this supplementary work of Pan Piao totalled sixty-five sections.

In the structure of his history Pan Piao departed in some respects from that of the "Historical Record." He had to discard the division of hereditary houses,[15] inasmuch as the class of feudal nobility which it included had disappeared with the unification of China. He omitted the divisions of special treatises and of tables, but retained the annals of emperors and the biographies of notable men.

Although the history written by Pan Piao is lost, some idea of his qualities as a historian may be gathered from the remarks of others, as well as from his own critical essay [16] preserved in his biography. Fan Yeh wrote that Pan Piao "gathered material both from early histories and from narratives heard on all sides of matters not reported in official documents, . . . but in his work he was cautious about the contents and systematic in literary style." The philosopher Wang Ch'ung in his "Critical Disquisitions" [17] praised his one-time teacher because "in continuing the work of the Grand Annalist (Ssû-ma Ch'ien) (he) . . . was not disturbed by sympathies, for the pen of such a writer cared for nothing but justice." Since Wang Ch'ung himself censured the scholars of his age for accepting blindly the teachings of the Western Han Confucianists, he must have been a great admirer of his master not to have seen Pan Piao's bias against any kind of Taoist opinion or indeed anything other than the most orthodox Confucian views. Pan Piao's survey of historical sources is a mere book-list of ancient authors, giving titles but no comment, except in the case of Ssû-ma Ch'ien, whose impartiality of treatment and independent opinions (all too few though they are) he condemned rather than praised. He did, however, recommend the use of critical judgment when it came to selecting a book upon which to model one's own writings, and from his statement of the defects which he found in the "Historical Record" it is possible to form a fair idea of the qualities at which he aimed in his own historical writings.

Although Pan Piao's continuation of the "Historical Record" and the greater part of his essays have long since been lost, there can be little doubt that they were employed, together with notes and comments not intended for publication, as source material by his son Ku, who like his father was a devoted student of ancient literature. The biographer of the son has left us the interesting detail that in the time of the emperor Chang (76–88 A. D.), who was a lover of literature.[18] Pan Ku lived at several different times in the Forbidden City in order to study,—sometimes spending night and day at his books. After his father's death in 54 A. D., "because Pan Piao's compilations from early histories were not detailed," Pan Ku studied quietly and thoughtfully,[19] desiring to finish the work of his father. Some one, however, laid before the throne an accusation against Pan Ku, that although a private individual he was venturing to correct and rewrite the history of the country. A mandate was sent down to the prefecture ordering that Pan

Ku be taken into custody. He was thrown into prison in the capital, and all books were taken from his home.[20]

"Because another man from Fu-fêng[21] . . . had died while imprisoned for writing falsely interpreted prophecies, Pan Ku's younger brother Ch'ao feared that Ku on examination by the local officials would not be able to make his case clear. He therefore rode in haste to the imperial city in order to petition the throne."

He obtained an imperial audience for which he prepared a statement clearly explaining the intention of Pan Ku's historical compositions. The writings themselves were also sent up by the prefect. The emperor Ming (58–75 A. D.) was so profoundly impressed by these writings that he commanded Pan Ku to join the Department of the Editing of Books in the imperial city, and appointed him to a post in the bureau of historiography.[22] With three others[23] he was commissioned to complete the imperial annals of Han Kuang-wu (25–57 A. D.); and he was also given a higher post with the task of editing the rare books of the palace.

At this time he wrote an account of the achievement of Kung-sun Shu[24] together with biographies of notable men and other records, in twenty-eight sections. Upon presenting this history to the emperor, Pan Ku was empowered to complete the edition of his former historical writings. Except for the work left by his father there existed no connected history of the period following the close of the "Historical Record." Pan Ku, who believed in the inheritance of the Fortune of Yao[25] by the House of Han, wished to present the early emperors of that line in a more favorable light[26] than that in which Ssû-ma Ch'ien had placed them. "He therefore investigated and compiled from former records; followed up and collected current reports in order to write the history of the Han dynasty." He began with a story of the miraculous birth of the founder, who having first fought his way to the position of King of Han[27] later proclaimed himself emperor (Han Kao Tsu, 202–195 B. C.), and ended with the death of Wang Mang the Usurper (9–22 A. D.), covering a period of two hundred and thirty years. He chronicled the events of twelve imperial rulers during twelve generations; "he gathered accounts of deeds and wove them together on the standard of the Five Classics.[28] From beginning to end his book was unified into one whole, following the chronological method: (I) imperial annals, (II) tables, (III) special treatises, and (IV) biographies of notables;[29] a total of one hundred chapters."

Unmolested in his researches, Pan Ku studied contentedly for more than twenty years, "beginning from the middle of the Yung-p'ing period (58–75 A. D.), when he received the command to write the history, until the middle of the Chien-ch'u period (76–83 A. D.), when it was completed. His work was considered invaluable in his time; among the learned of his generation there was none but read it."

In his history Pan Piao had retained only two of the divisions established by Ssû-ma Ch'ien: the imperial annals and the biographies of notables. Pan Ku, however, adopted as far as practicable the method of the "Historical Record" by adding tables and special treatises. The whole was organized on a chronological basis. In an edition [30] of sixteen volumes the imperial annals occupied one and a half volumes, while the biographies of eminent men and women required more than eight, or half of the whole.

Thus a total of nearly ten volumes is recorded as being the work of the son Ku. To Ku alone are also ascribed nine of the ten treatises which occupy nearly three more volumes, and which deal [31] with Mathematical Calculations in Measurement, Music, and Astronomy; Ritual and Music; Jurisprudence; Economics; State Sacrifices; the Five Elements; Geography; Land Drainage; and Literature.

Pan Ku's younger sister Chao shared in the compilation of the tenth treatise,[32] an essay on astronomy in which are preserved the Han theories of cosmogony. To Pan Chao is likewise ascribed the continuation of the eight tables which display in chronological perspective the nobles of pre-Ch'in feudal holdings; princes of the direct and collateral lines of the House of Han; [33] ministers of state; [34] princes of the empresses' families; high imperial officials; and notables of ancient times and of the Han dynasty. These occupy three and a half volumes. Thus the portion of the *Han Shu* on which Pan Chao worked, though consisting of less than one-tenth of the chapters (nine out of one hundred), amounts in bulk to nearly a quarter of the entire book.

The seventy chapters [35] of the *Han Shu* which are devoted mainly to biographies occupy slightly more than one-half of the whole. The first fifty-seven contain accounts of those who supported or opposed the founder of the dynasty in his struggle for the throne, of the imperial princes in chronological order, and of the ministers of state and officials of eminence in chronological order with contemporaries arranged in order of importance. Then follows a long chapter devoted to twenty-seven Confucian scholars. Next come two chapters portraying the life and work of six officials who sympathized with their people, and of twelve who were cruel and tyrannical in the exercise of their power. References to women are not infrequent; of a worthy man it is usual to record that he was blessed with a virtuous mother, and in the chapter following that which has just been described a woman [36] is actually included among the eleven prominent merchants whose lives are described. Two more chapters are devoted to seven wandering heroes and to seven eunuchs respectively. Three chapters differ in subject matter from the remainder of this division of the work in that they deal with the relations of the empire with neighboring peoples: the Hsiung-nu; the southwestern I; [37] the two Yüeh; [38] the Koreans; and the peoples of the western regions. One chapter contains a record of the families of the empresses, and another is devoted to the last empress of the line. The last chapter but one, divided into three sections, is devoted to Wang Mang the Usurper; and the last chapter gives in two parts an account of the Pan family,[39] thus ending the book with such information concerning the authors as a modern writer might include in a preface.

Although Fan Yeh stated in his biography of Pan Ku that in the middle part of the Chien-ch'u period [40] (76–83 A. D.) the history was completed and given to the Han world of scholars, yet in his biography of Pan Chao he recorded that "the 'Eight Tables' and the 'Treatise on Astronomy' were not finished at the time of Ku's death. Thereupon the emperor Ho (89–105 A. D.) commanded Pan Chao . . . to continue and complete the work." More curious still, he added later on "at the time when the *Han Shu* first appeared (whether in the middle of the Chien-ch'u period or later after Pan Chao's work on it was finished is not clear), most of the scholars could not comprehend it. Ma Rung . . . was allowed as a special favor to go to the library where he studied under Pan Chao. Afterwards an edict ordered Ma Rung's elder brother Hsü [41] to continue and complete Pan Chao's work."

Liu Chih-chi of the T'ang dynasty, followed by Chao Kung-wu of the Sung dynasty, assigned to Pan Chao a more important rôle than did Fan Yeh. Liu related that when Pan Ku was thrown into prison and died, his book was scattered, until his younger sister Pan Chao gathered it together, rearranged it, and continued it. Meanwhile, she had as pupils Ma Rung and others, ten men altogether. Before the "Eight Tables" and the "Treatise on Astronomy" were completed, she died, and Ma Hsü was ordered to continue them, and according to

Liu Chih-chi, Ma Hsü composed the eighth table, the "Lives of Ancient and Modern Notables." [42] But according to Hui Tung [43] (circa 1750 A.D.) the Chin scholar Yüan Hung (328–376) recorded that "Pan Ku wrote the *Han Shu* in one hundred sections (*p'ien*). Its 'Seven Tables' and the 'Treatise on Astronomy' were in (the form of) notes, without (full) text. (Ma) Hsü continued and completed them." Chou Shou-ch'ang (1814–1884) also said that Ma Hsü was ordered by mandate to continue the treatise on astronomy written by Pan Ku.

It thus seems reasonably certain that other hands than those of the Pan family have contributed at least in some degree to the book now known as Pan Ku's *Han Shu.* There can certainly be no doubt that after Pan Chao's death Hsü, the elder brother of her pupil Ma Rung, was commanded to continue and complete the work. With this exception, the rest of the work done on the history during the centuries which followed was mainly in the nature of commentation, a circumstance which is no doubt due to the fact that the plan of the record had been so definitely established by Pan Ku himself as to admit of little addition or alteration.[44]

A certain amount of information is available about these subsequent commentators. Yen Shih-ku [45] of the T'ang dynasty named in his preface twenty-three persons as commentators whose work followed that of the four original writers upon the text of the *Han Shu.* But concerning ten of these nothing more is given than the names, and the whole list is distributed in time from the Eastern Han through the later Wei, a period of five hundred years, at least two hundred and fifty of which were marked by internal anarchy accentuated by successive barbarian incursions from the north. Liu Chih-chi, writing somewhat later [46] in the same dynasty, mentioned twenty-five commentators. His list, which has not survived, presumably consisted of the twenty-three enumerated by Yen Shih-ku together with Yen Shih-ku himself and some other scholar now unknown. This unknown individual may have been a writer subsequent to Yen Shih-ku; but it is also possible that Liu Chih-chi may have included Pan Ku in the twenty-five, for some of the annotations on the chapters on geography and literature are known to have been written by the authors of the text and are invariably credited to Pan Ku alone.

Thanks to Ma Rung's device [47] of a double line of small characters for textual comments and explanatory notes, the genuineness of the text as it left the hands of Pan Chao and her pupils is substantially assured. Since the first printed edition of the history in the late tenth century (990–994 A. D.), the standard edition, including the comments of Yen Shih-ku, has been kept virtually the same even down to the present day.[48] Of the editions now available, the most complete in textual criticism and explanatory notes is that of Wang Hsien-ch'ien (1842–1918), a Ch'ing scholar who made an exhaustive textual study of the *Han Shu* in the closing years of the nineteenth century. This edition, which includes a large amount of information gathered from various previous workers in the same field, was published in Ch'ang-sha, Hunan Province, not earlier than 1900.[49]

The unique place occupied by this great history of the Western Han dynasty is due in the first place to its delimitation to a selected period of time. It is actually what it professes to be, namely, a dynastic history, the first of the long line of such works which, extending through the whole list of the dynasties of mediaeval and modern China, constitute the greatest historical record existing in any human tongue. The elder Pan appears to have been among the first to perceive that the narration of the gradual development during a historical era, and the depiction of the changing characteristics of succeeding ages, afford scope for creative literary workmanship. With this concept in mind he set to work to revise and continue the "Historical Record" of Ssû-ma Ch'ien, carefully examining and reorganizing the materials available, and writing in the continuation volume a new kind of history suited for a new age. The younger Pan, inheriting his father's work, perceived that it was still too scanty in detail for the needs of the rising generation, and embarked upon a fresh task of research for a new edition. But in the course of this research there came to him somehow, from somewhere, the idea of an independent and entirely novel creation—a unified history of the glorious House of Han. And so, after more than twenty years of patient and diligent labor, Pan Ku brought forth the first of China's dynastic histories.

Even then, the "Eight Tables" and the "Treatise on Astronomy" were incomplete, and it is possible also that the literary style was too difficult for ordinary comprehension. Meanwhile the widowed sister, Pan Chao, had probably been allowed to return to her parental home; if so, that event may have taken place even before her father's death in 54 A. D., but it is more likely to have occurred about the middle of the Chien-ch'u period (76–83 A. D.). She was a lover of learning, and it may be taken as almost certain that she helped her elder brother in his historical work; it may even have been for this very purpose that she was permitted to leave the home of her deceased husband's family.[50] It is certain that after her brother's untimely death in 92 A. D., she proceeded, on orders from the emperor Ho, to continue the "Eight Tables" and the "Treatise on Astronomy." She may have completed the tables and the treatise. It is even possible that she revised and reëdited the entire work.

NOTES

[1] Chavannes (*Mémoires,* I, pp. CCXL-CCXLI) translated this passage.

[2] For traditional texts with translation, see Legge: *Classics,* III and IV. The Chinese scholars of the Era of Han Learning, especially Yen Jo-chi, 閻若璩 (1636-1704, Giles: *Biog.,* no. 2466; Chavannes: *Mémoires,* I, p. CXIX, note), rejected the *"Ku-wên"* text of the Book of History, which with its commentaries credited to K'ung An-kuo, 孔安國 (second century B. C., Giles: *Biog.,* no. 1038), is a spurious text of the second half of the third century A. D. The *"Chin-wên"* text, except the first three sections, were short treatises composed about the eighth century B. C. (Rédaction, according to Karlgren: same, p. 50). The *Yü Kung,* 禹貢, is dated by Maspero (same, p. 100) at the end of the Western Chou dynasty; the original *Shun Tien* is lost, and in the fifth century A. D. the present text was taken from the *Yao Tien* (dated the end of the Western Chou dynasty), an introduction of twenty-eight characters added, and given the title of the lost section (Maspero: same, p. 438, note). The *Kao Yao Mo,* 皋陶謨, is dated by Maspero (same, p 436) in the seventh or sixth century B. C. Ku Chieh-kang (*Ku Shih Pien,* p. 134, Intro., p. 58) dates these sections of the Book of History as late as the period of the Contending States, and credits anything in the Book of History or the Book of Poetry, giving historicity to the legends of Yao, Shun, and Yü, and to the Golden Age to Confucian editors of these works.

[3] 楚之檮杌, 晋之乘, 魯之春秋, 其事一也.

Mencius IV, II, 21, 2, Legge: *Classics,* II, 327. Text of this quotation in *Hou Han Shu* shows a slightly different arrangement from that in Legge. Cf. Maspero: same, p. 589.

[4] 定公; 哀公.

左傳. The present arrangement of the *Tso Chuan* as a commentary on the *Ch'un-ch'iu* is considered to have been the work of Liu Hsin and his collaborators of the Han dynasty, or of Tu Yü, 杜預 (222-284 A.D., Giles: *Biog.,* no. 2072) of the third century A. D. Karlgren came to the conclusion (same, p. 65) that "it has nothing to do (at least directly) with the school of Lu, as its grammar is totally different from that of Confucius and his disciples and of Mencius. It is later than the year 468 B. C. (the last year treated in the work), and in any case anterior to 213 B. C., probably to be dated between 468 and 300 B. C."

Maspero from a historical study of the *Tso Chuan* arrived independently at practically the same date for the work: "de deux parties: (I) une histoire générale de la Chine de 722 à 450—, composée vers fin du IVe siècle a.C., et découpée au temps des Han, lors de la publication, pour servir de commentaire au *Tsch'ouen Ts'ieou*: (II) un commentaire rituel sur le *Tsch'ouen Ts'ieou*, de la même époque ou un peu plus récent." (See same, p. XII.)

If these conclusions are correct, then Tso Ch'iu-ming or Tso-ch'iu Ming, 左丘明, a scholar of Lu (see Legge: *Classics*, I, 182), did not write the *Tso Chuan*, nor the *Kuo-yü*, and this statement by Pan Piao, like a similar one by Ssû-ma Ch'ien, cannot be true. Cf. Karlgren: same, pp. 22-23, 49; Chavannes: same, pp. CXLVII-CL. For the text and translation of the *Tso Chuan*, see Legge: *Classics*, V.

5 國語. Karlgren (same, p. 64) dates pre-third century B.C., of the same general period as that of the *Tso Chuan*. Cf. Chavannes: same, pp. CXLVII-CL; Maspero: same, p. 595.

6 世本. Chavannes: *Mémoires*, I, p. CXLI with footnote. "The Genealogy of the Hereditary Nobles." This book has been lost, but has been largely reconstructed from numerous citations in various later collections. It was an important source used in the *Shih Chi* by Ssû-ma Ch'ien who failed to cite it by title. It is listed in the bibliographical section of the *Han Shu* (*chüan* 30).

戰國策. Karlgren (same, p. 63) dates third century B.C. By an unknown author (Maspero: same, p. 595). See Chavannes: same, p. CLII.

7 太中大夫陸賈. Giles: *Biog.*, no. 1404; *Shih Chi, chüan* 97; *Han Shu, chüan* 43; Chavannes: same, pp. CLVII-VIII. A native of Ch'u, and a great statesman and author of the Han period, 楚漢春秋.

8 太史令. Title of 司馬遷. See Chavannes: same.

9 刪. Chavannes translated (same, p. CCXL) "fit une récension."

10 Or *ch'i-lin*, 麒麟. Han Wu Ti. Yüan-shou, 元狩, first year. Cf. *Shih Chi, chüan* 12, p. 5a; *chüan* 130, p. 12a; *Han Shu, chüan* 6, 元狩, first year and 太始, second year. For dates of the *Shih Chi*, see Liang Ch'i-ch'ao: same; Chavannes: same. Although Chavannes dated the capture of the *ch'i-lin* 122 B.C. on p. XXIII, he erroneously placed this event in 95 B.C. on p. CCXL. Wang Hsien-ch'ien's edition of the *Hou Han Shu* (*chüan* 40a) has this same mistake, as does also the Ch'ien-lung (1739) edition (*chüan* 70).

11 本紀, 世家, 列傳, 書, 年表.

12 The commentary lists among the names those of Liu Hsin and Yang Hsiung, see Liang Ch'i-ch'ao: same, p. 47; *Shih T'ung T'ung Shih, chüan* 12, 古今正史. Cf. p. 17.

13 數十篇.

14 661–721 A.D. *Shih T'ung* first issued 710 A.D. *Shih T'ung T'ung Shih, chüan* 12. Cf. Also *Hou Han Shu, chüan* 40a, commentary on the passage.

15 *Shih-chia*, 世家. *Shu, piao, chi, chuan,* 書, 表, 紀, 傳.

16 *Hou Han Shu, chüan* 40a. (Cf. Liu Chih-chi: *Shih T'ung T'ung Shih, chüan* 8, 書事; Chavannes: same, I, pp. XLIX ff.)

17 王充: 論衡, 佚文 (*chüan* 20), the translation by Forke: *Lun-Hêng* (pp. 279-280) in the edition printed in Berlin, 1911, but omitted (Chapter IX, note 73) in the edition of 1907.

18 See p. 28.

19 潛精, "immersing himself" in, and 研思, "grinding at" his studies.

20 Probably his own writings, but Hui Tung (c. 1750 A.D.) quoted Yüan

Hung: "Sought out, collected, and sealed up books of his home," *Hou Han Shu, chüan* 40a, 注.

[21] The home prefecture of Pan Ku.

[22] *Lan-t'ai Ling-shih,* 蘭臺令史 (Giles: *A Chinese-English Dictionary,* ed. 1912, no. 6721); see *Shih T'ung T'ung Shih, chüan* 11, 史官建置, and *Tz'û Yüan,* 申, p. 107.

[23] See Appendix, p. 158. Beside these three, according to his biography (*Hou Han Shu, chüan* 24) Ma Yen, 馬嚴, elder cousin of the empress Ma, nephew of the celebrated general Ma Yüan, 馬援, and father of Ma Rung, after an imperial audience in 72 A. D., was ordered to work with Pan Ku and others.

[24] 公孫述 (d. 36 A. D.). An aspirant for the imperial throne, who in control of Ssûch'uan was himself conquered and his family exterminated by the founder of the Eastern Han dynasty. (See Giles: *Biog.*, no. 1033.)

[25] 運. The fortunate or happy destiny which Yao possessed. As Chavannes (*Mémoires,* I) indicated, Ssû-ma Ch'ien displayed in personal notes, vital though all too brief, a scepticism towards the traditional legends concerning the origin of his race. Fan Yeh, like all the other writers of the dynastic histories, was too blinded by the exaggerated respect for antiquity fostered by the scholars of the Confucian lore to follow his great predecessor, Ssû-ma Ch'ien.

[26] For a criticism of this, see Liu Chih-chi: same, *chüan* 8, 書事.

[27] 漢中, Han-chung. Its territory bordered on the Han River, at the far-distant southern mouth of which has grown up the modern metropolis known as Han-kow, 漢口.

[28] Literally "alongside he threaded them on the woof of the Five Classics."

[29] 帝紀, 表, 志, 列傳.

Pan Ku altered the titles of two divisions of the "Historical Record" without changing their content: 本紀 became 帝紀; 書 became 志. He retained the exact number of *chüan* in each division established by Ssû-ma Ch'ien: 12, 10, 8, and 70 respectively, although inverting the number of tables and treatises.

[30] Containing text of *Han Shu* and annotations by Yen Shih-ku, 顏師古 (581-645).

[31] 律歷, 禮樂, 刑法, 食貨, 郊祀, 五行, 地理, 溝洫, 藝文. Berthold Laufer ("Multiple Births Among the Chinese," *New China Review,* II, 1920, p. 110) wrote that "Beginning from the Annals of the Former Han Dynasty (漢書), a novel departure from the old practice was instituted inasmuch as the natural events were detached from the general narrative to be relegated to a special section, entitled 'Records relating to Five Elements' (五行志). The majority of official annals have adopted this practice. These chapters contain most interesting information, not for the historian, but for the scientist. They give detailed lists, with exact reference to date and place, of great catastrophes, such as famines, droughts, locust pests, inundations, hailstorms, landslides, earthquakes, conflagrations, excessive cold, electric storms in the winter, etc., abnormal phenomena and monstrosities in domestic animals and human beings, cases of insanity, abnormal customs and practices, etc."

Commentaries on 地理志 and 藝文志 were written by authors of the

Han Shu. They are credited to Pan Ku in all traditional accounts.

[32] 天文志, 八表.

[33] Their surname was *Liu,* 劉, see p. 5. Fill two Tables.

[34] Fill two Tables.

[35] A *chüan,* 卷, or roll in an ancient book corresponds to a chapter or section or part in a modern book. A *chuan* 傳 or biography may occupy a whole *chüan* or only part of one.

[36] 巴寡婦清.

[37] 夷. Uncivilized peoples of the southwest regions.

[38] 粵. Two peoples of the south and southeast with whom the Chinese had intermarried after their conquest by Han Wu Ti.

[39] See Chapter III.

[40] According to the commentary, at the beginning of *chüan* 100 (*Han Shu,* Wang Hsien-ch'ien edition): "Ancient copies of the *Han Shu* stated that Pan Ku presented his work in the Yung-yüan period, sixteenth year (73 A. D.), fifth moon, twenty-first day, but modern copies do not contain any entry of a year, moon, or day." Cf. *Ssû-k'u Ch'üan Shu Tsung-mu,* 四庫全書總目 first ed.), *chüan* 45, p. 18, where the date of presentation is stated to have been 67 A. D. Both the editors of the *Ssû...k'u* and Wang Hsien-ch'ien question the accuracy of the date given for presentation.

[41] Cf. p. 41. The Ma brothers perhaps owed their preferment in part to their family connection with the later Han emperors. The daughter of the great general Ma Yüan had been consort of the emperor Ming (58-75 A. D.) and died in the very year of Ma Rung's birth (79 A. D.). The biographies of the general and the empress (*Hou Han Shu, chüan* 24 and 10) have been sketched by Giles (nos. 1490 and 1471) and by Mayers (nos. 478 and 469). According to Wang Hsien-ch'ien (*Hou Han Shu, chüan* 16, p. 14a), quoting the Ch'ing scholar, Hui Tung, in 109 A. D., Ma Rung joined the household of General Têng Chih, elder brother of the empress Têng, and the next year he was made a *lang-chung,* 郎中.

[42] Chao I, 趙翼, the Ch'ing scholar, in his "Notes on the Twenty-two Histories," 廿二史劄記 (*chüan* 2), wrote that the *Han Shu* is the result of the work of four persons. While he does not give names in this connection, he leaves the impression that the four were the Pan family, father, son, and daughter, and Ma Hsü.

[43] Wang Hsien-ch'ien quoted these scholars in an annotation on the scope of Ma Hsü's scholarship, *Hou Han Shu, chüan* 24, biography of Ma Yen, 馬嚴.

周壽昌, *Chinese Biog.,* p. 542.

[44] See Liu Chih-chi: same, *chüan* 12.

[45] 顏師古, 581-645 A. D. (see Giles: *Biog.,* no. 2472).

[46] Liu Chih-chi, 661-721 A. D.

[47] See Giles: *Biog.,* no. 1475.

[48] See discussion of the trustworthiness of the *Hou Han Shu* by Hirth (*China and the Roman Orient,* pp. 7-10).

[49] 王先謙: 前漢書集解 (1900). See Appendix, pp. 155 ff.

[50] As is well known it is not even yet customary for the young widow to return to her parental home to live after the death of her husband. A semi-historical narrative of the Han dynasty, 東漢演義, follows the account of

the death of Pan Ku with the statement that Pan Chao's husband died early, and while newly a widow she turned to study and to work on the *Han Shu*, 早卒而昭居新寡. Wang Hsien-ch'ien, in commenting on 早卒, did not think that the usual impression that Pan Chao was very early left a widow is necessarily correct. See *Hou Han Shu*, biography of Pan Chao, *chüan* 84.

BIBLIOGRAPHY

Han Shu, edition of 1900 by Wang Hsien-ch'ien (1842-1918), text with commentaries, thirty-one volumes, 100 *chüan* of which twenty are divided into two parts, introductory *chüan*, preface dated Changsha, 1900. Also an earlier edition containing only the text and comments by Yen Shih-ku (581-645 A.D.), sixteen volumes, 100 *chüan*.

Hou Han Shu, edition of 1915 by Wang Hsien-ch'ien, text with commentaries, preface dated Changsha, 1915, *chüan* 40, 47, and 84, biographies of Pan Piao, Pan Ku, Pan Ch'ao, and Pan Chao.

Liu Chih-chi: *Shih T'ung*, edition of 1885 by P'u Ch'i-lung, *chüan* 1, 8, 12.

Chao Kung-wu: *Chün Chai Tu Shu Chih* (1151 A.D.), *chüan* 5.

Chavannes: *Mémoires*, I. The comments on the *Han Shu*, etc., and the translation of Pan Piao's criticism of Ssû-ma Ch'ien (Appendix II).

Liang Ch'i-ch'ao: *Yao Chi Chieh-t'i Chi Ch'i Tu-fa.*

Chao I: *Êrh-shih-êrh Shih Cha-chi*, *chüan* 2.

(*Hui-hsiang*) *Tung Han Yen-i* (undated). A semi-historical popular account in simple style of the events of the period of the Eastern Han dynasty, *chüan* 2. Ch'ing edition (see above, Chapter IV, note 52).

CHAPTER VI

Two Memorials

A. THE PACIFICATOR OF DISTANT COUNTRIES

Memorial in Behalf of Pan Chao's Elder Brother Ch'ao (circa 101 A.D.)

Your handmaiden's [1] own [2] elder brother, Governor-general of the Western Regions, the Marquis of Ting-yüan,[3] (Pan) Ch'ao, has had the good fortune to obtain for his trifling achievement the special distinction of a great reward: he has been ennobled a marquis, a rank with an allowance of two thousand piculs [4] of grain. This imperial favor truly far surpasses what a small official ought to receive.

When Ch'ao first went (beyond the frontier), he dedicated himself, body and life (to his work), in the hope of accomplishing a small service in order to demonstrate his devotion. Consequently at the time of the revolt against Ch'ên Mu,[5] although communications were interrupted, Ch'ao by himself alone made the rounds of the Western Regions, and informed [6] all the states; used their soldiers; and in every battle unhesitatingly took the lead. Often wounded by metal weapons,[7] he did not flee from death itself. Relying upon the divine power [8] of the Throne, he has attained a prolonged life in the sandy desert until now there have accumulated thirty years.

He has been separated from those of the same bone and flesh [9] (so that they) no longer recognize each other. All those who went out with him, both high and low in rank, have already passed away; Ch'ao is extremely aged. He is now seventy; decrepit, old, and ill; head without a single black hair; both hands powerless; [10] ears and eyes no longer keen; and able to walk only by leaning upon a staff. Although he desires to exert himself to the utmost in order to repay the imperial favor, he is hard pressed by old age, and like a horse or dog (that has long served its master) he has lost his teeth.

Now the barbarian tribes [11] are stubborn by nature, and rude to the old. Ch'ao, moreover, from morning to evening expects death [12] (at any moment). If it is a long time before he is relieved, (your handmaiden) fears [13] that there will be a springing up of conspiracies to incite a spirit of rebellion and disorder. Now all the great ministers at court care only for things of the moment,[14] but no one of them is willing to plan for the future. Should trouble arise among the barbarian soldiers, Ch'ao's physical strength would not be able to follow the wishes of his heart. And it may happen that from the point of view of the dynasty the work of several generations would be injured; and from the point of view of the people the strenuous labors of a faithful official would be lost. This would surely be grievous.

For that reason from his post ten thousand *li* away Ch'ao himself has made plain his bitterness and his anxiety,[15] and with outstretched neck has been longing for his return. Up to the present for the last three years [16] he has received no official mandate. Your handmaiden has heard it said that the ancients had the following custom: [17] at fifteen a man received the arms of the soldier, at sixty he returned them; and also he had periods of rest with no responsibility. Because Your Majesty has governed the empire with utmost filial piety, (the Throne) has won the happy hearts of ten thousand tributary states, and has not neglected officials of small kingdoms.[18] How much less can (Your Majesty) fail Ch'ao who has obtained the rank of marquis?

In behalf of Ch'ao (your unworthy subject) dares face death in order to beg commiseration for him. She pleads for his release during the remaining years of his life, that he may return alive and see again the Imperial Court. Thus the state will never have disturbances on the frontiers, and the Western Regions will not have troublesome revolts. At least may Ch'ao receive the grace which Wên Wang [19] bestowed upon the (unearthed) bones by burial; [20] or the pity which Tzû-fang [21] had for the aged (horse). The "Book of Poetry" says: [22]

> "The people are indeed heavily burdened,
> But perhaps a little relief may be secured for them.
> Let us cherish the Middle Kingdom
> To secure the repose of the Four Quarters of the Empire."

(Pan) Ch'ao has sent a letter in which while yet alive he bids farewell to your handmaiden. He fears that the two of us will never see each other again. Your handmaiden is really distressed about Ch'ao. He gave his vigorous years in loyal service in the sandy desert,[23] and now exhausted by old age for him to die in the distant wilds would be heartbreaking.

Unless (Your Majesty) saves and helps Ch'ao he will one morning encounter a sudden change. (In such an event) may the (Pan) family hope to receive the same favor (as that granted) because of the petitions made beforehand by Chao Mu[24] and by Wei Chi. Unsophisticated and stupid, ignorant of the great principle of righteousness, in thus addressing[25] (Your Majesty) your handmaiden is guilty of great transgression in the use of a sacred name.

B. YIELDING PLACE TO OTHERS

A Memorial[26] to the Empress Têng (circa 110 A.D.)

Below the steps of the Throne, (the unworthy writer) prostrates herself before the Great Empress, the beauty of whose overflowing virtue fills up the measure of the imperial rule of Yao and Shun.[27] (Your Majesty) opens the gates to the four quarters of the empire, takes knowledge of all events in the four directions,[28] and chooses (to follow) unintelligent words of irresponsible persons who offer deliberations of straw and stubble.[29] Your handmaiden Chao is both stupid and old, (but she is fortunate)[30] to happen (to live in this) prosperous and brilliant age, and dares not but reveal her inmost self,[31] if only to render (the minutest service—a proportion of) one to ten-thousand.

Your handmaiden has heard it said that there is no virtue greater than the custom of yielding place[32] (to others). Therefore the Great Classics[33] narrate its excellence, and the gods of Heaven and Earth shower blessings (upon those who practise it). In ancient times I and Ch'i[34] withdrew from the State (rather than dispute its inheritance); and the empire[35] bows before their exalted self-denial.[36] T'ai-po turned away from the Pin[37] State, and Confucius acclaimed his threefold refusal (of its throne). Consequently the luster of their outstanding virtue has spread their fame to future generations. The "Analects"[38] say: "(If a ruler) is able to govern his state by courtesy and by yielding place (to others), what difficulty will he have in administration?" From these we may say that sincerity in yielding place[39] (to others) is the farthest reaching (virtue).

At this time (Your Majesty's brothers), the Four Uncles,[40] maintaining their loyalty and filial piety, seek to retire [41] (from office), but because the frontiers are not yet peaceful, (Your Majesty) is opposed and will not grant permission. (If the Four Uncles be not allowed to retire, when) in the future there are trivial episodes [42] added to this (occasion, then your unworthy subject) sincerely fears that they may never again gain the name and fame for yielding place (to others).

Because (your handmaiden) has come to this conclusion, she ventures at the risk of her life (to write this opinion to Your Majesty. To reach this conclusion your humble servant) has exhausted her stupid self, both in mind and in emotions.[43] Although she herself knows that her words are not worth the consideration (of Your Majesty), nevertheless they reveal the deep feeling [44] of your handmaiden, worm that she is.

NOTES

[1] This humble designation for herself by Pan Chao, as well as the extremely depreciative expressions elsewhere, especially at the close of the memorial, was the conventional usage in a petition to the throne in the age in which she lived.

[2] The Chinese text reads 同產, "born of the same mother."

[3] According to the *Tung Kuan Han Chi* this locality was in the prefecture of Han-chung (the territory where the founder of the Han dynasty became King of Han, and the native place of Chang Ch'ien, see *Shih Chi, chüan* 123), on the southern border of the modern province of Shensi, see commentary in *Hou Han Shu* biography of Pan Ch'ao, *chüan* 47. It seems much more reasonable, however, that the title became the designation of the locality from which Pan Ch'ao's remuneration was drawn than that his title was taken from the name of the district, strangely enough, still known as Ting-yüan, 定遠 (see *Tz'û Yüan,* 寅, p. 47).

[4] Cf. *Tz'û Yüan,* 子, p. 110; Chavannes: *Mémoires,* II, 527.

[5] 陳睦. Ch'ên Mu was Pan Ch'ao's predecessor, holding the title of 都護 Tu-hu, see *Hou Han Shu, chüan* 47, Pan Ch'ao's biography, and *chüan* 88, 西域傳. He was killed in 76 A. D. (see *chüan* 2), and Pan Ch'ao was appointed in 91 A. D.

[6] Made the position of China as represented by himself clear to the several states, and thus held their friendship and submission.

[7] For a description of the equipment and life of the Han troops in the Western Regions see Chavannes: *Documents chinois,* Intro., pp. IX ff. On pp. XV-XVI he wrote that the discoveries by M. Aurel Stein "seem to prove that the garrison troops in the time of the Han were armed with cross-bows and not with bows. The arrows must also have been for cross-bows. They are of two kinds—either type could have been fitted with the bronze tips of which M. Stein himself was able to collect many specimens (see *Ruins of Desert Cathay,* London, 1912, I, 366; II, 65, 127). The arrows were kept in quivers.

We have no special information about the swords, and their actual form must be studied on the Shantung bas-reliefs. (See Chavannes: *La sculpture sur pierre en Chine.*) These troops were armed with swords and cross-bows." Translated by Mm. Chavannes and H. Wilford House, *New China Review,* IV (1922), 431 ff. See also *Serindia,* pp. 758-759; Chavannes: *Documents,* no. 39-40; B. Laufer: *Chinese Clay Figures,* Part I (Chicago, 1914), Chapter 3.

[8] For the character, 靈, on the Honan bone relics, see L. C. Hopkins, "The Shamen or *Wu,*" *New China Review,* II (1920), 423-433.

[9] "Bone and flesh" instead of western "flesh and blood."

[10] Here 仁 is used in the realm of the physical.

[11] Chavannes (*Mémoires,* I, 68) noted that "les Ti, 狄, les Man, 蠻, les Jong, 戎, et les I, 夷 (sont)—les peuples barbares des quatre points cardinaux."—(p. 149) "les Man sont les barbares du sud et les I ceux de l'est." Maspero (same, p. 5, note 1) remarks that ancient Chinese has no general term to express the idea of "barbarians."

Huai-nan Tzû wrote that the Ti "despise the old (man) and respect the strong (one)," 賤長, 貴壯, 淮南 鴻烈解 (Preface, 1580 A. D.), *chüan* 1.

[12] 入地. Literally "to enter the ground."

[13] 恐. It is feared by the writer, his sister.

[14] Wang Hsien-ch'ien suggested that 一切 means 權宜, "temporary."

[15] 自陳苦急. This term refers to Pan Ch'ao's petition, *Hou Han Shu, chüan* 47; cf. p. 31.

[16] According to the biography of Pan Ch'ao in *Hou Han Shu* he wrote his petition in the twelfth year (100 A. D.), and he arrived in Lo-yang in the fourteenth year, eighth moon, dying the following moon (102 A. D.). This then would be the three years. But according to the commentary Pan Ch'ao sent his petition by his son Yung along with a tribute-bearing train from Parthia. The *Hou Han Shu, chüan* 88, 西域傳, records that this nation sent tribute in the thirteenth year (101 A. D.). The *T'ung-chien,* 通鑑 (*chüan* 48), dates Pan Ch'ao's petition the fourteenth year of Ho Ti (102 A. D.), but the commentator noted that there was some discrepancy in dates as these events did not fit into a proper chronological order, because Pan Ch'ao arrived in Lo-yang in the fourteenth year, eighth moon, dying the following moon (102 A. D.), according to the *Hou Han Shu.* Since in the petition of the sister she said that Pan Ch'ao was seventy years old, and since he was born in 32 A. D., her petition, then, according to Chinese reckoning of age, was written in 101 A. D.

[17] The *Chou Li,* 周禮 (*chüan* 3, 地官司徒,卿大夫), says that within the cities and towns, 國中, when the young man reached a height of seven feet (the foot measure was nine English inches, see Chapter VIII, note 38), he was enlisted and served until he was sixty years old; in the suburbs and rural districts, 野外, when a height of six feet, he was enlisted, and served until he was sixty-five years old. According to the commentator this meant in the first case from twenty to sixty years of age, and in the second case from fifteen to sixty-five years of age. Thus Pan Chao used the second date for the enlistment age and the first for the retirement age.

[18] For 小國, see Hirth: *Ancient History,* p. 68; Mencius, I, II, 3 and 15; *Classics,* II, 155 and 176.

[19] For Wên Wang, 文王, see Giles: *Biog.,* no. 2308; Hirth: same, pp. 57-62; *Shih Chi, chüan* 4, 周本紀; Book of Poetry, *Classics,* IV, III, I, Decade of King Wan, 427-464; *Li Ki,* Legge: *Classics, SBE,* XXVII, 343-363, Intro., pp. 22-23.

[20] See *Hsin Hsü,* section under *chüan* 5, 新序, 雜事, *Hsin Shu,* section under *chüan* 7, 新書, 論城; for translation see J. J. M. de Groot: *The Religious System of China* (Leyden, 1892-1894), III, 915-917, both (1) *Hsin Hsü* by Liu Hsiang, and (2) *Hsin Shu* by Chia I, 賈誼 (201-169 B.C.; Giles: *Biog.,* no. 321; *Han Shu, chüan* 48; *Shih Chi, chüan* 84). From such traditions doubtless the burial of the uncared-for corpses came to be regarded through all dynasties as the business of the government. According to one account, in preparing the foundation for a building, some bones of the dead were unearthed, whereupon Wên Wang had them reïnterred with proper ceremonies.

[21] Mentioned as a teacher (*Shih Chi, chüan* 44, 魏世家) of a prince of the House of Wei. One day seeing an old horse which the prince had abandoned, T'ien Tzû-fang, 田子方 (*Chinese Biog.,* p. 197), took it in charge and cared for it until it died, saying that the horse having been used while it was strong, should be cared for in its old age; see commentary in *Hou Han Shu.*

[22] *Classics,* IV, III, II, 9, 495, Legge makes 中國 refer to the capital, but here Pan Chao seems to mean the "Middle Kingdom," while the "Four Quarters" refer to the border lands, especially the Western Regions.

[23] This gives another item to add to the story of the Desert of Gobi in Chinese life, history, and poetry.

[24] 趙母. This mother petitioned the king (259 B.C.) not to send her son out in command of an expedition, as she did not think that he would be able to succeed. The king would not agree, but he promised the mother that if the son failed, the mother and family would not be punished for the crime done. For the story see "Biographies of Eminent Women," *chüan* 3, 列女傳; and *Shih Chi, chüan* 81, 列傳第 21.

衛姬. In the Ch'un-ch'iu period this concubine of a ruler of a small state (685-643 B.C.) interceded to prevent her native state Wei, 衛, from being invaded by forces from Ch'i, 齊. She so far succeeded in her plea that she was raised in rank among the women of the palace. For the story see the "Biographies of Eminent Women," *chüan* 2.

[25] For French translations of this memorial see Chavannes, *T'oung Pao,* VII (1906), 240-243, and Georges Margouliès: *Le Kou-wên chinois* (Paris, 1926), pp. 106-109.

[26] The setting for this memorial is given in Chapter IV, p. 41. In the memorial there are a dozen or so words and phrases which without doubt show conventional usage in a petition to the throne. As such they are the reflection of the age in which Pan Chao lived rather than the portrayal of her personality. Note 伏; 陛下; 采 . . . 慮; 妾; 愚; 敢; 萬一; 昧死; 言不足采; 蟲螘; 赤心.

[27] The traditional Golden Age; pp. 5-7. Also see Hirth: *Ancient History,* p. 55; and Chavannes: *Mémoires,* I, p. CXL. Cf. Analects 8:20, of which Legge (*Classics,* I, 215) wrote that "The style of the whole chapter is different from that of any previous one, and we may suspect that it is corrupt."

[28] See the Book of History, II, I, 5: 15, *Shun Tien, chüan* 1, Legge: *Classics,* III, 41-42; 闢四門—達四聰, "(how) to throw open all the doors (of communication between the court and the empire) and sought—to hear with the ears of all."

[29] The theory that the Will of Heaven is manifested in the Will of the

people, cf. Book of Poetry, *Classics,* IV, III, I, 9:2; same, III, II, 9:1, 459, 495.

[80] The phrases in parenthesis are added for clearness of meaning in translation.

[81] Literally "unroll her liver and her gall."

[82] Compare the use of 謙讓 in "Lessons," pp. 83, 88 ff. See an excellent essay on this subject by Ts'ui Shu, 崔述 (1740-1816), the late eighteenth century historical critic, who made the point that such courteous yielding is possible only when the two parties are on equal footing, see 崔東壁遺書, 無聞集, 爭論, *chüan* 2.

[83] According to tradition these "Great Classics," 三墳五典, of ancient China were lost long before Liu Hsiang, and his son Hsin catalogued the books of the Han dynasty. They are mentioned in the *Tso Chuan, chüan* 38, Chao Kung, 昭公, twelfth year, Classics, V, 638, 641.

[84] 伯夷叔齊. See Giles: *Biog.,* no. 1657; Mayers, no. 543. For some material to supplement Giles, see L. C. Arlington, "Sinological Notes," *New China Review,* IV (1922), 135. See also *Chinese Biog.,* pp. 283, 523: *Shih Chi, chüan* 61. (For a modern Chinese study of the *Shih Chi,* see Liang Ch'i-ch'ao: same, pp. 23-66.) A summary of the story of the two brothers may also be found in the *Tz'û Yüan;* Legge: *Classics,* I, 181, note. Also "they were celebrated for their purity, and aversion to men whom they considered bad, but Confucius (Analects 5:22) brings out their generosity." Cf. Mencius, I, II, 22:3, *Classics,* II, 194; Analects 7:14, *Classics,* I, 199, note 14; Analects 16:12, 18:8, pp. 315, 336.

For an account of a Han stone monument to these brothers, sons of one of the last kings of the Shang dynasty period, see B. L. Ancell, "An Ancient Monument," *New China Review,* I (1919), 233-236.

Wang Ch'ung (*chüan* 10, "Mencius Satirized," 論衡, 刺孟篇) criticized the self-denying death of these worthies credited as a praiseworthy act by his generation of Han Confucianists (see Forke: *Lun-Hêng* [ed. 1907], p. 430).

Ku Chieh-kang (*Ku Shih Pien,* pp. 43-44, 132-133), writes: 伯夷, 叔齊, 態度不明, 恐不可信. Their *jang* came forth from conscience, the *t'ui-jang,* 推讓, or unselfishness of a family, not between prince and minister. Out of this in the middle of the Contending States period rose the *shan-jang,* 禪讓, or principle of abdication (p. 7), and was by the Confucianists ascribed to the Golden Age.

[85] This use was projecting Han geography and customs back into the Shang period.

[86] Today a motto over many an official's office, 公正廉明, has brought the letter of this old Chinese idealism down to the present day.

[87] 太伯. For summary of the story of his threefold refusal, see L. C. Arlington, "Sinological Notes," *New China Review,* IV (1922), 138-139. Cf. Mencius, I, II, 15:1, Legge: *Classics,* II, 176; Analects 8:1, *Classics,* I, 207; Hirth: *Ancient Hist.,* pp. 68-69. They really left Chou not Pin, 邠, but because Pin was the home of their ancestors (Maspero: same, p. 48, note 3, pp. 53, 55), it is used here. Pin was near the western boundary of the modern province of Shensi; for life in Pin, see the Odes of Pin, Book of Poetry,

I, XV. *Classics,* IV, 226-243, with comments by J. Edkins, *JRAS, NCB,* XXIV (1889-1890), 260-261.

[38] Analects 4: 13, Legge (*Classics,* I, 169) translated: "Is (a prince) able to govern his kingdom with complaisance proper to the rules of propriety, what difficulty will he have?"

Pan Chao in quoting added the phrase, 於從政, between 國 and 乎, which is not found in Legge (cf. Chapter VII, note 69).

[39] *Tso Chuan* (*chüan* 15, Wên Kung, first year, 左傳文公) has 卑讓, 德之基也, translated by Legge (*Classics,* V, 230): "Humble complaisance is the foundation of virtue."

[40] A polite form of address for the brothers of the empress. Cf. Chapter IV, note 7. See the biography of General Têng, *Hou Han Shu,* 鄧騭傳, *chüan* 16, and compare with the biography of the empress, 和熹鄧皇后注, *chüan* 10a. In the fourth year of the emperor An, 110 A. D., on account of the illness of their mother the four Têng brothers together sent up a petition asking that they might be retired in order to take proper care of their mother, who in this illness died. According to the biography of Pan Chao (see p. 41) it was only the general who was refused permission to retire.

[41] 引身自退. Literally "lead themselves, themselves retire."

[42] 豪毛. Literally "A hair, or a feather."

[43] Here 情 seems to include the whole self, mind as well as emotions.

[44] *K'ang-hsi Dictionary,* Character 丹: 詩秦風: 赤心無僞, "The simple heart is without falsity."

CHAPTER VII

Lessons for Women [1]

INSTRUCTIONS IN SEVEN CHAPTERS FOR A WOMAN'S ORDINARY WAY OF LIFE IN THE FIRST CENTURY A. D.

Introduction

I, the unworthy writer, am unsophisticated, unenlightened, and by nature unintelligent, but I am fortunate both to have received not a little favor from my scholarly father,[2] and to have had a (cultured) mother and instructresses upon whom to rely for a literary education as well as for training in good manners. More than forty years have passed since at the age of fourteen I took up the dustpan and the broom [3] in the Ts'ao family. During this time with trembling heart [4] I feared constantly that I might disgrace my parents, and that I might multiply difficulties for both the women and the men [5] (of my husband's family). Day and night I was distressed in heart, (but) I labored without confessing weariness. Now and hereafter, however, I know how to escape (from such fears).[6]

Being careless, and by nature stupid, I taught and trained (my children) without system. Consequently I fear that my son Ku [7] may bring disgrace upon the Imperial Dynasty [8] by whose Holy Grace [9] he has unprecedentedly received the extraordinary privilege [10] of wearing the Gold and the Purple, a privilege for the attainment of which (by my son, I) a humble subject never even hoped. Nevertheless, now that he is a man and able to plan his own life, I need not again have concern for him. But I do grieve that you, my daughters,[11] just now at the age for marriage, have not at this time had gradual training and advice; that you still have not learned the proper customs for married women. I fear that by failure in good manners in other families you will humiliate both your ancestors and your clan. I am now seriously ill, life is uncertain. As I have thought of you all in so untrained a state, I have been uneasy many a time for you. At hours of leisure I have composed in seven chapters these instructions under the title, "Lessons for Women." In order that you may have something wherewith to benefit your persons, I wish every one of you, my daughters, each to write out a copy for yourself.

From this time on every one of you strive to practise these (lessons).

Chapter I

Humility

On the third day after the birth of a girl the ancients [12] observed three customs: (first) to place the baby below [13] the bed; (second) to give her a potsherd with which to play; [14] and (third) to announce her birth to her ancestors by an offering.[15] Now to lay the baby below the bed plainly indicated that she is lowly and weak, and should regard it as her primary duty to humble herself before others. To give her potsherds with which to play indubitably signified that she should practise labor and consider it her primary duty to be industrious.[16] To announce her birth before her ancestors clearly meant that she ought to esteem as her primary duty the continuation of the observance of worship [17] in the home.

These three ancient customs epitomize a woman's ordinary way of life and the teachings of the traditional ceremonial rites and regulations. Let a woman modestly yield to others; let her respect others; let her put others first, herself last. Should she do something good, let her not mention it; should she do something bad, let her not deny it. Let her bear disgrace; let her even endure [18] when others speak or do evil to her. Always let her seem to tremble and to fear. (When a woman follows such maxims as these,) then she may be said to humble herself before others.

Let a woman retire late to bed, but rise early to duties; let her not dread tasks by day or by night. Let her not refuse to perform domestic duties whether easy or difficult. That which must be done, let her finish completely, tidily, and systematically.[19] (When a woman follows such rules as these,) then she may be said to be industrious.

Let a woman be correct in manner and upright in character in order to serve her husband. Let her live in purity and quietness (of spirit), and attend to her own affairs. Let her love not gossip and silly laughter. Let her cleanse and purify and arrange in order the wine and the food for the offerings to the ancestors.[20] (When a woman observes such principles as these,) then she may be said to continue ancestral worship.[21]

No woman who observes these three (fundamentals of life) has ever had a bad reputation or has fallen into disgrace. If a woman fail to observe them, how can her name be honored; how can she but bring disgrace upon herself?

Chapter II

Husband and Wife

The Way of husband and wife is intimately connected with *Yin* and *Yang*,[22] and relates [23] the individual to gods and ancestors. Truly it is the great principle of Heaven and Earth, and the great basis of human relationships. [24] Therefore the "Rites" [25] honor union of man and woman; and in the "Book of Poetry" the "First Ode" [26] manifests the principle of marriage. For these reasons the relationship cannot but be an important one.

If a husband be unworthy then he possesses nothing by which to control his wife. If a wife be unworthy, then she possesses nothing with which to serve her husband. If a husband does not control his wife, then the rules of conduct manifesting his authority are abandoned and broken.[27] If a wife does not serve her husband, then the proper relationship (between men and women) and the natural order of things are neglected and destroyed. As a matter of fact the purpose of these two (the controlling of women by men, and the serving of men by women) is the same.

Now examine the gentlemen of the present age. They only know that wives must be controlled, and that the husband's rules of conduct manifesting his authority must be established. They therefore teach their boys to read books and (study) histories. But they do not in the least understand that husbands and masters must (also) be served,[28] and that the proper relationship and the rites should be maintained.

Yet only to teach men and not to teach[29] women,—is that not ignoring the essential relation between them? According to the "Rites," it is the rule to begin to teach children to read at the age of eight years,[30] and by the age of fifteen years they ought then to be ready for cultural training.[31] Only why should it not be (that girls' education as well as boys' be) according to this principle?

Chapter III

Respect and Caution [32]

As *Yin* and *Yang* are not of the same nature, so man and woman have different characteristics.[33] The distinctive quality of the *Yang* is rigidity; the function of the *Yin* is yielding. Man is honored for strength; a woman is beautiful on account of her gentleness.[34] Hence there arose the common saying: [35] "A man though born like a wolf may, it is feared, become a weak monstrosity; a woman though born like a mouse may, it is feared, become a tiger."

Now for self-culture [36] nothing equals respect for others. To counteract firmness nothing equals compliance. Consequently it can be said that the Way of respect and acquiescence is woman's most important principle of conduct.[37] So respect may be defined as nothing other than holding on to that which is permanent; and acquiescence nothing other than being liberal and generous. Those who are steadfast in devotion know that they should stay in their proper places; those who are liberal and generous esteem others, and honor and serve (them).

If husband and wife have the habit of staying together, never leaving one another, and following each other around [38] within the limited space of their own rooms, then they will lust after and take liberties with one another. From such action improper language will arise between the two. This kind of discussion may lead to licentiousness. Out of licentiousness will be born a heart of disrespect to the husband. Such a result comes from not knowing that one should stay in one's proper place.

Furthermore, affairs may be either crooked or straight; words may be either right or wrong. Straightforwardness cannot but lead to quarreling; crookedness cannot but lead to accusation. If there are really accusations and quarrels, then undoubtedly there will be angry affairs. Such a result comes from not esteeming others, and not honoring and serving (them).

(If wives) suppress not contempt for husbands, then it follows (that such wives) rebuke and scold (their husbands). (If husbands) stop not short of anger, then they are certain to beat (their wives). The correct relationship between husband and wife is based upon harmony and intimacy, and (conjugal) love is grounded in proper union. Should actual blows be dealt, how could matrimonial relationship be preserved? Should sharp words be spoken, how could (conjugal) love exist? If love and proper relationship both be destroyed, then husband and wife are divided.

Chapter IV

Womanly Qualifications

A woman (ought to) have four qualifications:[39] (1) womanly virtue; (2) womanly words; (3) womanly bearing; and (4) womanly work. Now what is called womanly virtue need not be brilliant ability, exceptionally different from others. Womanly words need be neither clever in debate nor keen in conversation. Womanly appearance requires neither a pretty nor a perfect face and form. Womanly work need not be work done more skilfully than that of others.

To guard carefully her chastity; to control circumspectly her behavior; in every motion to exhibit modesty; and to model each act on the best usage, this is womanly virtue.

To choose her words with care; to avoid vulgar language; to speak at appropriate times; and not to weary others[40] (with much conversation), may be called the characteristics of womanly words.

To wash and scrub filth away; to keep clothes and ornaments fresh and clean; to wash the head and bathe[41] the body regularly, and to keep the person free from disgraceful filth, may be called the characteristics of womanly bearing.

With whole-hearted devotion to sew and to weave; to love not gossip and silly laughter; in cleanliness and order (to prepare) the wine and food for serving guests, may be called the characteristics of womanly work.

These four qualifications characterize the greatest virtue of a woman. No woman can afford to be without them. In fact they are very easy to possess if a woman only treasure them in her heart. The ancients[42] had a saying: "Is Love[43] afar off? If I desire love, then love is at hand!" So can it be said of these qualifications.

Chapter V

Whole-hearted Devotion [44]

Now in the "Rites" is written the principle that a husband may marry again, but there is no Canon that authorizes a woman to be married the second time.[45] Therefore it is said of husbands as of Heaven, that as certainly as people cannot run away from Heaven,[46] so surely a wife cannot leave [47] (a husband's home).

If people in action or character disobey the spirits of Heaven and of Earth,[48] then Heaven punishes them.[49] Likewise if a woman errs [50] in the rites and in the proper mode of conduct, then her husband esteems her lightly. The ancient book, "A Pattern for Women," (*Nü Hsien*)[51] says: "To obtain the love of one man is the crown of a woman's life; to lose the love of one man is to miss the aim in woman's life." [52] For these reasons a woman cannot but seek to win her husband's heart. Nevertheless, the beseeching wife need not use flattery, coaxing words, and cheap methods to gain intimacy.

Decidedly nothing is better (to gain the heart of a husband) than whole-hearted devotion and correct manners. In accordance with the rites and the proper mode of conduct, (let a woman) live a pure life. Let her have ears that hear not licentiousness; and eyes that see not depravity. When she goes outside her own home, let her not be conspicuous in dress and manners. When at home let her not neglect her dress. Women should not assemble in groups, nor gather together, (for gossip and silly laughter). They should not stand watching in the gateways. (If a woman follows) these rules, she may be said to have whole-hearted devotion and correct manners.

If, in all her actions, she is frivolous, she sees and hears (only) that which pleases herself. At home her hair is dishevelled, and her dress is slovenly. Outside the home she emphasizes her femininity to attract attention; she says what ought not to be said; and she looks at what ought not to be seen. (If a woman does such as) these, (she may be) said to be without whole-hearted devotion and correct manners.

Chapter VI

Implicit Obedience [53]

Now "to win the love of one man is the crown of a woman's life; to lose the love of one man is her eternal disgrace." [54] This saying advises a fixed will and a whole-hearted devotion for a woman. Ought she then to lose the hearts of her father- and mother-in-law? [55]

There are times when love may lead to differences of opinion [56] (between individuals); there are times when duty may lead to disagreement. Even should the husband say that he loves something,[57] when the parents-in-law say "no," this is called a case of duty leading to disagreement. This being so, then what about the hearts of the parents-in-law? Nothing is better than an obedience which sacrifices personal opinion.

Whenever the mother-in-law says, "Do not do that," and if what she says is right, unquestionably the daughter-in-law obeys. Whenever the mother-in-law says, "Do that," even if what she says is wrong, still the daughter-in-law submits unfailingly to the command.

Let a woman not act contrary to the wishes and the opinions of parents-in-law about right and wrong; let her not dispute with them what is straight [58] and what is crooked. Such (docility) may be called obedience which sacrifices personal opinion. Therefore the ancient book, "A Pattern for Women," says: "If a daughter-in-law (who follows the wishes of her parents-in-law) is like an echo and a shadow,[59] how could she not be praised?"

Chapter VII

Harmony with Younger Brothers- and Sisters-in-law

In order for a wife to gain the love of her husband, she must win for herself the love of her parents-in-law. To win for herself the love of her parents-in-law, she must secure for herself the good will of younger brothers- and sisters-in-law. For these reasons the right and the wrong, the praise and the blame of a woman alike depend upon younger brothers- and sisters-in-law. Consequently it will not do for a woman to lose their affection.

They are stupid [60] both who know not that they must not lose (the hearts of) younger brothers- and sisters-in-law, and who cannot be in harmony with them in order to be intimate with them. Excepting only the Holy Men, few are able to be faultless. Now Yen Tzû's [61] greatest virtue was that he was able to reform. Confucius praised him (for not committing a misdeed) the second time.[62] (In comparison with him) a woman is the more likely (to make mistakes).

Although a woman possesses a worthy woman's qualifications, and is wise and discerning by nature, is she able to be perfect? Yet if a woman live in harmony with her immediate family,[63] unfavorable criticism will be silenced (within the home. But) if a man and woman disagree, then this evil will be noised abroad. Such consequences are inevitable. The "Book of Changes" [64] says:

> "Should two hearts harmonize,
> The united strength can cut gold.
> Words from hearts which agree,
> Give forth fragrance like the orchid."

This saying may be applied to (harmony in the home).

Though a daughter-in-law [65] and her younger sisters-in-law are equal in rank, nevertheless (they should) respect (each other); though love (between them may be) sparse, their proper relationship should be intimate. Only the virtuous, the beautiful, the modest, and the respectful (young women) can accordingly rely upon the sense of duty to make their affection sincere, and magnify love to bind their relationships firmly.

Then the excellence and the beauty of such a daughter-in-law becomes generally known. Moreover, any flaws and mistakes are hidden and unrevealed. Parents-in-law boast of her good deeds; her husband is satisfied with her.[66] Praise of her radiates, making her illustrious in district and in neighborhood; and her brightness reaches to her own father and mother.

But a stupid and foolish person as an elder sister-in-law uses her rank [67] to exalt herself; as a younger sister-in-law, because of parents' favor, she becomes filled with arrogance. If arrogant, how can a woman live in harmony with others? If love and proper relationships be perverted, how can praise be secured? In such instances the wife's good is hidden, and her faults are declared. The mother-in-law will be angry, and the husband will be indignant. Blame will reverberate and spread in and outside the home. Disgrace will gather upon the daughter-in-law's person, on the one hand to add humiliation to her own father and mother, and on the other to increase the difficulties of her husband.

Such then is the basis for both honor and disgrace; the foundation for reputation or for ill-repute. Can a woman be too cautious? Consequently to seek the hearts of young brothers- and sisters-in-law decidedly nothing can be esteemed better than modesty and acquiescence.

Modesty is virtue's handle;[68] acquiescence is the wife's (most refined) characteristic. All who possess these two have sufficient for harmony with others. In the "Book of Poetry" it is written that "here is no evil; there is no dart."[69] So it may be said of (these two, modesty and acquiescence).[70]

NOTES

[1] After this translation was made the writer noted that the title "Lessons for Women" had been given to this treatise by MacGowan (see *Imperial History,* second edition, Shanghai, 1906, p. 120, note).

Pan Chao's successors in the field of moral writings have been so much more widely quoted than herself that modern China as well as the west has failed to appreciate the ethical value of this treatise. The classical style of the composition has likewise prevented a widespread knowledge of the contents except as interpreted through traditional teachings. Apparently it is these traditional interpretations which have been the sources for the so-called translations (see Cordier: *Bibliotheca Sinica,* Histoire, I, col. 675) in western literature. A detailed study of the text itself shows that it contains much which could be of permanent value to modern womanhood.

[2] Pan Chao here alluded to her father as 先君.

[3] This expression for the marriage of the girl, 執箕帚, is found in the *Han Shu* (*chüan* I, 高帝紀上) where the father of the future empress Lü, 呂后, offered her to the future founder of the House of Han. Although the term was perhaps originally used to designate the duties of a girl in her husband's home, this could not be said to be true in the case of the empress Lü. It had become conventionalized, as an expression for the inferior position of the daughter-in-law in relation to her parents-in-law, see commentary on the passage.

While according to tradition fifteen years was the age of marriage for girls, and Pan Chao was married at fourteen, twenty, and even twenty-three is given in the *Li Chi,* see Legge: *Li Ki, SBE,* XXVII, 479.

[4] 戰戰兢兢 is translated by Legge (Book of Poetry, II, V, 2:6, *Classics,* IV, 333): "We should be apprehensive and cautious"——; and 而今而後, 吾知免夫. (Analects 8:3, same, I, 208), "Now and hereafter, I know my escape."

In a note (same, IV, 333) is found 戰=恐, "to be afraid," 兢=戒, "to be cautious"; and (I, 209) 而=自, "from."

Legge (*Classics,* I, 252) noted that "懼 is fear when the troubles have arrived."

[5] The husband's place is without, the wife's place is within, the home. Below, in Chapter VII (p. 89) of "Lessons"), Pan Chao used 外內 as well as 中外.

[6] Or such faults.

[7] Fan Yeh in the biography of Pan Chao called the son Ch'êng, 成. The commentator, Wang Hsien-ch'ien, wrote that while elsewhere it is recorded that the personal name of the son was Ch'êng, and the style Ku, 穀, or Tzû-ku, 穀子, it was strange for the mother to call her son by the style, 字, rather than by the personal name, 名 (*San Fu Chüeh Lu, chüan* 1, p. 1, *Êrh-yu T'ang Ts'ung Shu,* 1821, cf. Chapter III, note 19.) See also *Ch'ung-ting Wên Hsüan Chi P'ing, chüan* 2, 重訂文選集評, 曹大家東征賦 (1778), by Yü Kuang-hua, 于光華.

[8] 清朝, "Pure Dynasty." This was chosen by the Manchus for the name of the recent dynasty, 1644-1911.

[9] E. H. Parker ("The Educational Curriculum of the Chinese," *China Review,* IX [1880-1881], 5) wrote that as late as the Manchu dynasty the successful candidates for *hsiu-ts'ai,* 秀才, at the graduation ceremony *kotow* thrice to his Majesty, and this is called 謝聖恩.

[10] According to the *Han Shu* (*chüan* 19, 百官公卿表) this allowed two thousand piculs of grain, the gold seal, and the purple robe. See biography of Pan Chao, p. 41; the memorial in behalf of Pan Ch'ao, p. 74; *Tz'û Yüan,* 子, p. 109, 戎, p. 4.

[11] Not necessarily only her own daughters, but girls of her family. This term, 諸女, seems to deny the assertion both of the French missionaries and of S. Wells Williams that these "Lessons for Women" were written to the empress who was a pupil of Pan Chao. In (*Hui-hsiang*) *Tung Han Yen-i* (*chüan* 4, 繪像東漢演義, 第 58 回) the writer had Pan Chao herself call her daughters into her presence for them to read these "Lessons," and for her to explain to them the difficult passages, and had Ma Rung to order the wives and daughters of his family to study with the daughters of Pan Chao. See p. 41.

[12] Pan Chao does not indicate that any such custom existed in her time, it was the custom of ancients—people who were "ancient" more than eighteen hundred years ago.

[13] That is: "on the floor, or the ground," cf. Maspero: same, pp. 128-129.

[14] In the Book of Poetry (II, IV, 5:8-9, *Classics,* IV, 307) it is written that "Daughters shall be born to him——. They shall have tiles to play with." W. Scarborough ("Chinese Modes of Address," *Chinese Recorder,* X [1879], 267) wrote that "the birth of a daughter is (1879) politely spoken of as 弄瓦."

S. Wells Williams ("Education of Woman in China," *Chinese Recorder,* IX [1880], 45) stated that "The tile is here used as an emblem of weaving, because women prepare the fibres of the nettle-hemp and grass-cloth for the loom by rubbing them on tiles, even to this day." (1880).

Giles (*Adversaria Sinica,* p. 312) wrote of "'tiles as playthings for girls' from which it has been too hastily inferred that the Chinese have themselves admitted their absolute contempt for women in general. Yet this idea never really entered into the mind of the writer—the tile, so far from being a mere potsherd implying discourtesy was really an honorable symbol of domesticity, being used in ancient times as a weight for the spindle." See also B. Laufer: *Jade, A Study in Chinese Archaeology and Religion* (Chicago, 1912), p. 100.

[15] Legge (*Classics,* I, 198 and 232) noted that 齋 means "to fast," or rather denotes "the whole religious adjustment enjoined before the offering of sacrifice, . . . Sacrifices presented in such a state of mind were sure to be acceptable."

L. C. Hopkins ("Working the Oracle," *New China Review,* I [1919], 113) wrote that "Lo Chên-yü, 羅振玉, in his *Yin Hsü Shu-ch'i K'ao-shih,* 殷虛書契考釋, or 'Critical Interpretation of the Records of the Tumulus of Yin,' Introduction to the sixth section, on 'The Oracle Sentences,' says there are inquiries as to (1) the sacrifice known as *tsi,* 祭 (see below, note 17; (2) that known as *kao,* 告, announcement——; and (4) ordinary journeys, literally 出入, going out and entering."

[16] Legge (Analects 13:19, *Classics,* I, 271) translated 執事敬, "In the management of business, to be reverently attentive." Note the use of 執 above, note 3.

[17] For women's place in the family group in the *Li Chi,* see Legge, *SBE,* XXVII and XXVIII; in the Chou dynasty, see Maspero: same, pp. 120, 121, 123-128; in ancestral worship, same, p. 264.

In the *Chinese Repository* (I, 1832, 500) an observer wrote of "rites, performed at the tombs of ancestors, parents, and friends—(that) the practice is universal, and when the men are absent from their families, the women go to perform the rates." J. G. Andersson (*The Dragon and the Foreign Devils,* Boston, 1928, pp. 110-111) gives an account of a mother and her son making an offering to the memory of the lately deceased father of the family, who "had been the headman of his village, and as a mark of honor toward the deceased and his widow, the boy——had been made his father's successor in office with his mother as assistant."

S. Wells Williams ("The Perpetuity of Chinese Institutions," *Chinese Recorder,* XIII, 1882, 84) related that "Underlying these (Chinese national) characteristics is one general idea——. This is the worship and obedience due to parents and ancestors—(an) indirect result of which has been to define and elevate the position of the wife and mother. As there can be only one 'Illustrious consort' (of the father), 先妣, named on the tablet, there is of course only one wife, 妻, acknowledged in the family. There are concubines, 妾,——but this acknowledged parity of the mother with the father, in the most sacred position she can be placed, has done much to maintain the purity and right influence of women."

L. C. Hopkins ("Working the Oracle," *New China Review,* I 1919, 249) stated that of "Various sacrificial services now known as *tsi*—— Lo observes on the evidence of the Bone inscriptions that the word *tsi* or *chi* denoted only one of the total number of sacrificial ceremonies, and not, as it became later, the general term for all." See above, note 15.

[18] 含垢. Literally "Let her hold filth in her mouth, let her swallow insult."

[19] 整理. Pan Chao here used a term which in modern writings carries the reader from the concrete picture of a woman tidying up self and home as she goes about her tasks to the fact of the disorder in Chinese historical records calling for a scientific study of all source materials, see article by Hu Shih in 古史討論集, pp. 198 ff; as well as other articles in the same

book. See preface by Liang Ch'i-ch'ao to his lectures (1925): same; also Ku Chieh-kang's *Ku Shih Pien,* Preface (pp. 1-103), pp. 30-59 ff. Hu Shih (*China Year Book,* 1924, p. 650) calls **整理國故** the "systematization of the national heritage."

[20] G. Jamieson, "Translations from the *Lu-li,* or General Code of Laws," *China Review,* X (1881-1882), 97:" But the wife had special duties to perform in the periodical sacrifices. She was a sort of priestess assisting her husband, and ——. It was her duty to prepare the sacrificial cakes, the rice, the millet, and the fruits, and to see them served up upon the proper vessels."

[21] Same, VIII (1879-1880), 197: "The 宗, *Tsung,* correspond precisely to the group known as the Agnates (from the point of view of a woman) of the Civil Law, except they do not include adopted strangers by blood." For table of *Tsung,* see same, p. 200.

Legge (*Classics,* I, 271, in note 20) wrote that "宗族 is a designation for all who form one body having the same ancestor (note the use of the term in Introduction above)—being all of the same surname from the great-great grandfather to the great-great grandson—the circle of his relatives." For Chinese Family Nomenclature, see H. P. Wilkinson: *New China Review,* III (1921), 159-191. For a description of a clan, see P. G. von Möllendorf: "The Family Law of the Chinese," *JRAS, NCB,* XXVII (1892-1893), 170-171.

G. Jamieson (same, VIII [1879-1880], 201) noted that the custom of ancestral sacrifices is in harmony with the system of succession. "Every family has its own particular *sacra,* consisting of the ancestral tablets, which are handed down from father to son, increasing in number as one generation is added to another, and it is the duty of the eldest son or the adopted successor to take charge of these, and to perform the customary Rites with all due reverence."

The *Li-Chi, Hwan I,* Legge, *SBE,* XXVIII, 428) says that "The ceremony of marriage was intended to be bond of love between two (families of different) surnames, with a view, in its retrospective character, to secure the services in the ancestral temple, and in its prospective character, to secure the continuance of the family line."

G. Jamieson (same, X, 1881-1882, p. 97) quoted the following comment on the above passage from the *Li Chi*: "The superior man marries so that when he sacrifices to his ancestors he may—have some one to assist him in the worship—and when a wife is divorced the formula says, 'So-and-so is not intelligent. She is incompetent to assist me in serving up the offerings at the sacrifices.'"

Herbert Chatley (Magical Practice in China," *JRAS, NCB,* XLVIII, 1917, pp. 16-17) wrote that "it is perfectly clear that the Chinese behave and have behaved for millennia as if the soul of each clan were a continuous organism, having an annual pulse, incarnate in the living descendants, transfusable into women brought into the clan by marriage and into children co-opted by adoption, immanent in all lives associated with the family, and present at the tombs, the ancestral temple, and the family altar." Confucius certainly believed that a worshipper should behave as if the ancestors were present (Analects 3:12, Legge, I, 159).

For a modern scholar on ancestral rites, see E. T. C. Werner's translation of an article by Hu Shih, "Reform in Chinese Mourning Rites," *New China Review,* II (1920), 225-247; *Hu Shih Wên Ts'un, chüan* 4, pp. 132 ff. (cf. Chapter IV, note 11).

[22] Léopold de Saussure ("On the Antiquity of the *Yin-Yang* Theory," *New China Review,* IV, 1922, 457-459) noted that "If this idea has been little understood up to now, it is simply because the unity and the value of the astronomico-cosmological system of Chinese antiquity have not been sufficiently recognized. The fundamental basis of the Chinese conception lies in the revolution of the seasons, in the alternation of heat and cold, of darkness and light. The two antithetic principles were later" named *Yin-Yang.*

The *Yin* and *Yang* according to Maspero (same, p. 482, note 1) appeared for the first time in a philosophic sense in the *Hsi Tz'û,* 繫辭, a work which he dates about the end of the fifth century B.C. The definition of *Yin* and *Yang* as forces he considers to be an introduction of modern ideas into ancient Chinese thought (same, note 2).

Li Ju-chên's "Flowers in the Mirror," 李汝珍: 鏡花緣 (c 1825) is an early nineteenth century protest against the inequality of man and woman, and a declaration for equality of the sexes, see Hu Shih's edition, I, 19-49, together with Hu Shih's comments in an article, "A Chinese Declaration of Rights for Woman," *Chinese Soc. and Polit. Science Review,* VIII (1924), 100-109.

[23] Compare 通達神明 with 通于明神, pp. 117, 118.

[24] Mencius (V, I, 2:1, *Classics,* II, 346) said, 男女居室, 人之大倫也, "that male and female should dwell together, is the greatest of human relations."

G. Jamieson (same, X, 1881-1882, 96) stated that "Marriage has always been considered by the Chinese as the most solemn and important act of life. It is the root and origin of future existence. An unholy union is like want of harmony between heaven and earth." For the Five Relationships, see Mayers, II, no. 149.

S. Wells Williams ("Education of Woman in China," *Chinese Recorder,* XI, 1880, 47) wrote that "It is well known that the language has one character, 妻, for wife; and quite another, 妾, for the other woman brought into the family. The relation between the two is acknowledged in the eyes of Chinese law, but our terms of first and second wives, or wife and concubine, do not exactly convey the native idea. The *Tsieh,* 妾, is not a wife at all, of which there can be only one, ——. The relation between the two is like that of Sarah and Hagar in Abraham's household, but the *tsieh* cannot be summarily ejected with her children from the family. She is taken into it by a kind of purchase and without the formalities of the first marriage,—yet the children of the *tsieh* are regarded as legal heirs of the family."

[25] After the Han dynasty there were three Chinese classics into which the name *Li,* 禮, entered: (1) 周禮, (2) 儀禮 (3) 禮記. They are often called "The Three Rituals," see Wylie: *Notes,* p. 4; Mayers, II, no. 42. For the significance of the character, and a discussion of the Classics, see Legge: *SBE,* XXVII, Intro., 2-11; also *Li Chi,* Legge's translation, *Hwan I, SBE,* XXVIII, 428-434. Maspero (same, pp. XII, 579, 591) dates *Chou Li,* fourth and third centuries B.C., with revisions and interpolations at the time of the Han; *I Li,* a Han work from earlier sources, and *Li Chi,* fourth to first century B.C. treatises compiled under the Han scholars.

Legge (same, p. 430): "Whence it is said, 'The ceremony of marriage is the root of the other ceremonial observances.'"

[26] Legge: *Classics,* IV, 1-5.

[27] See the Book of Poetry, I, IV, 8, *Classics,* IV, 85.

[28] Analects 20:3 (*Classics*, I, 354): 不知禮, 無以立也, "Without an acquaintance with the rules of propriety, it is impossible for the character to be established." And note that this is from the section where the genuineness of the text is questioned, and thus would reflect the more Han Confucian thought.

E. H. Parker ("The Philosopher Sün-tsz," fifth chapter, *New China Review*, IV, 1922, p. 14) translated 禮義, "courtesy and equity." Cf. Dubs: *Hsüntze*, Chap. VIII, "*Li*: The Rules of Proper Conduct."

[29] The Analects (15:38, *Classics*, I, 305; cf. 275) records 有敎無類, "The Master said, 'In teaching there should be no distinction of classes.'" Yet nowhere do Confucius' sayings show any interest in teaching women.

The opening sentence of the "Doctrine of the Mean" is: 天命之謂性, 率性之謂道 修道之謂敎, which Legge (*Classics*, I, 383) translated: "What Heaven has conferred is called The Nature; an accordance with this nature is called The Path (of duty); the regulation of this path is called Instruction."

Leonard Hsü of Yenching University, Peiping, translates this:

"What God has endowed is nature;
The pursuit of nature is the Way;
The cultivation of the Way is education."

[30] *Li Chi, chüan* 5, 內則: 八年出入門戶 (*SBE*, XXVII, 478.)

[31] Legge (*Classics*, I, 196, note 4) translated 學, "liberal education." And in a note on Analects 1:6 (same, p. 140) he wrote that "after the performance of these things, 則以學文, 'he should employ them in polite studies'—not literary studies merely, but all the accomplishments of a gentleman also: ceremonies, music, archery, horsemanship, writing, and numbers." Cf. Maspero: same, p. 131.

[32] The Analects (8:2) says that 愼而無禮則葸, which Legge translated (*Classics*, I, 208): "Carefulness without the rules of propriety becomes timidity."

The Analects (7:12) also says that 子之所愼, which Legge (*Classics*, I, 198) translated: "The things in reference to which the Master exercised the greatest caution."

[33] See note 22 above.

The Chinese have a common expression, "Woman is woman; man is man"—the two being different, they are not comparable.

[34] I. T. Headland ("Chinese Women from a Chinese Standpoint," *Chinese Recorder*, XXVIII, 1897, 14) quoting, translated this passage: "The *Yin* and *Yang*, like the male and the female, are very different principles; the virtue of the *Yang* is firmness; the virtue of the *Yin* is flexibility. So man's strength is his honor; woman's weakness is her beauty."

From the "Great Plan" of the Book of History, Legge (V, IV, 17, *Classics*, III, 333) translated that "for the reserved and retiring there is the strong, 剛, rule; for the lofty and intelligent there is the mild, 柔, rule."

In the hexagrams of the *I Ching*, 易經, the two elemental lines correspond to the two primordial substances *Yin* and *Yang*, and the unbroken lines are called "*Kang*" or "hard" lines, and the broken ones "*jou*" or "soft" lines, cf Maspero: same, p. 483.

Mencius (VII, II, 25:5, translated by Legge: *Classics*, II, 490) said that

"He whose goodness has been filled up is what is called a beautiful man," 充實之謂美.

Huai-nan Tzû's 陰以柔爲用, (*chüan* I, p. 10b), F. H. Balfour ("The Principle of Nature," *China Review*," IX, 1880-1881, 288) translated 柔勝出於已者其力不可量, "weakness can overcome what is far stronger than itself." See also same, p. 289, and Lao Tzû's *"Tao Tê Ching,"* Chap. 61, 謙德, P. Carus: *Lao Tsze's Tao-Teh-King* (Chicago, 1898), p. 128.

Giles (*Dict.*, no. 8139) translated 男以疆爲貴, "strength is the glory of man"; and (no. 8419) 女以弱爲美, "weakness is woman's charm."

[35] Giles (*Dict.*, no. 8139) translated "if you have a son like a wolf, you still fear lest he should be a weakling"; and (no. 8419) "if your daughter is (timid) as a mouse, you still fear lest she should turn out a tigress."

[36] The "Great Learning," translated by Legge (*Classics*, I, 359), says that "All must consider the cultivation of the person the root of everything besides." Cf. Mencius VI, I, 16; VII, I, 1-3, *Classics*, II, 419, 449-450.

This term, 修身, was used for the name of the ethics which was given a place with textbook even in the primary grades of the government schools of China for the first few years of the Republic.

[37] Mencius (III, II, 2:2, *Classics*, II, 265) said: 以順爲正者, 妾婦之道也, "to look upon compliance as their correct course is the rule for women."

[38] 周旋. Literally "follow around"; idiomatically, "to pay attention to."

[39] *Li Chi*, Legge: *SBE*, XXVIII, 432; "she was taught here (three months before her marriage) the virtue (德), the speech (言), the carriage (容), and the work (功), of the wife." Cf. Maspero: same, p. 133.

[40] In the Analects (14:14, *Classics*, I, 280) it is found that "My Master speaks when it is time to speak, and 人不厭其言, so men do not get tired of his speaking."

[41] Legge (*Classics*, I, 284, note 22) wrote that "Properly, 沐, is to wash the hair with the water in which rice has been washed, and 浴 is to wash the body with hot water."

[42] Analects 7:29, *Classics*, I, 204: 仁遠乎哉,我欲仁, 斯仁至矣. "The Master said: 'Is virtue a thing remote? I wish to be virtuous, and lo! virtue is at hand.'" This is the one place where Pan Chao gave a direct quotation from the Analects or from Confucius without crediting it to its source.

[43] On Analects 1:2, Legge (*Classics*, I, 139, note 2) stated that "仁 is explained as 'the principle of love,' 'the virtue of the heart.' 仁 is man,'—'benevolence' often comes near it."

Léopold de Saussure, "On the Origin of Ideo-phonetic Characters," *New China Review*, III (1921), 392, note) wrote that "仁, *jên* (humanity), is merely a special meaning of the word 人, *jên* (man). Though deprived of accurate views on the etymological evolution, the Chinese scholars point out this phonetic identity in the saying: 仁者人也: 'Humanity is man.'" Cf. *T'oung Pao* (1910), p. 244 (1913), p. 808; Dubs: same. Maspero (same, pp. 464-465) prefers "l'Altruisme," which must be distinguished from "l'Amour Universel" preached by Mo Ti.

[44] This is just the meaning of the western rime:

"All that you do, do with your might,
Things done by halves are never done right."

Chapter V of "Lessons" applies this spirit in the broad field of the relationship of man and wife.

[45] This sentence was written about the same time that the Corinthian Christians were asking Paul what his advice was about widows. Cf. *Li Chi* (Legge, *SBE,* XXVII, 439): "Once mated with her husband, all her life she will not change (her feeling of duty to him) and hence, when the husband dies she will not marry (again)."

[46] Analects 3:13, Legge (*Classics,* I, 159): "He who offends against Heaven has none to whom he can pray."

[47] Not even after the death of a husband does the worthy wife yet leave her husband's home.

[48] G. M. H. Playfair ("One Phase of Chinese Superstition," *China Review,* XVI, 1887-1888, 232) wrote that "a belief in the personal intervention of their gods in human affairs is a deep-rooted tenet of Chinese faith." Cf. The poem "Travelling Eastward," pp. 117-118.

[49] For three Chinese stories to illustrate, see G. C. Stent, "The Double Mail Murderers," *China Review,* X (1881-1882), 41-43; G. M. H. Playfair, "The Wicked Mother-in-law," same, XI (1882-1883), 173; Anonymous, "The Restoration of the Jadestone Ring," same, XIII (1884-1885), 247-250.

[50] P. G. von Möllendorf ("The Family Law of the Chinese, and Its Comparative Relations with that of Other Nations," *JRAS, NCB,* XIII, 1878, 111, 115) wrote that "the wife comes into the power of her husband,—though she shares the rank and the position of her husband,—the husband has the right to inflict corporal punishment on her."

[51] 女憲. This is thought, even by contemporary Chinese historical critics, to be the title of a long lost book. Both Liang Ch'i-ch'ao (died January, 1929) and Ku Chieh-kang told the writer this was their opinion.

[52] The full translation is as follows: "To become of like mind with one man may be said to be the final end; to fail to become of like mind with one man may be said to be the eternal end."

[53] See *Li Chi,* Legge: *SBE,* XXVIII, 430-431. M. F. C. ("The Chinese Daughter-in-law," *Chinese Recorder,* V [1874-1875], 207-214) aptly remarked that "Those who with native ability combine patience and shrewdness, adroitly manage the whole family, while seeming to be everyone's servant. They are so conciliating, and so winning, so wise, and yet so modest," that they win their way.

[54] A repetition of the quotation above; see note 52.

[55] Hu Shih ("The Social Message in Chinese Poetry," *Chinese Soc. and Polit. Science Review,* VII, 1923, 72) wrote that "in the Chinese family system where children are morally bound to live together under the same parental roof, there often arise troubles between the mother-in-law and the daughter-in-law, between sister-in-law and the younger brothers and sisters. There is in the Han literature of social problems a long poem entitled 'The Wife of Chiao Chung-ch'ing' (孔雀東南飛, *K'ung-ch'üeh Tung-nan Fei*) which tells the story of a faithful wife who was loved by her husband, but whose mother-in-law disliked her so much that she was forced to return to her own home." For translation of this poem see Waley: *The Temple,* pp. 113-125.

[56] The commentary suggests that 離 should be written 麗 which according to an earlier authority means 著. So instead of "differences," the reading would be "agreements."

[57] 云爱 has the idea 云是, but to Pan Chao it was impossible to have the son say "yes" when just below the mother says "no."

[58] Analects 8:2 is translated by Legge (*Classics*, I, 208): 直而無禮則絞, "straightforwardness, without the rules of propriety, becomes rudeness."

[59] This term, 影響 in modern usage has come to mean "influence."

[60] Note the use of 蔽, above, p. 84.

[61] 顏, 子 or 回, was the favorite disciple of Confucius; see Legge: *Classics*, I, Prolegomena, 112-113; Giles: *Biog.*, no. 2465; Mayers, no. 913; Analects 6:2, 11:6-10, Legge: same, I, 185, 239-240.

Ssû-ma Ch'ien (*chüan* 61, 伯夷列傳) said of Yen Tzû: 附驥尾而行益顯 (translated by Mayers, no. 913), "Clinging (as a fly) to the swift courser's tail his progress was thereby the more brilliant." In the Confucian temple at Ch'ü-fu, 曲阜, is an incised slab which represents Confucius followed by Yen Tzû, and is after the design by Ku Kai-chih, see Waley: *Chinese Painting*, p. 63.

Wang Ch'ung (IX, 28, "Confucius Interrogated," 論衡, 問孔, translated by A. B. Hutchinson, *China Review*, VII, 1878-1879, 43, 89, 170, 171, 173, here and elsewhere references to Wang Ch'ung can be found in the later translation [Berlin, 1907, 1911], of *Lun-Hêng* by Alfred Forke) said of Yen Tzû, that he was one of the principal disciples of Confucius, an advocate of education as the proper regenerator. He surpassed in wisdom and in quickness of perception.

[62] Analects 6:2 (*Classics*, I, 185): 不貳過, "he did not repeat a fault." According to this passage Yen Tzû had two virtues: (1) he never visited his anger upon another, 不遷怒; (2) he never repeated a fault.

[63] Literally "the people in the same room." In China today the daughter-in-law often lives in the same room, 室, but not necessarily the same compartment, with her mother-in-law in the women's courtyard, while the husband has his room up in front in the men's courtyard.

[64] See Legge's translation, *SBE*, XVI, 易繫辭 (Maspero: same, p. 480, dates about end of fifth century B.C.). Legge (The Great Appendix, p. 362) incorrectly translated:

> "But when two men are one in heart,
> Not iron bolts keep them apart;
> The words they in their union use,
> Fragrance like orchid plants diffuse."

The idea is rather that in loving unity there is strength and beauty as the two (or the group) meet life's responsibilities.

[65] Chang Chü-chêng, 張居正 (1525-1582 A.D., Giles: *Biog.*, no. 41; *Nü Chieh Chih Chieh*, 女誡直解, *Chang Wên-chung Kung Ch'üan Chi* 5, 張文忠公全集五, 1901), considered *sao*, 嫂, an error, and substituted *shu*, 叔, and interpretated this passage to mean that "although younger brothers- and sisters-in-law are of the same rank (as the daughter-in-law), since those of one rank fall into groups, there should be mutual respect, and although love between these may be sparse," etc. In this interpretation he makes *ti*, 敵, to mean *hsiang-têng*, 相等.

[66] 嘉美. Literally "praises the beauty of her character."

[67] The *Li Chi* gave the power of control of other sons' wives to the eldest daughter-in-law, see Legge, *SBE*, XXVII, 457-458.

[68] In the Book of Changes, *Hsi Tz'û* (Legge: same, p. 397), is found: "*Li* shows us the foundation of virtue, *Ch'ien* its handle," 謙德之柄也.

[69] This quotation from the 周頌 section of the Book of Poetry differs from the text of Mao, 毛詩; see Legge (*Classics*, IV, 585) who translated as follows:

在彼無惡 "There (in their States), not disliked;
在此無斁 Here (in Chou), never tired of."

The Li Hsien commentary, 唐太子李賢註, of the T'ang dynasty, says that 射, instead of 斁, followed the Han text, 韓詩, one of the well-known texts of the Book of Poetry in the Han dynasty (see *Classics*, I, Prolegomena, 8-10).

[70] In "Die Lebensgeschichte des Philosophen Mongtse" (*Chinesische Blätter für Wissenschaft und Kunst*, Veröffentlichung des China-Instituts zu Frankfurt am Main, I, 2, 1926, Darmstadt, Germany) Richard Wilhelm (died, 1930) included nine scenes from a scroll of a Sung painting (1101-1126 A.D.) illustrating Pan Chao's "Lessons for Women," which he also translated in part (pp. 83-87). These scenes were photographically reproduced (1913) from a scroll now in the possession of a former high official of the Chinese Government.

CHAPTER VIII

Three Short Poems

A. THE BIRD FROM THE FAR WEST[1]
(circa 101 A. D.)

Pan Chao's elder brother, Governor-general in East Turkestan, the Marquis of Ting-yüan, Pan Ch'ao, presented a (strange) large bird[2] to His Majesty (the emperor Ho, 89–105 A. D.).[3] His Majesty commanded Pan Chao by mandate to compose verses suitable to the occasion of the presentation of the gift, and she wrote:

Congratulations to haunts of the Bird (from the Far West);
Miraculous[4] that peak of the K'un-lun[5] which gave him birth:
He differs greatly from a small one of like name.[6]
Lo! he belongs to the ranks of the Imperial Phoenix.[7]

In his breast he cherishes virtue,[8] he seeks the Righteous One;[9]
Soaring ten thousand *li* he has come, travelling (eastward).
Alighting at the imperial court, he halts, resting;
He delights in the Spirit of Harmony, so at leisure here he roams.

(All ranks at court,) high and low, dwell in mutual love;
They listen to the harmony of music in its refined praise.[10]
(Themselves) from east and west, from south and north;[11]
All think[12] of submitting, and coming to serve and live.

大雀賦

大家同產兄西域都護定遠侯班超獻大雀詔令大家作賦曰

嘉大雀之所集生崑崙之靈丘同小名而大異乃鳳皇之匹疇懷有德而歸義故翔萬里而來遊集帝庭而止息樂和氣而優游上下協而相親聽雅頌之雍雍自東西與南北咸思服而來同

B. THE CICADA [13]

(Let us sing to:) [14]
That one [15] which of somber-colored [16] insects is least [17] and lowliest; [18]
Yet which also derives its life [19] from Heaven and Earth.
Just at the climax of summer's [20] heat,
Mounted [21] high upon a tree,[22] it vents [23] itself.
Following the warm breeze,[24] it roams this way;
Then, when autumn withers and oppresses,[25] it vanishes.

(Let us sing to:)
(That one which) drinks the clear dews [26] of the scarlet [27] garden;
And perched proudly on a high branch, plumes [28] itself.
It extols the glorious light of the adorable Imperial Dynasty,
The dazzling, brilliantly blinding, and luminous August One! [29]

(Let us sing to:)
(That one which) at the height of happiness [30] unsatisfied, (is cut off).
So it leaves behind only dullness and sadness on the horizon.

蟬賦

伊玄蟲之微陋亦攝生于天壤當三秋之盛暑陵高木之流響融

風被而來遊商焱厲而化往吸清露于丹園抗喬枝而理翮崇皇

朝之輝光映豹豹而灼灼復丹款之未足畱滯恨乎天際

C. THE NEEDLE AND THREAD

Strong [31] Spirit of Pure (Steel),[32] from autumn's metal cast; [33]
(Incarnate) body (of Power), slight and subtle, straight and sharp!
To pierce, then to enter gradually in, that is your nature; [34]
Things far apart all strung into one,[35] (that is your task).

Only your ordered footprints, (you wonderful) Needle and Thread,
Attest the quantity, the variety, the universality (of your work).
You retrace, you sway, you twist [36] (in your path) to mend flaws,
Until the results resemble the pure wool of the lamb.[37]

What measure [38] or basket suffices to count (the pieces of your work)?
All, all together these are your memorials.[39]
(They are found in the village home;)
They ascend [40] into the stately hall.[41]

鍼縷賦

鎔秋金之剛精形微妙而直端性通達而漸進博庶物而一貫惟
鍼縷之列迹信廣博而無原退逶迤呂補過侶素絲之羔羊何斗
筲之足算咸勒石而升堂

THE BIRD FROM THE FAR WEST: NOTES

[1] The title in Chinese is literally "Verses to the Great Sparrow."

[2] Literally, "great sparrow." The *Kuang Chih,* 廣志 (*P'ei-wên Yün-fu,* 佩文韻府, 1711, *chüan* 99, 雀), said that "the great sparrow is the ostrich of today," 卽今之駝鳥也; and (*I-wên Lei-chü,* 藝文類聚, *chüan* 92, 雀) that "Parthia's great sparrow lifts its head eight or nine feet (the foot-measure was probably nine English inches; see below, note 38), opens its wings more than ten feet, eats wheat, and lays eggs as (large as) a jar, 甕." (Cf. *Hou Han Shu, chüan* 88, 條支國, *Han Shu, chüan* 96a.) Similar comments with explanatory notes in the section for T'iao-chih Kuo are made upon the entry of the gift of a *ta ch'üeh,* 大雀. The Chinese name for this gift, "bird of Parthia," implies a Parthian origin, but Chavannes (*T'oung Pao,* VIII, 1907, 176-178) advanced the theory that "these birds originated from T'iao-chih, that is, Desht Misan or Mésène (the theory is disputed, however, by Laufer in footnote 2, *Chinese Clay Figures,* pp. 125-126), where ruled Arabic princes who had all facilities for obtaining ostriches from Arabia." The Chinese texts which the author of this study has examined seem to agree with Chavannes' theory, the writers naming T'iao-chih Kuo as the origin of the Parthian bird. According to the *Tung Kuan Han Chi* in "101 A. D. (Yung-yüan, thirteenth year), the King of Parthia sent up the gift of a great sparrow from T'iao-chih Kuo." See also *I-wên Lei-chü,* same; and *T'ai-p'ing Yü-lan,* 太平御覽, *chüan* 922, 大雀.

[3] According also to the *Hou Han Shu* (*chüan* 88, 安息國), in the thirteenth year of the reign of the emperor Ho (101 A. D.) Parthia sent tribute to the Chinese court. According to the *Tung Kwan Han Chi* (*chüan* 16, 班超) Pan Ch'ao sent his son Yung with the tribute train from Parthia (101 A. D.). Hui Tung, 惠棟 (c. 1750), quoting Yüan Hung, 袁宏, of the Chin dynasty (see Appendix, p. 159), added that this son brought the "great sparrow" to the emperor the tenth moon of the thirteenth year of Ho Ti, and Pan Chao was ordered to compose verses suitable to the occasion of the presentation of the gift (see Wang Hsien-ch'ien's edition, 1915, of the *Hou Han Shu*). The *T'ung Chien,* 通鑑 (*chüan* 48, 漢紀, 和帝, fourteenth year), dated these events 102 A. D., but the commentator noted the discrepancy in events thus dated, see p. 50; Chapter VI, note 16. This poem then can only be dated "*circa* 101 A. D."

[4] See Legge (*Classics,* IV, 456): "Some take it, 靈, in the sense of 'royal'; others as marvellous, a name of admiration." See Chapter VI, note 8, pp. 74, 78.

[5] The name is found in the "Tribute of Yü" (of the Book of History, *Classics,* III, 127) dated by Ku Chieh-kang (*Ku Shih Pien,* Intro. p. 58, p. 134) not earlier than the period of the Contending States (481-221 B. C.). It is also mentioned in the *Shan Hai Ching,* 山海經, which according to Ku Chieh-kang, is of the same or a bit later period. Maspero (same, p. 100, note 1, p. 610), however, credits the *Yü Kung* to a time probably prior to the end of the Western Chou, eighth century B. C.; and the first treatise of the *Shan Hai Ching* he places at the end of the Eastern Chou, fourth century B. C. (same, p. 611, notes 1 and 2). With the K'un-lun then and later were associated countless fictions. (For pre-Han foreign influence in China, see Maspero: same, pp. 607-621.) After the expedition of Chang Ch'ien to the West, 139-126

B.C., and the gradual opening of East Turkestan to Chinese intercourse, first in the Han dynasty, and then in the T'ang, Yüan, and Ch'ing dynasties, the name was applied to the range of mountains stretching east and west south of the Tarim Basin and lying north of Tibet, which was connected with the T'ien-shan on the north by the mighty eastern rim, the Pamirs. Here at the same time the name seems to be used in its mythological value as being the region where Hsi-wang-mu, 西王母 (Giles: *Adversaria Sinica,* pp. 1-19), reigns. It indicates that the bird being compared with a phoenix comes from the supernatural country of the Immortals.

[6] "One of like name" means the "sparrow," 雀.

[7] While, 鳳凰, *fêng-huang* is usually translated "phoenix," Florence Ayscough (*Fir-Flower Tablets,* Boston, 1921, Introduction, p. LV) translates "crested love-pheasants." Really, however, since it is a mythical creature, there is no adequate non-Chinese term for the *fêng-huang.*

Since the days of Confucius (see Analects 9:8, *Classics,* I, 219) it has occupied an important place both in Chinese literature and in Chinese thinking where its appearance signifies the reign of a Saint. For a description of the fabulous bird, see *Chinese Repository,* "Notices of Natural History," VII (1838-1839), pp. 212, 250 ff; C. A. S. Williams, "Chinese Metaphorical Zoology," *JRAS, NCB,* vol. L (1919), 26-27; Giles: *Dict.,* no. 3560; Mayers, I, no. 134, II, no. 94; Book of Poetry, III, II, 8:7, 8, and 9, *Classics,* IV, 493-494; *Shan Hai Ching, chüan* 1, 丹穴之山; *Huai-nan Tzû,* 淮南鴻列解說林訓, *chüan* 17. For a discussion of the Chinese character, *fêng,* see L. C. Hopkins, "The Wind, The Phoenix, and a String of Shells," *JRAS* (April, 1917), pp. 377-383.

[8] Virtue, 德, harmony, 和, and similar expressions need to be interpreted in terms of the idealism of the Han Confucianists, who would unite and pacify by the civilizing influence of virtue, 德化, see pp. 5-7.

[9] That is: since he appears whenever there is a Sage Ruler. The poem thus contains the highest compliment to the rule of the emperor.

[10] This line refers to court music and songs. For the place of music in Han thinking see the *Li Chi,* "The Record of Music," with notes by John Chalmers in *China Review,* XV (1886-1887), 9-10; Legge: *Li-Ki, Yo-Ki, SBE,* XXVIII, 92-131; B. Jenkins, *JRAS, NCB,* V (1868), 30-57, a complete translation of the "Memorial of Music," under the title, "Notions of the Ancient Chinese Respecting Music." Contemporary Chinese scholarship (see p. 14) recognizes this "Record of Music" as the work of the Han Confucianists based upon earlier material, chiefly that of Hsün Tzû, 荀子, so it doubtless reflects Han conceptions of the art.

[11] A use of "The Fame of Wên Wang," Book of Poetry, see *Classics,* IV, 463: 自西自東, 自南自北. 無思不服, 皇王烝哉.

> "From the west to the east, from the south to the north,
> There was not a thought but did him homage."

In the submission of his seventy disciples to Confucius because of his virtue, the excerpt is the same, but Legge translated the third phrase: "There was not one who thought of refusing submission," see Mencius, II, I, 3:2, *Classics,* II, 197.

[12] 無思不服 of the quotation above from the Book of Poetry, *i.e.,* under the Sage rule of the emperor.

THE CICADA: NOTES

[13] The cicada, or broad locust is common all over China, and has many names. L. C. Arlington noted in *New China Review* (IV, 1922, 412-413) that "it is a small green insect common in the seventh moon; a small black one which appears during the fifth moon, and also a large black one." The *Tz'û Yüan* describes the cicada as "born in the summer and autumn," and of many names and varieties. Of the five ancient Chinese fables translated by C. Arendt (*China Review*, XIII, 1884-1885), the fable of "The Cicada and The Mantis" seems to be one of the two earliest known. The most ancient source for this apologue is Liu Hsiang's, 劉向, version in his "Garden of Stories" (*Shuo Yüan*, 說苑, BK. 9, fol. 3, first century B. C.). A second source is the *Wu Yüeh Ch'un-ch'iu*, 吳越春秋 (BK. 3, fol. 14), a semi-historical work belonging to the first century A. D. (see Wylie: *Notes*, p. 40). Based doubtless, said Arendt, on this second source, the apologue is found in the "History of the Various States under the Eastern Chou Dynasty," 東周列國志. (Bk. 18, chap. 82), a late Ming or early Ch'ing dynasty historical narrative (see Wylie: *Notes*, p. 203). For a translation of a poem "The Cicada" by Ou-yang Hsiu, see Waley: *The Temple*, pp. 99-102.

[14] "Let us sing to" is added in order to make something of a whole of the three fragments of Pan Chao's poem, in translation arranged in three stanzas of unequal length.

[15] 伊, this, that; he, she, it, etc., is noted by J. Edkins ("Evolution of the Pronoun," *China Review*, XVI, 1887-1888, 49-53) as one of the root pronouns, a demonstrative. "That one which" is supplied as introductory for stanzas two and three as well as for one.

[16] J. Edkins ("The *Yi King* and Its Appendices," *China Review*, XIV, 1885-1886, 306) wrote that this word, 玄, somber-colored, "the dark principle, constitutes the base of the operations of the universe, and it is convertible with (the Way), 道 of Lao Tzû." See *Tao Tê Ching*, Paul Carus, pp. 148, 97, 337. According to *Kung-kuei Wên Hsüan*, 宮閨文選 (*chüan* 1), the first three characters are 伊鳴蜩, and the reading would be, "That one which is of chirping creatures a small and lowly one."

E. R. Eichler (*China Review*, XV, 1886-1887, 74) translated 玄冥, "the spirit of water." So the cicada is the 玄蟲, "the spirit of Insect Life," in these fragments from the brush of Pan Chao.

[17] 微, "small," note its use in the *Tao Tê Ching*, Carus, Chap. 14, pp. 103, 165.

[18] 陋, "lowly." The *Tz'û Yüan* (戌, p. 113) says: 地位卑賤曰陋.

[19] The modern term for 攝生 is 衛生, "to preserve your health." There is the suggestion of the Taoist "simple life" as preached by Chuang Tzû.

[20] 三秋 usually means the three autumn moons, seventh, eighth, and ninth. It is also a name for the ninth moon. From approximately the first week in August to the first week in November is the period known as autumn in China. As the ninth moon (late September—early October of the western calendar) is rather cold for cicadas anywhere in China, certainly in Honan Province, here 三秋 is taken to mean 三伏, or the Three Decades of Heat (see Mayers, p. 316).

秋 not infrequently means 時, "time." Since the Three Decades of Heat cover the hottest part of the season, 三秋, is translated "the climax of the summer."

[21] 陵. See *Tz'û Yüan*, 戎, p. 123.

[22] The *Tz'û Yüan* says that the female cicada lays eggs in the branches of the trees, and when hatched the young fall to the ground, and burrow below the surface where they feed on the moisture from the roots. The larva becomes a pupa, emerges from the ground, mounts the trees, and from this pupa issues the cicada. This process covers not more than two years. As soon as the cicada comes forth, it seeks a mate. If male, it then usually dies immediately; if female, it lays and hatches eggs, then dies. The life period of the cicada, male or female, is not generally more than a few days, though specimens are known to have lived as long as two years. (For the western species, see *Encyclopedia Britannica*, Article, Cicada.)

C. Arendt (*China Review*, XIII, 1884-1885, 23), translating from "The Cicada and The Mantis," wrote: "The song of a cicada from the boughs of a high tree,—the cicada singing the protracted notes of its ditty in the breeze of the morning" (東周列國志, BK. 18, Chap. 82). Same, p. 27: "In the garden there is a tree, on which a cicada was perched. The cicada was sitting there on high, singing the mellow tones of its ditty, and drinking the dew." (Liu Hsiang's "Garden of Stories," BK. 9, fol. 3.)

[23] Both the *Encyclopedia Britannica*, Article, Cicada; and the *Tz'û Yüan*, Character 蟬, agree that "Cicadas are chiefly remarkable for the shrill song of the males, which in some cases may be heard in concert at a distance of a quarter of a mile or more,—no auditory organs have been found in the females."

The *Li Chi* (Legge, *SBE*, XXVII, 275) under the record for the first moon of summer says that "Cicadas begin to sing."

[24] The *Shuo Wên*, 說文, defined this term, 融風, as a "northeast wind." At the beginning of spring, 立春節, comes this wind; at the arrival of autumn it goes. The use of 被 (Giles: *Dict.*, no. 8709) here shows that the cicada is under the influence of the wind; or wrapped, as it were, in the wind.

[25] After autumn begins, 立秋節, the early mornings in north China bring a breeze which withers and exhausts both plant and animal life. In the summer of 1926 in Peking the writer saw her last cicada of the season during the week following the beginning of autumn, which occurred that year on August eighth.

[26] Chuang Tzû's 吸淸露 (莊子集釋, *chüan* 1a, 逍遊) is translated by Giles (*Chuang Tzû, Mystic, Moralist, and Social Reformer*, London, 1926, Chap. I, p. 7): "lives on air and dew."

C. Arendt (*China Review*, XIII, 1884-1885, 26) wrote that "In the 'Annals,' 吳越春秋, the cicada is prettily described as 'drinking the dew of the morning,' 飲淸露."

[27] *Tan*, 丹, has a Taoistic connotation: "the elixir of life."

[28] A barbershop in Peking is called 理髮館.

[29] Legge (*Classics*, IV, 12, in his note on the use of 灼 in the Book of Poetry, I, I, 6, line 2) said that "灼灼 is descriptive rather of the brilliance of the flowers than of their luxuriance."

[30] 丹款之未足. "The scarlet entertainment had not been enjoyed to the limit.

According to the *Shuo Wên*, 欵 means that which is desired," 意有所欲也. According to the *Po Ya*, 博雅, it means 愛也.

Note the use of 足 in *Tao Tê Ching*, Carus, Chap. 44:3 and 8; 46:3, pp. 217, 219, 120-121, as "Contentment."

[31] Strong 剛, literally "firm" or "hard" (in "Lessons for Women," p. 85), slight, 微 (in "The Cicada," p. 103), straight, 直 (in "Lessons for Women," p. 88), to pierce, 通達 (see 通 in "Travelling Eastward," p. 113), illustrate the use of terms in this poem which convey with their descriptive power psychological meaning that no doubt carried weight with Pan Chao in her selection of them.

[32] Hirth (*Ancient History*, pp. 235-237) wrote of the probability of steel being known as early as the time of King Kou-chien, 勾踐 (496-465 B.C.), of Yüeh State, 越國. Maspero (same, p. 43) writes that iron was not used until the end of Chou.

[33] Metal, 金, *"chin"* is one of the Five Elements, 五行 (see Maspero: same, p. 439, note 3), or the perpetually active principles of Nature (see *Shu King*, Legge: *Classics*, III, 325). The later speculations and enlargements on them were derived from the disquisitions of Tsou Yen, 騶衍 (fourth century B.C., Chavannes: *Mémoires*, I, p. CXLIV; Maspero: same, pp. 613-615), followed by the *Wu-hsing Chih*, 五行志, of Liu Hsiang, and the *Po-hu T'ung*, 白虎通, of Pan Ku (see p. 28). The nature of the element *Chin* (see Mayers, II, no. 127, 135) is coolness, 涼. Of the Five Metals (see Mayers, II, no. 139), the fifth is iron. The grain of the Five Grains which corresponds with metal is hemp, 麻. Metal is overcome by earth, 土. According to Chang Hêng, 張衡 (78-130 A.D., see p. 17), Venus was the Metal Planet, 金星, of the Five Planets (see Mayers, II, no. 162.) The *Yin*, 陰, principle (pp. 84, 85) corresponds to metal.

As Spring is under the rule of wood, Summer of fire, and Winter of water, so Autumn is under the metal element.

[34] In translation F. H. Balfour (*China Review*, IX, 1880-1881, 288-289) quoting from "The Principle of Nature," a chapter from "The History of Light," said that Huai-nan Tzû wrote: "It is always the man who does a thing for the first time, who has the difficulties to contend with; to those who come after him the fight is easy—the point (of the spear) encounters dangers; —yet the virtuous and wise are unable to avoid being always in the position of the point."

Huai-nan Tzû (see *T'ai-p'ing Yü-lan, chüan* 830, 鍼) also wrote a short verse on "The Needle and Thread" to show their mutual need for accomplishment of results.

"First the thread, then the needle,
Fails to fashion garments.
First the needle, then the thread,
May complete a curtain;
May fill enough earth baskets
To build a city wall."

[35] The meaning of this character, 貫 (Giles: *Dict.*, no. 6378), is "to run a thread through; to string; to connect," and doubtless Pan Chao had reference to its use in the "Analects." See Analects 4:15, *Classics*, I, 169; Analects

15:2, same, p. 295. The first use in 吾道一以貫之; the second in 予一以貫之. Legge's explanation (same, note 2, p. 295) is wrong. The unity in knowledge is the point. It means "to string together" as used by Pan Chao.

[36] Note the use of these ideas in the field of morals in "Lessons for Women," Chapter VII.

[37] In China the lamb is associated with filial piety. 羊跪乳, "The mother sheep stands and the lamb kneels." Thus for example the practice of filial piety is enforced by the reference to the lamb which always kneels when it is suckled by the dam.

If, however, Pan Chao meant the line to be an allusion to a similar line in the Book of Poetry, I, II, 7, (see *Classics*, IV, 28-29), the wording might be changed to read: "Until the results resemble court garments." These garments of skin, as explained by Legge, were seamed with white silk thread.

[38] In 1924 when the Ch'ing imperial family was driven out of the Forbidden City, Peking, there was discovered in the K'un-ning, 坤寧, Palace the original standard measure of capacity, a bronze *hu*, 斛, cast by order of Wang Mang. This measure of capacity unquestionably fixes the length of the foot measure of the Wang Mang period (9-22 A. D.) at slightly over nine English inches length; and determines the depth of the Han *tou*, 斗, "peck," to be slightly over nine-tenths of an English inch. (Wang Kuo-wei, 王國維, 1877-1927, in a lecture, "The Foot Measure in Various Chinese Dynasties," July, 1926, delivered in Yenching School of Chinese Studies, Peking). "The Coin-Foot-Measure of the Wang Mang period has the same length as that made in the Chien-wu, 建武, period (25-55 A. D.) of the later Han dynasty, and is also the same length as the foot measure of the Chou dynasty." (Translation by A. W. Hummel, cf. *JRAS, NCB*, LIX, 1928, 112-113.)

While Pan Chao probably had in mind the expression in the "Analects," her use here seems also, especially on the surface, that of an ordinary measure of capacity. See Analects 13:20, *Classics*, I, 272: 斗筲之人, "peck and hamper people—mere utensils, fit to fulfill a given function and no more."

[39] According to the *K'ang-hsi Dictionary*: 勒叉刻也. Giles (*Dict.*, no. 7316): 勒石, "to carve upon stone." So here taken to mean that the quantities of the pieces of work are the memorial stones to the needle and thread. The Sung dynasty commentator, Chang Ch'iao 章樵 (1232 A. D.), of the *Ku Wên Yüan*, 古文苑 (1886 A. D.), *chüan* 3, 賦, interpreted 石 to tell of quantities only, without the thought of "memorial stones." From a small beginning a great number is gradually made as a result of work.

[40] While 堂 may mean a stately hall, undoubtedly Pan Chao had in mind the expression of Confucius about Tzû-lu from the Analects 11:12, *Classics*, I, 242): 升堂. He "has ascended the hall, though he has not yet passed into the inner apartments." Legge (same, note 14:2) wrote, "This contains a defense of (Tzû-lu), and an illustration of his real attainments"; given at a time when the other disciples began not to respect him.

[41] For purposes of bibliographical record it may be mentioned that the translation of this poem into English was done by the author in 1926-1927 at which time there existed, so far as she knows, no translation of it into any western language. The admirably poetical translation by Professor W. E. Soothill which appeared in Lady Hosie's *Portrait of a Chinese Lady* in 1929 was made from a Chinese text supplied to the translator by the present author in 1928.

For a discussion of the poems see Chapter XII.

They are about the same in construction. The longest is that of "The Bird from the Far West," which having one phrase of seven instead of six characters, exceeds the poem of "The Cicada" in length by one character. These two poems, however, are exactly the same length in phrases, each having twelve. The shortest of the poems is that of "The Needle and Thread," which has ten phrases, and so a total of only sixty characters. Each of the three poems uses about the same characters for the lightly stressed conjunctions, prepositions, and enclitics. In "The Bird from the Far West" are found 而 in seven phrases, 之 in four phrases, and 與 in one phrase. In "The Cicada" are found 而 in four phrases, 之 in five phrases, 于 in two phrases, and 乎 in one phrase. In "The Needle and Thread" are found 而 in five phrases, 之 in four phrases, and 以 in one phrase. The first part of the long poem also uses about these same characters: namely, 而 thirty-two times, 之 twenty-two times, 乎 three times, 其 twice, 于 twice, and 以,與,欲,爲,多, once each, see next chapter.

CHAPTER IX

Travelling Eastward

Pan Chao's son Ku was appointed an official in Ch'ên-liu.[1] While travelling with him from the capital [2] to his post, Pan Chao composed an essay in rime,[3] "Travelling Eastward."

It is [3] the seventh year of Yung-ch'u; [4]
I follow my son in his journey eastward.
It is an auspicious [5] day in Spring's [6] first [7] moon;
We choose this good hour, and are about to start.
Now I rise to my feet and ascend my carriage.[8]
At eventide we lodge at Yen-shih: [9]
Already we leave the old and start for the new.
I am uneasy in mind, and sad at heart.[10]

Dawn's first light comes, and yet I sleep not; [11]
My heart hesitates as though it would fail me.[12]
I pour me out a cup of wine [13] to relax my thoughts.[14]
Suppressing my feelings,[15] I sigh and blame myself;
I shall not need to dwell in nests, nor (eat) worms from dead trees.[16]
Then how can I not encourage myself to press forward? [17]
And further, am I different from other people?
Let me but hear Heaven's command and go its way.[18]

Throughout the journey [19] we follow the great highway.[20]
If we seek short cuts, whom shall we follow?
Pressing [3] forward, we travel on and on;
In abandonment our eyes wander, and our spirits roam.
We pass through the Seven [21] Districts, watching, gazing;
At Kung Hsien [22] we experience difficulties,[23]
Further on we watch the Lo [24] unite with the Great River;
We see Ch'êng-kao's [25] "Farewell Gate."

Just when we have left behind lofty heights,
We reach and pass Ying-yang [26] and the nearby villages,[27]
We find food and rest enough at Yüan-wu.[28]
(One night) we lodge at Yang-wu, the mulberry center.[29]
Wading (a stream near) Fêng-ch'iu, again we tread the highway.[30]
Secretly I sigh for the Capital City I love, (but)
To cling to one's native place characterizes a small nature,[31]
As the histories have taught us.

Going forward on the highway but a little ahead,
We come to a low hill's [32] north side.
When we enter [3] K'uang City [33] I recall far distant events.[34]
I am reminded of Confucius' [35] straitened activities
In that decadent,[36] chaotic age [37] which knew not the Way; [38]
And which bound and awed [39] even him, that Holy Man! [40]
As I muse upon such vexing thoughts, (our train) has long halted;
Unobserved the sun has come to eventide, and dusk descends.

We arrive at the borders of Ch'ang-yüan,[41]
Where we study the natives of that agricultural land.
At P'u Ch'êng [42] we note its worn city walls
Upon which riotously thrive wild thorns.
Startled, aroused, I wake; thinking back, I wonder!
(Then) I recall the awe-inspiring spirit of [43] Tzû-lu,
Whom the people of Wei [44] did praise,
And to this day yet name for his brave sense [45] of duty.
In the district southeast of this city,
The people still honor the grave of Ch'ü Yüan,[46]

In fact genuine virtue cannot [47] die; [48]
Though the body decay,[49] the name lives on.
So what the Classics always praise
And honor are truth and virtue,[50] love [51] and merit.
Wu Cha [52] said this district had many princely men; [53]
For the truth of his words there was evidence.[54]
Afterwards came misfortune and a decadent age;
Whereupon (virtue) lapsed, and (its principle) prospered no more.[55]

東征賦

子穀為陳留長大家隨至官作東征賦

惟永初之有七兮余隨子乎東征時孟春之吉日兮撰良辰而將行乃舉趾而升輿兮夕予宿乎偃師遂去故而就新兮志愴悢而懷悲明發曙而不寐兮心遲遲而有違酌鐏酒吕弛念兮喟抑情而自非諒不登櫟而椓蠡兮得不陳力而相追且從衆而就列兮聽天命之所歸遵通衢之大道兮求捷徑欲從誰乃遂往而徂逝兮聊游目而遨魂歷七邑而觀覽兮遭鞏縣之多艱望河洛之交流兮看成皋之旋門既免脫于峻嶮兮歷滎陽而過卷食原武之息足宿陽武之桑間涉封丘而踐路兮慕京師而竊歎小人性之懷土兮自書傳而有焉遂進道而少前兮得平丘之北邊入匡郭而追遠兮念夫子之厄勤彼衰亂之無道兮乃困畏乎聖人悵容與而久駐兮忘日夕而將昏到長垣之境界察農野之居民睹蒲城之丘墟兮生荊棘之榛榛惕覺寤而顧問兮想子路之威神衛人嘉其勇義兮訖于今而稱云蘧氏在城之東南兮民亦尚其丘

I know that man's nature and destiny rest with Heaven,[56]
But by effort [57] we can go forward and draw near [58] to love.
(Muscles) stretched, head uplifted, we tread onward to the vision.[59]
With unfailing loyalty and reciprocity, in our dealing with men,[60]
Let us love uprightness,[61] and turn not back.
And thus our spirits [62] will communicate [63] with the spirits above.[64]
The (magic) mirror [65] of all the Spirits of the Earth
Protects the pure and the good, and helps [66] the faithful.

The *Luan* [67] says:

The thoughts [3] of the princely man
Ought to be written down.[68]
But why not also each say one's own opinion? [69]
As we admire the ancients,[70] (so I attest that)
Every action [71] of that virtuous one, (my father,) [72]
Meant a literary creation.[73]
Even though I am not wise,[74]
I dare not but follow him.[75]

Honor and dishonor, poverty and wealth,[76]
These may not be sought.[77]
With body erect,[78] let us walk the Way!
And bide the proper time.[79]
Our turn of life may be long, (or it may be) short,[80]
The stupid and the wise are alike in this.
Let us be quietly reverential; resigned to our Destiny,
Regardless whether a good or an evil one.[81]
Let us respect, be careful,[82] and not be indolent; [83]
Let us think of being humble and temperate; [84]
Let us be pure and calm, and want litttle,[85]
Like the Master Kung Ch'o.[86]

墳唯令德為不朽兮身既沒而名存惟經典之所美兮貴道德與
仁賢吳札稱多君子兮其言信而有徵後衰微而遭患兮遂陵遲
而不興知性命之在天由力行而近仁勉仰高而蹈景兮盡忠恕
而與人好正直而不回兮精誠通于明神庶靈祇之鑒照兮祐貞
良而輔信亂曰君子之思必成文兮盍各言志慕古人兮先君行
止則有作兮雖其不敏敢不法兮貴賤貧富不可求兮正身履道
以俟時兮脩短之運愚智同兮靖恭委命唯吉凶兮敬慎無怠思
嗛約兮清靜少欲師公綽兮

開平關宗軾書

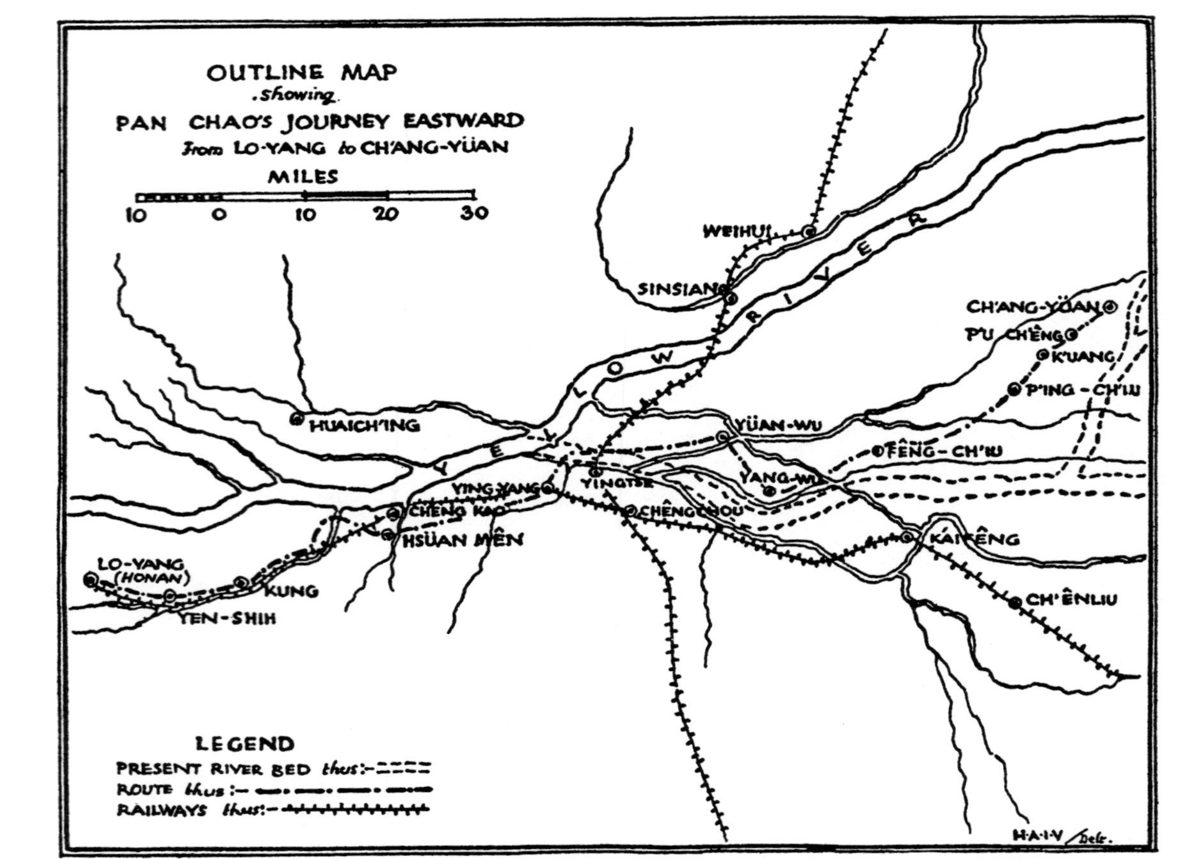
OUTLINE MAP
showing
PAN CHAO'S JOURNEY EASTWARD
from LO-YANG to CH'ANG-YÜAN
MILES
10 0 10 20 30
WEIHUI
SINSIAN
YELLOW RIVER
CH'ANG-YÜAN
P'U CHÊNG
K'UANG
P'ING-CH'IU
HUAICH'ING
YÜAN-WU
FÊNG-CH'IU
YANG-WU
YING YANG
YINGTSE
CHÊNG CHOU
CHÊNG KAO
HSÜAN MÊN
KAI FÊNG
CH'ÊNLIU
LO-YANG
(HONAN)
KUNG
YEN-SHIH
LEGEND
PRESENT RIVER BED thus:-
ROUTE thus:-
RAILWAYS thus:-
H.A.I.V. Delt.

NOTES

[1] According to the commentator in the *Wên Hsüan,* 文選李善註, the "Collected Works of Pan Chao," 曹大家集, gave the post of her son to which she accompanied him as a district official, 長垣長, in the prefecture of Ch'ên-liu, 陳留. But this district, 長垣, later was changed to the control of a prefecture in Chihli Province, 直隸大名府.

According to the *Hsü Han Shu* (Chavannes, *T'oung Pao,* VIII, 1906, 214; Appendix, p. 159 ff.), *chüan* 21, 續漢書, 郡國志, 陳留郡, the distance of Ch'ên-liu from Lo-yang was 530 *li*—that is, about 180 English miles.

[2] The journey began at the capital, 京師, which in 95 A. D. was Lo-yang, known in the Chou dynasty as Lo-i, 雒邑, or Wang Ch'êng, 王城 (cf. Maspero: same, pp. 25, 81, 148). The Western Han dynasty had made Ch'ang-an, 長安, the capital, but the Eastern Han rebuilt the fortifications of Lo-yang, and there erected a palace making Lo-yang the capital.

The journey eastward was practically that from modern Honanfu, in Honan Province, through Yen-shih-hsien, 偃師, Kung-hsien, 鞏縣, Ying-yang-hsien, 滎陽, all west of modern Chêng-chow, the juncture of the two railroads, Peking-Hankow and Lung-hai—and northeastward to Ch'ang-yüan-hsien, 長垣, which is now north of the Yellow River in Chihli Province, so that between Ying-yang (modern name Hsing-yang) and Yüan-wu, 原武, the river must be crossed. When Pan Chao made the journey the course of the Yellow River was such that Ch'ang-yüan-hsien was south of it, and belonged to the prefecture of Ch'ên-liu, east and southeast of modern K'aifêngfu, the provincial capital of Honan. See any modern map of Honan, Shantung, and Chihli Provinces, as well as accompanying map, p. 118.

[3] According to the rime of the essay its first portion falls into three sections. These sections are indicated in the translation by the repetition of the figure 3 in the first line of each of them. The arrangement of the translation into paragraphs is due to the arbitrary decision of the translator.

[4] The seventh year of Yung-ch'u, 永初, was 113 A. D. This reign period from 107 to 113 A. D. was under the emperor An, 安帝. *Tung Kuan Han Chi* said that Yung-ch'u was a reign period under the emperor Ho. As the Ch'ing scholar Yüan Yüan, 阮元 (1764-1849), reasoned it out, the poem must have been written in Yung-yüan, 永元 period, seventh year, or 95 A. D. See p. 49.

[5] J. Edkins ("*Yi King* and Its Appendices," *China Review,* XIV, 1885-1886, 303-304) wrote that "The first time we meet the term lucky day, 吉日, is in the 'Odes,' and it is connected with prayers. In the *Han Shu* it is found in conjunction with fasting, 歷吉日以齋戒. From this it appears that the word lucky has not in it enough of religious sentiment to render it an exact equivalent of the Chinese—religious day. About 60 A. D., in the time of Ming Ti (57-75 A. D.)—the officers in charge of sacrifices chose a happy day to present a written announcement in the ancestral temple (see *Hou Han Shu,* 明帝紀). Such examples of the phrase 'lucky day' bring it in close relationship with worship and self-purification."

In (*JRAS, NCB,* XXIV, 1889, 256-257) "Chinese Architecture," he also remarks that "There was in ancient times no *fêng-shui,* 風水. This is a recent superstition. But it was required to have lucky portents and begin laying out a city upon a lucky day."

A list of auspicious days is yet (1928) given in the official almanac issued annually, by the Government of the Republic of China.

[6] According to the Chinese calendar, spring includes the first, second, and third moons after Chinese New Year, which occurs usually in the last week of January or the first week of February.

[7] First, second, and third, 孟仲季, were used in connection with the three moons of each season. These were also the names of the three rival houses of the states of Lu in the days of Confucius.

[8] Legge (*Classics,* I, in a note to Analects 15:5, p. 296) noted that 輿 "is properly the bottom of a carriage, planks laid over wheels."

[9] This night-stop was Yen-shih, 偃師, which district may be found on any modern map of Honan Province. From Lo-yang to Yen-shih now by rail is about sixty *li* or twenty miles.

[10] All characters in this line except the 而 for caesura have for radical 心, the heart. Note Pan Chao's use of 志, in her memorial to the emperor Ho, p. 74. As a comment on this line in the *Wên Hsüan,* Li Shan, 文選李善註, quoted from *Ch'u Tz'û*: 楚辭：愴怳懭悢兮，去故而就新.

[11] In the Book of Poetry is the passage, 明發不寐 (II, V, 2:1), translated by Legge (*Classics,* IV, p. 333): "When the dawn is breaking, and I cannot sleep."

[12] For comparison with 有違, see 行違 in "Lessons," p. 87, note 50. In the Book of Poetry (I, III, 10:2) is the passage, 行道遲遲，中心有違, translated by Legge (*Classics,* IV, 55):

"I go along the road slowly, slowly,
In my inmost heart reluctant."

J. Edkins (Notes in *China Review,* XVII, 1888-1889, 180) said that the origin of 遲 is "in constant deflection from the path, thus leading to delay."

[13] He also (Notes in *China Review,* XV, 1886-1887, 309) stated that Legge in the *Li Chi* "translates 酒 (*chiu*) by liquor and occasionally by spirits. Neither of these words sounds quite so well as wine. The ancient Chinese wine was fermented, not distilled, and was intoxicating.—The Chinese first knew spirits in the T'ang dynasty,—Northern Chinese in the Yüan dynasty learned to distil on a large scale. Chinese (*chiu*) corresponds to the Japanese *sake,* which means any brewed liquid of intoxicating quality."

For the *tsun,* 罇, which has come down from Han times, see S. W. Bushell: *Chinese Art* (London, 1921), I, figures 51, 53, 55; Albert J. Koop: *Early Chinese Bronzes,* (London, 1924), pp. 8-15, plates 6-17; J. C. Ferguson: *Outlines of Chinese Art* (Chicago, 1919), pp. 50, 58, 33-65.

[14] 弛, "to unstring a bow; to relax" (Giles: *Dict.,* no. 9931). The commentator on this passage in the *Wên Hsüan,* 文選李善註, quoted from the *Êrh Ya,* 爾雅：念思也. Legge (*Classics,* I, 171, note 21 on Analects 4:21) translated 念念不忘意, "the meaning of unforgetting thoughtfulness."

[15] The seven emotions usually given under 情 are joy, 喜, anger, 怒, sorrow, 哀, fear, 懼, love, 愛, hatred, 惡, and desire, 欲 (Giles: *Dict.,* no. 2187).

[16] The *K'ang-hsi Dictionary* uses this clause from Pan Chao to illustrate that 樔又作巢. See also 朱珔 (1769-1850), 文選集釋, *chüan* 11, 東征賦.

Legge translated a passage from the *Li Chi* (*SBE,* XXVII, 369) to read that "Formerly the ancient kings had no houses. In winter they lived in caves— and in summer in nests,—ate the fruits of plants and trees, the flesh of birds and beasts." See also the note on this passage in *Wên Hsüan*, 文選李善註, 東征賦, and cf. Mencius, III, II, 9:3, *Classics*, II, 279.

E. J. Eitel (*China Review*, XVII, 1888-1889, 330) translated from Liu Hsin's address to the throne, on the presentation of the *Shan Hai Ching*, that "At that early time (of Yao and Shun) mighty inundations, with their continuous floods, engulfed the Empire of China in extensive destruction, the people being deprived of their substance, and having to take refuge on hills and mountains, or to nest in trees."

[17] The use of the term, 陳力, may, like that in Analects 16:1, have reference to the assumption of official responsibility since Pan Chao was en route with her son to his official post. Legge (*Classics*, I, 307) translated: "When he puts forth his ability." Here, however, it seems best to render the term from the personal rather than the official view-point.

[18] Hear=obey; 所歸 is the contents of Heaven's command. The free will aspect of the question of determinism versus free will in early Chinese thinking is well illustrated by the extraordinary faculties which the "superior man," 君子, can attain. See E. J. Eitel, "Fragmentary Studies in Ancient Chinese Philosophy," *China Review*, XV (1886-1887), 338 ff; Herbert Chatley, "Studies in Chinese Psychology, II, Fate and Fortune," *New China Review*, I (1919), 145-148.

The most outspoken declaration against Fate or Destiny as the controlling influence in a person's life was most interestingly made by Mo Ti, see 淸孫詒讓 (1848-1908): 墨子閒詁, 非命, *chüan* 35, 36, 37; with translation made by Forke: *Mê Ti*, Kapitel 35-37, Verdammung des Fatalismus, pp. 374-375; Alexandre David: *Le Philosophe Meh-Ti et l'idée de solidarité* (London, 1907), Chapter IV, Le Déstin, pp. 156 ff; and Liang Ch'i-ch'ao: *Mo Tzû Hsüeh-an*, 墨子學案.

For a discussion of the decree of Heaven by Wang Ch'ung, see the translation by A. D. Hutchinson, "The Critical Disquisitions of Wang Ch'ung," *China Review*, VII (1878-1879), 89-91, 170, 240-242, 308; VIII (1879-1880), 46; by Forke: *Lung-Hêng, Ming-lu*, 命祿, *Ch'i-shou*, 氣壽, and *Ming-yi*, 命義.

For the popular interpretation, "What must be, must be; you cannot escape that which the gods have ordained for you," see Charles Kliene, "The Marriage Maker," *JRAS, NCB*, LII (1921), 139-155; Evan Morgan, "Destiny, Fate," same, LI (1920) 25 ff.; Hu Shih, "The Social Message in Chinese Poetry," *Chinese Soc. and Polit. Science Review*, VII (1923), 79; R. W. Hurst, a translation of a "Story of a Chinese Cinderella," *China Review*, XV (1886-1887), 221-233.

For a criticism against the Chinese custom of deciding cases of marriage by fortune-telling, see Li Ju-chên's "Flowers in the Mirror," Hu Shih's edition, Vol I, Preface, 22, together with Hu Shih's comment on fate in "A Chinese Declaration of Rights of Women," *Chinese Soc. and Polit. Science Review* (1924), VIII, 100-109.

According to Analects 20:3 (*Classics*, I, 354): "Without recognizing the ordinances of Heaven, it is impossible to be a superior man," 君子; and according to Analects 16:8 (same, p. 313): "A *chün-tzû* stands in awe of, and a 小人 does not know 天命." (These two quotations are passages in that part of the Analects [16-20] the genuineness of which has been so questioned that contemporary Chinese scholarship rejects the most of the five sections. They would then the more reflect Han ideals.) Analects 2:4 (Legge: same, p. 146): Confucius said that 五十而知天命, "At fifty I knew the decree of Heaven."

[19] Note the use of 通 in the "Needle and Thread" poem, pp. 105, 106.

[20] J. C. Hall ("The Confucian Reformers of Japan in the Eighteenth Century," a translation, see *JRAS, NCB,* XLI [1910], 15) wrote that "The natural and spontaneous Way of mankind—is like the great highway, 大道—the thoroughfare between the ordinary town and the Capital City—there may be those who do not make use of the highway but take some short cut."

[21] According to a commentary quoted from Hsü Kuang, 徐廣 (352-425 A. D., Giles: *Biog.,* no. 778), in the *Shih Chi* (*chüan* 4, 周本紀) on the destruction of the Chou dynasty, 滅東西周, the conquered districts were seven, 周比亡之時凡七縣, namely, Ho-nan, 河南, Lo-yang, 洛陽, Ku Ch'êng, 穀城 P'ing-yin, 平陰, Yen-shih, 偃師, Kung, 鞏, and Hou Shih, 緱氏. In all probability it was to these historical "Seven Districts," 七邑, that Pan Chao referred because she passed through this region, and even named some of them. See also 文選旁證, *chüan* 12, 東征賦, 注七縣; 文選集釋, *chüan* 11, 東征賦.

Legge wrote of 邑 (note 27 to Analects 5:27, *Classics,* I, 183): "The designation of the place where men are collected together; and may be applied from hamlet upwards to a city." For a discussion of the origin of the character see L. C. Hopkins, "Pictographic Reconnaissances," Pt. 2, *JRAS* (July-August, 1918), p. 417.

[22] This is approximately the modern Kung-hsien, 鞏縣, found on any modern map of Honan Province, about twenty miles east of Yen-shih-hsien. It is mentioned both in the *Han Shu, chüan* 28, 地理志, and *Hsü Han Shu, chüan* 19 and 21, 郡國志.

[23] Just what this "distress" was is not clear. While it may have been the difficulties of a bad road, very likely it may have been the distress of the people from some cause now unknown.

[24] A note in the *Shan Hai Ching,* 山海經, says: 洛水至東河南鞏縣入河, "The Lo stream flows east until it enters the Yellow River at Kung-hsien in Honan." See *Shui Ching,* 水經注, *chüan* 15.

The Yellow and the Lo Rivers, two of the three rivers of ancient China, see Mayers, II, no. 13, 21, 267. This designation, *ho,* was first applied to the Yellow River exclusively, but in time to rivers in general.

The fairy ladies of the River Lo (曹直, 192-232 A. D., 洛神賦; 顧愷之, third century A. D., 洛神圖, J. C. Ferguson: "Stories in Chinese Paintings," *JRAS, NCB,* LVI (1925), 119-120; Waley: *Chinese Painting,* pp. 60-62), and the legends of the *Lo Shu,* 洛書 (mentioned in the Book of History, cf. Maspero: same, p. 439), and of the *Ho T'u,* 河圖, rose in detail after the Han dynasty, being based upon the spurious text of the Book of History rejected by early Ch'ing scholarship. See also the Book of Changes, 繫辭.

[25] This place is mentioned in *Han Shu, Honan Chün, chüan* 28; in *Shui Ching, chüan* 15; the *Tz'û Yüan;* and is given on Map 12, 中國地理沿革圖,

1922. Chang Hêng (see p. 17) said in a poem, 東京賦: 西阻九阿, 東門于旋. From a note, 文選李善註, on this line it may be seen that Ch'êng-kao was a strategic centre in the struggles of the Contending States (481-221 B.C.) as well as in the Han dynasty. (See Ch. Piton, "The Fall of the Ts'in Dynasty and the Rise of that of Han," *China Review,* XI, 1882-1883, 230-231.) About twenty miles west of Ying-yang, 滎陽. Ten odd *li* out southwest from Ch'êng-kao was 旋門, the East Gateway. This is shown as a place on Map 12 (same, see above), but since 旋 carries with it the idea of return, and every large town usually yet has ten *li* out on the main roads tea houses from which point officials turned back when escorting departing officials, it is rendered "Farewell Gate."

[26] For 免脫, "to avoid," of the text, Dr. Kiang Kang-hu suggests that perhaps in the original the more picturesque term 兔脫 (see *Tz'û Yüan,* 子, p. 256), "to skip by," was used.

Of the places mentioned, Yen-shih, Kung-hsien, Ying-yang (Giles: *Dict.,* no. 5741, Jung-yang), Yüan-wu, Yang-wu, Fêng-ch'iu, and Ch'ên-liu all may be found in the *Tz'û Yüan* (Supplement), located in Honan. They are also all mentioned both in the *Han Shu, chüan* 28, and in the *Hsü Han Shu, chüan* 19, 21. See also the map on p. 118.

[27] There is a place by the name, 卷, mentioned in both the *Han Shu, chüan* 28, and the *Hsü Han Shu, chüan* 19. It was the native place of Chou P'o, 周勃 (d. 169 B.C.), faithful supporter of the direct imperial line of the Western Han dynasty, see Giles: *Biog.,* no. 422. It is rendered simply "nearby villages."

[28] Yüan-wu is now north of the river, as are all the other places mentioned below: Yang-wu, Fêng-ch'iu, Ping-ch'iu, K'uang, Ch'ang-yüan and P'u Ch'êng. The *Tz'û Yüan* lists five changes in the course of the Yellow River. At the time of the Eastern Han dynasty, its course was such that Pan Chao did not cross the river in her journey but kept to the southern bank of it. For the route followed by Pan Chao see *Li-tai Yü-ti Yen-ko Hsien-yao T'u,* 歷代輿地沿革險要圖 (續漢郡國志., 後漢, 郡國圖司隸河南尹, 南二西一. p. 34), 1906, by Yang Shou-ching, 楊守敬 (1839-1915); also the map, p. 118.

[29] For China's silk trade in the Eastern Han dynasty, see *Serindia,* I, Chapter XI, 373: "A find of a silk bale from the Kingdom of Jên Ch'êng, 任城 (in present Shantung), established 84 A.D."; II, Chapter XIX, 700 ff.: "A relic of the ancient silk trade"; IV, Plate XXXVII, the picture of the silk bale found, which belongs to the last part of the first century or the early part of the second century A.D.; Chavannes: *Documents,* no. 539, pp. 116 ff; F. H. Andrews: *Ancient Chinese Figured Silk* (London, 1920), Intro. by Stein; cf. p. 30. On exhibit in the British Museum (King's Library) are two specimens of these finds in silk: two strips of an uncoloured silken fabric—the date cannot be much later than 100 A.D. (T, XV, a. 1). See also Harada: *Lo-Lang,* and references Chapter III, note 39.

For open trade routes see Carter: *Invention of Printing,* pp. 85-86, 88.

For a popular presentation of the importance of silk in Han times, see Samuel Merwin: *Silk, A Legend* (London, 1924).

[30] The use of 涉一踐路 pictures the cart drivers "wading water" and then

"stamping their feet" dry as they again tread the highway. So "a stream near" is supplied for the translation.

[31] Analects 4:11, Legge: *Classics,* I, 168: 小人懷土, "The superior man thinks of virtue; the small man thinks of comfort."

[32] 平丘, "a low hill," is a place mentioned in both the *Han Shu* and in the *Hsü Han Shu,* same. The translation is used in order to avoid too many proper names in the English version.

[33] 匡郭, K'uang City is a historic place, K'uang, where Confucius, mistaken for some one else, was in danger for the time. See below, note 39.

[34] Analects 1:9, Legge: *Classics,* I, 141: 追遠, "Let them be followed when long gone (by the proper ceremonies of sacrifices)."

[35] 夫子, Confucius, see Legge: *Classics,* I, Prolegomena, Chapter V, "Confucius and His Immediate Disciples," pp. 56-127. Cf. Ssû-ma Ch'ien, *chüan* 47 and 67; and Maspero: same, pp. 454-468.

[36] Analects 7:5, Legge: *Classics,* I, 196: 甚矣吾衰也. "Extreme is my decay." See also Analects 18:3; 6:14; 15:1; 15:25: same, pp. 334, 190, 294, 301.

[37] G. G. Warren ("The First League of Nations," *New China Review,* I, 1919, 356-359) wrote of representatives of fourteen nations meeting in 546 B.C. at the capital of Sung—practically the location of the modern Kweitehfu, Honan,—"to stop the wars of the barons by treaty." The Big Four were Chin, 晉, Ch'u, 楚, Ch'in, 秦. and Ch'i, 齊, "five years before this Peace Conference, *i.e.,* 551 B.C. (according to Chinese traditional reckoning) Confucius was born."

[38] According to the Analects (6:22, Legge: *Classics,* I, 192, note), 道 is 先王盡善盡美之道, "the entirely good and admirable ways of the former kings." 無道 is when "right principles of government do not prevail," Analects 8:13, same, p. 212. And according to Analects 16:2, same, p. 310, "When bad government prevails in the Empire, ceremonies, music, and punitive military expeditions, 禮樂征伐, proceed from the princes, 諸侯."

[39] For Confucius' unpleasant experience at K'uang, see Analects 9:5, *Classics,* I, 217: 子畏於匡, "The Master was put in fear in K'uang"; also note, p. 217; Analects 11:22, p. 245 with note; *Shih Chi, chüan* 47, on Confucius.

[40] T. T. Meadows (*The Chinese and Their Rebellions,* London, 1856, p. 348) wrote that "The first occidental sinologues, all missionaries, naturally shrank as professional theologians from applying the word 'Holy' to any heathens, and hence rendered 聖 by 'Sage,'—*Holy, Heilig, and Saint* are the only words in English, German, and French, that at all express the perfect moral purity and wisdom which is attributed to the 聖人."

E. H. Parker ("The Philosopher Sün-Tsz," *New China Review,* IV, 1922, 13, 362, 364) rendered "the perfect man."

For the view of L. C. Hopkins, see Notes, *China Review,* X (1881-1882), 144.

For the Confucian Holy Man, see Mencius, VII, II, 25, *Classics,* II, 490; the translation by J. C. Hall, *JRAS, NCB,* XLI (1910), 1-25.

For the Taoist Holy Man, see Maspero: same, pp. 484-485; Huai-nan Tzû, "The Principle of Nature," translated by Frederic H. Balfour: *China Review,* IX (1880-1881), 281-297; *Chuang Tzû,* translated by Giles: *Tao Tê Ching,* translated by Carus.

[41] 長垣. This place is mentioned in both the *Han Shu* and the *Hsü Han Shu,* same. See above note 1.

[42] 蒲城. This place is mentioned in the *Ch'ên-liu Chün* (*chüan* 21), in the *Hsü Han Shu,* and the commentator added a note on its connection with the history of both Confucius and his disciple Tzû-lu.

[43] 子路, Tzû-lu, whose name was Chung Yu, 仲由 (543-480 B.C.), was a native of the State of Lu, but as stated by Legge (*Classics,* I, 115), "For some time was chief magistrate of the district of P'u, where his administration commanded the warm commendations of the Master." Also see Legge: same, pp. 86-87, 114-115; *Shih Chi, chüan* 67; Couling: *Encyclo. Sinica,* Chung Yu, p. 116; Giles: *Biog.,* no. 522; Mayers, no. 91.

According to tradition, to the "Historical Record," and to the *Tso Chuan,* he was unwilling to die with the tassel of his cap out of place. See *Classics,* I, 151: *Tso Chuan.* Ai Kung, fifteenth year, 左傳, 哀公, fifteenth year, 479 B.C.; *Shih Chi, chüan* 67; *Classics,* V, pp. 842-843, *Chinese Biog.,* p. 221.

For references to him in the Analects, see Analects 2:17; 11:12; 17:23; *Classics,* I, 151, 241, 329.

A picture of his tomb, together with an account of its having been rebuilt by officials during the Ch'ing period may be seen in the Gazetteer of the district of Ch'ang-yüan (see note below on 蘧, Ch'ü) 長垣縣志 (1809), *chüan* 1, section, 圖考.

He is among the nineteen disciples depicted on the Shantung bas-reliefs, 武梁司; see Chavannes: *La Sculpture sur pierre en Chine,* Plate IX, pp. 39-40.

Tzû-lu "stands out a sort of Peter in the Confucian school, a man of impulse, prompt to speak and prompt to act. He gets many a check from the Master, but there is evidently a strong sympathy between them. Tzû-lu uses a freedom with him on which none of the other disciples dares to venture, ——. A pleasant picture is presented to us in one passage in the 'Analects' (Bk. 11:12)—Tzû-lu looking bold and soldierly; ——. The Master was pleased, but he observed, 'Yu (Tzû-lu's name) there! he will not die a natural death.'" This prediction was verified. In 479 B.C. a revolution broke out in the State of Wei. Tzû-lu would not forsake his chief who had treated him well. He threw himself into the fight, and was slain. See *Classics,* I, Prolegomena, 86.

[44] 衛, a feudal state; for early Chou times, see map by Legge: *Classics,* IV, Prolegomena, 126; for late Chou times, same, V, Prolegomena, 112.

In the reign of Prince I, the Wei Kingdom was taken by the 狄, Ti barbarians, and the total population, male and female, of 730 persons, then moved eastward, so the location of the Wei of early Chou and of late Chou is different. It became so encircled by rival states that it had no way to expand (see p. 4). Lü Shih's "Spring and Autumn Annals," 呂氏春秋, says: "Between the Yellow River, 河, and the Chi River, 濟, is Wei Chou, 衛州," or the Wei Kingdom.

Modern Wei-hui-fu, 衛輝府, Honan Province, preserves in name and general location the ancient Wei Kingdom.

See the "Odes of Wei," Book of Poetry, *Classics,* IV, 91 ff.

[45] Giles (*Dict.,* no. 13,457): 見義不為, 無勇也, "to see what is right, and not to do it is want of courage." See *Classics,* I, 322, 329, 330.

J. Edkins ("A sketch of the Life of Confucius," *JRAS, NCB,* Old Series, II, no. 1, 1860, 14) wrote that "China honours her sages by the preservation of their places of burial; ancestral tombs are built to them; while their descendants receive titles and emoluments from the state. In travelling through the country, many a spot is found to have a special interest belonging to it, from the reminiscences clustering round it, of the great statesmen, poets, sages, or warriors of past times. The more remarkable, such as those which commemorate the acts of Confucius, are under the charge of the central government, ——; while the less important are cared for by the local government and the inhabitants of the neighborhood."

Herbert Chatley ("The Dead Hand in China," *JRAS, NCB,* LV, 1924, 57) wrote that "The practical bearing of worship of death is an important sociological question. The recent war (1914-1918) with its immense cemeteries, cenotaphs, and cult of 'the unknown warrior' shows that the same tendencies persist. The repugnance to cremation and the desire to have the dead in an accessible cemetery bear like testimony.—— In so far as there are in all of us memories—funeral rites will probably always have a strong social effect."

[46] 蘧瑗, Ch'ü Yüan has a prominent place in the gazetteer of the district of Ch'ang-yüan, which reproduces a picture of both his tomb and a temple erected to his memory, together with this reference to his grave by Pan Chao. His tomb was rebuilt by officials of the Ch'ing dynasty, by whom also was erected not far away a temple which included a school. See *chüan* 11, section 周, first biography, and *chüan* 1, section 圖考 (see note 43 above).

Ch'ü Yüan was officer of Wei, 衛, a friend and not a disciple of Confucius, and so he is not listed among those most intimate with the Master despite his frequent appearance in both the "Analects" and in "Mencius," see Legge: *Classics,* I, Prolegomena, 112-127. Nor is he, therefore, listed among the disciples of Confucius in the "Historical Record," *chüan* 67. See Giles: *Biog.,* no. 501.

[47] The use of 唯 implies that no contradiction can be made to the statement.

[48] See an article under this title, 不朽, by Hu Shih, *Wên Ts'un,* 文存, vol. II, *chüan* 4, 105 ff.

The *Tso Chuan* has a passage, 大上有立德, — 此之謂不朽, for the same idea, see Hsiang Kung, twenty-fourth year, *chüan* 30, 左傳, 襄公, *Classics,* V, 505, 507.

[49] Analects 9:5, *Classics,* I, 217: 文王旣沒, "After the death of King Wan."

Lao Tzû: *Tao Tê Ching,* Carus, p. 105: 沒身不殆, "The end of the body, it is not dangerous."

Wang Ch'ung, Chapter XI, translation by A. B. Hutchinson, *China Review,* VIII (1879-1880), 45: "The body will decay like grass and herbs, the reputation like the sun and moon, will remain brilliant."

[50] See *Shih Chi, chüan* 63, Lao Tzû, Chuang Tzû, etc.; Paul Carus: same, pp. 51-52, 95-96, 142-146: 老子修道德. "Lao Tzû practised reason and virtue."

[51] 仁, rendered "love"; see also Lionel Giles: *The Sayings of Confucius* (London, 1920), Introduction, pp. 21-22; Leonard A. Lyall: *The Sayings of Confucius* (second ed., London, 1925), Preface. Cf. Chapter VII, note 43.

[52] 吳札, Wu Cha, or 季札, Chi Cha, a royal prince of the State of Wu (in the lower Yang-tzû valley, the section of the Wu dialects of modern China). Wu Chi Cha "was sent the rounds of the Chinese states as special ambassador, charged, under the convenient cloak of seeking civilization, ritual,

and music, with the duty of acquiring political and strategical knowledge. This prince so favorably impressed the orthodox statesmen (of the Chinese states) that he was everywhere received as an equal: his tomb is still in existence, about ten miles from the treaty-port of Chinkiang (Kiangsu Province), and the inscription upon it, in ancient characters," has long been ascribed to Confucius, who, "though a boy of eight (seven western reckoning) when the Wu prince visited Lu in 544 B.C., died only six years after the death of Wu Chi Cha, who lived to be 90 years old." See E. H. Parker: *Ancient China Simplified* (London, 1908), pp. 73, 81, 98, etc., mentioned in Index, Ki-chah, p. 324; Giles: *Biog.*, no. 287; Couling: *Encyclo. Sinica*, pp. 93-94; Mayers, no. 243.

Wu Chi Cha was given as fief the territory in Kiangsu province which is in general the modern Wu-chin Hsien, 武進縣, see the provincial gazetteer of Kiangsu and Anhui, 江南通志 (1729), *chüan* 32, p. 4.

[53] For a similar picture, see Hugh Cranmer-Byng's Introduction, *Yang Chu's Garden of Pleasure* (*The Wisdom of the East Series*, London, 1912, p. 7), when "to the capital of Liang, in the State of Wei, came all the Philosophers, just as they came to Athens." Compare with this the account of the visit of Wu Chi Cha a century earlier as given in the *Tso Chuan*, Hsiang Kung, twenty-ninth year, *chüan* 32, *Classics*, V, 544, 547, 549-551: . . . "there are many superior men in Wei"—and one mentioned by him was Ch'ü Yüan.

[54] This expression credited in the *Tso Chuan*, Chao Kung, eighth year, *chüan* 37, to one Yang-shê Hsi, 羊舌肸 (*Chinese Biog.*, p. 278), Shu-hsiang of the State of Chin, 晋叔向, Legge: *Classics*, V, 620, 622: "The words of a superior man are true and supported by evidence." The evidence here is Tzû-lu, Ch'ü Yüan, etc.

[55] If the reference is made to the Kingdom Wei instead of to "virtue," then the meaning is: "So the Kingdom (of Wei) fell, and never rose again."

[56] See above, note 18 on 命; and Mencius, VI, I, *Classics*, II, 394-421, on 性. See also Analects 17:2, with note, Legge, I, 318, 383.

Analects 12:5, *Classics*, I, 253; 死生有命, 富貴在天, "Death and life have their determined appointment; riches and honours depend upon Heaven." Compare with the use of 富貴 and of 修短 below in the first three couplets of the last stanza.

Pan Chao's great-aunt Pan Chieh-yü used the words from the Analects in her defense of herself before the emperor Ch'êng when accused by Chao Fei-yen, see *Han Shu*, *chûan* 97.

[57] 力行, as here used by Pan Chao, shows the influence of Mo Ti's teachings in Han times. Cf. the "effort" he called for in his censure of the belief in Fate or Destiny binding the people in their every walk of life; see his chapters, 非命, especially the third, *chüan* 37, Forke: *Mê Ti*, Chapters 35-37.

[58] The *Chung Yung*, *chüan* 20 (*SBE*, XXVIII, 314) has the expression: 好學近乎知,力行近乎仁, "To be fond of learning is near to wisdom; to practise with vigor is near to benevolence." 仁 rendered "love" instead of benevolence.

[59] The Book of Poetry (II, VII, 4:5, *Classics*, IV, 393) has the couplet: 高山仰止, "The high hill is looked up to; 景行行止, The great road is easy to be travelled on."

[60] Legge (*Classics*, I, 170, note) said that "忠 is duty-doing, on consideration, or from the impulse, of one's own self; 恕 is duty-doing, on the principle

of reciprocity." See also Analects 1:4, 5:18, 7:24, 9:20, 15:23, 4:11, *Classics*, I, 139, 179, 202, 223, 301, 177, 251, 170; and 忠恕違道不遠 (*SBE*, XXVIII, 305), "If one maintains his integrity and practises the reciprocal duties, he is not far from the path."

[61] Book of Poetry, II, IV, 3:5, *Classics*, IV, 366:

好是正直，神之聽之，介爾景福.

"Loving the correct and upright
So shall the spirits hearken to you,
And give you large measures of bright happiness."

[62] Note the use of 精 in "Needle and Thread" poem, p. 105. 誠, "actually and fully accomplished." See note by Legge: *Chung Yung, SBE*, XXVIII, 317.

[63] Note the use of 通 above, note 19, and also in "Needle and Thread," p. 105

[64] Analects 7:20, *Classics*, I, 201; 神, "One of the four subjects on which the Master did not talk."

Book of Poetry, III, III, 4:6, *Classics*, IV, 533: 敬恭明神，宜無悔怒, "Reverent to the intelligent Spirits, I ought not to be thus the object of their anger."

J. Edkins ("Chinese Architecture," *JRAS, NCB*, XXIV, 1889, 256) wrote of 神明, "spirits and bright intelligences. This phrase is much used—for worshipping beings who are believed to come and throng round the spots where sacrifices are offered and prostrations made. They also scrutinize and reward or punish the actions of mankind."

[65] Note the use of 靈 both in "The Bird from the West," Chapter VIII, note 4, and in the memorial to the emperor Ho, p. 98; and the use of 祇 with 神 in "Lessons," p. 87. One of Mo Ti's teachings was that of the intervention of spirits of the dead in affairs of this world in favor of the good, see Maspero: same, p. 470.

That is: "watchfulness." For Heaven's Looking Glass in Taoism, see J. Dyer Ball, *China Review*, XI (1882-1883), 210-211.

[66] 輔, poles used to prevent carts from upsetting, or as levers to raise the wheels, etc. (Giles: *Dict.*, no. 3627).

[67] Here there is a change from the six character phrases, broken by *hsi*, 兮, to four character phrases with *hsi* as the last character of the second phrase.

The *K'ang-hsi Dictionary* has 樂之卒章日亂. Legge (*Classics*, I, 213) translated: "The last part in the musical services is called *lwan*.—The name *lwan* was also given to a sort of refrain, at the end of each song."

[68] *Yang Hsiung Fa Yen*, 楊雄法言: 君子言則成文，動則成德.

Analects 7:24, Legge: *Classics*, I, 202, 文, "Letters"—one of the four things taught by Confucius. Cf. Analects 6:16, *Classics*, I, 190.

[69] Analects 5:25, *Classics*, I, 182: "The Master said: 'Come, let each of you tell his wishes.'"

Giles (*Dict.*, no. 3959): "Why doesn't each of you speak his mind?"

A. B. Hutchinson ("The Critical Disquisitions of Wang Ch'ung," IX, 28, 8, Confucius Interrogated, *China Review*, VII, 1878-1879, 44) translated: "I say there are those living in our times possessed of great talents and exalted wisdom, who are capable of answering any one seeking an explanation of difficulties, and by those my present day investigation deciding the right and the wrong will certainly be regarded with esteem."

[70] While the Han Confucianists "loved antiquity," unfortunately they mixed

in with their *Ku-wên* so much for which no evidence can be found that contemporary Chinese scholars are having a very difficult time to separate the facts of history from their creations of ideals.

[71] Mencius (I, II, 16:3, *Classics,* II, 179) said: 行或使之，止或尼之，行止非人所能也，"A man's advancement is affected, it may be, by others, and the stopping him is, it may be, from the efforts of others. But to advance a man or to stop his advance is (really) beyond the power of other men."

Book of Changes (*SBE,* XVI, Appendix I, Hexagram LII:1, 256) has the passage: (易經：下經艮, Hexagram 52): 時止則止，時行則行，動靜不失，其道光明，"Resting when it is time to rest, and acting when it is time to act. When one's movements and restings all take place at the proper time for them, his way (of proceeding) is brilliant and intelligent."

[72] 先君，Pan Chao means again her own father; see p. 82.

[73] As referred to on p. 63, Wang Ch'ung (*Lun-Hêng,* Lost Texts, *chüan* 20, by Forke, XX, 2, as Chapter XXV, 1911, 279-280) wrote of Pan Piao that "the pen of such a writer cares for nothing but justice. Worthies and sages having confided their thoughts to the pen, many strokes of the pen form a word, and a number of words bring out a sentiment, the reading of which enables later ages to distinguish between right and wrong, for why should a false statement be made?—from reading the words, one learns to know the character of the person described."

[74] Note the use of 不敏 in "Lessons," p. 82.

[75] Pan Chao's father wrote a "Travelling Northward" poem (北征賦, *Wên Hsüan, chüan* 9), 23-24 A.D., when a fugitive from the capital, writing en route from Ch'ang-an, 長安, to An-ting, 安定, Shensi.

[76] Analects 4:5, *Classics,* I, 166: "The Master said: 'Riches and honours are what men desire. If it cannot be obtained in the proper way, they should not be held. Poverty and meanness are what men dislike. If it cannot be obtained in the proper way, they should not be avoided.'" See also Analects 7:15, same, p. 200; and above, note 56.

[77] Legge (Analects 1:14, note, *Classics,* I, 143) explained that "With what mind one aiming to be a *chün-tzû,* 君子，pursues his learning. He may be well, even luxuriously, fed and lodged, but, with his higher aim, these things are not his seeking—無求."

[78] 正身, literally "erecting the body," came to mean "rectifying the person."

[79] F. H. Balfour (translating Huai-nan Tzû, *China Review,* IX, 1880-1881, 289) commented that "Wherefore the Holy Man preserves the principle of quiescence,—He waits till the changes bring about the time for action,—never being premature or precipitate; soft, pliant, and at rest,—easy, tranquil, and secure,—he storms, as it were, a great (citadel) and lays a strong (town) in ruins, nothing in the world being able to withstand him!"

[80] Wang Ch'ung (translation by A. B. Hutchinson, *China Review,* VIII, 1879-1880, 46) wrote that "Man's life has a determined length: man, like insects, has a time to be born and a time to die. Who by reflecting upon his years, can detain them?" See also Analects 6:2 (Legge's note), *Classics,* I, 185.

Hu Shih discusses the intelligence of Neo-Mohism in his "Logical Method," (pp. 87-92), and his conclusions are disputed by Maspero in *T'oung Pao,* XXV, (1927), 59-64.

[81] Note the use of 吉 above, note 5.

Lionel C. Hopkins ("Working the Oracle," *New China Review,* I, 1919, 3-9) noted that the Chinese scholar, Lo Chên-yü, 羅振玉, in his "Critical Interpretations of the Records of the Tumulus of Yin" has established "the fact that there was no great difference between the divination methods of the Shang and Chou dynasties.— (but) the Han scholars were already unable to grasp clearly the mode of divination practised under the Shang and Chou dynasties."

[82] 敬愼威儀. In the Book of Poetry, III, II, 9:3, Legge (*Classics,* IV, 497) translated: "Let us be reverently careful of our demeanor." Note the use of 敬愼 as the title of Chapter III of "Lessons," p. 85.

[83] 無怠, 無荒, 四夷來王. In the Book of History, II, II, 1:4, 大禹謨, Legge (*Classics,* III, 55) translated: "Attend to these things without idleness or omission, and from the four quarters the barbarian tribes will come and acknowledge your sovereignty." (This quotation is taken from the spurious section of the Book of History, cf. Karlgren: same, p. 52.)

[84] J. Edkins ("Ancient Physics," *China Review,* XVI, 1887-1889, 75) wrote that "Temperance and moderation are essential to health, and here medicine and Taoism are identical in practice, and the book (素問, see Wylie: *Notes,* pp. 96-97) in its first chapter becomes a teacher of Taoism."

[85] 不欲以靜. Lao Tzû in the *Tao Tê Ching,* Carus translated (p. 205): "There being no desire, thereby there is rest."

The "Historical Record" (*chüan* 63, 老子莊子等): 無為自化, 清靜自止.

[86] 公綽 or 孟公綽. See Analects 14:12 and 13, Legge: *Classics,* I, 279: 公綽之不欲, "the freedom from covetousness of Kung-ch'o"; (note 12) "Kung-ch'o was the head of the Mang, 孟, or Chung-sun, 仲孫, family, and, according to the 'Historical Record' was regarded by Confucius more than any other great man of the times in Lu." The comment to the Chinese text of Analects 14:12 says: 廉靜寡欲, 而短於才者也.

PART IV

PAN CHAO: A REPRESENTATIVE CHINESE WOMAN

CHAPTER X

The Moralist

Pan Chao holds a unique place in the history of Chinese philosophy, as the first thinker to formulate a single complete statement of feminine ethics. Despite its brevity, her "Lessons for Women" not only contains an elucidation of the science of the perfecting of womanly character—a system of theoretical moral principles,—but also lays down rules for the practical application of these principles. Although the basis of this science is an unchanging moral code, which is affirmed in the most absolute manner, many of its rules are such as could easily be restated in new terms to meet the conditions of a new age, so that the work may be considered as involving in some degree the concept of relative ethics.

According to the *Mémoires concernant les Chinois,* followed by S. Wells Williams in his article, "Education of Woman in China," Pan Chao composed the "Lessons" in her position as instructress to the young consort of the emperor Ho (89–105 A. D.), intending them also, however, "for the improvement of her sex at large." [1] Perhaps there is, or was, a Chinese written source for these statements; but Pan Chao's own explanation, given in her introduction, is that the book was intended for "unmarried girls," whom she asked to make, each for herself, a copy for personal use.[2] The term *chu nü* could never be interpreted to include the empress. That she wrote primarily for the girls in her own family seems to be clear from the fact that a reference to her son is followed by the reflection that "a man is able to plan his own life . . . but I do grieve that girls just at the age of marriage have not at this time training and advice." In writing the treatise she may well have had in view also "the improvement of her sex at large;" but she does not say so in any definite statement. However the work was handed, as soon as it was completed, to Ma Rung, who so highly approved of its contents that he "ordered the wives and daughters (of his family) to practise it."

Indisputably the "Lessons" were designed to meet the needs of the women of the period, as Pan Chao saw them. By the use of the phrase *chih mien êrh,*[3] "I know how to escape (from my fears or my faults)," she suggested her desire that her daughters, and no doubt young women in general, should be spared the terrors which she had herself experienced as a young bride in a strange house. Although the Classical Writings which she knew and loved are filled with moral teachings illustrated by precept and example, there existed then no treatise[4] especially devoted to the practical everyday life of woman in the home. It was from her own studies and experiences that Pan Chao evolved her ethical system with its homely rules for training girls in personal deportment and right appreciation of family relationships.

In this system the cardinal virtue of the ideal young woman is precisely that humility which is now so strongly condemned by modern Chinese youth. Pan Chao made no attempt to raise the question of the equality of the sexes. She assumed the superiority of man over woman as a matter of course, just as she did that of the old over the young, whether man or woman. Through her interpretation of the symbolic customs of the ancients at the time of the birth of a girl she inculcated humility, and formulated practical rules of conduct implying that the young woman must claim nothing for herself. While strength was the chief glory of man, the beauty of woman's character lay in gentleness, and the most important lesson for woman to learn was that of respectful acquiescence. In the home, however, woman should fill her place as perfectly as man fills his in the larger and perhaps more important world of affairs. "That which must be done, let her finish completely, tidily, and systematically." Probably implying that she must bear sons for this purpose, Pan Chao assigned to the woman the duty of ensuring the continuance of worship in the home, as well as the tasks of preparation for the rites. She went so far as to say that boys and girls are equally important, and though it must be the woman who should seek to win[5] her husband's heart, she "need not use flattery, coaxing words, and cheap methods of intimacy." It was the modest and obedient gentlewoman who would become illustrious in her district and win honor and fame for herself and her parents.

The conduct of such a woman would be dictated by her own respect for her husband. In the high place accorded to her as his consort in the family line of ancestors and descendants, she should take upon herself as a sacred duty the preparation of the offerings of food and wine for worship. The routine tasks which ensure cleanliness in person, food, and household must be carefully and systematically performed, with no waste of time in gossip and silly laughter. In quietness of spirit, attending to her own affairs, thinking before speaking, the wife should follow the correct way in thought, action, and speech. With full control of self, and with mind at peace, she must be content.

The gentlewoman should be industrious. "Late to bed, but early to rise" meant long hours, with many tasks, some easy, some difficult. Always ready and willing to serve others, orderly and neat in her work, giving her whole heart to the duties of the household, she would have neither leisure nor inclination to stand in the gateway or to gossip in the courtyard. She would find her joy in the womanly vocations of sewing and weaving, sanctified by her illustrious predecessors in the homes of her forbears.

Tucked away in chapter two of Pan Chao's treatise is her remarkable plea for the education of girls, a plea which would of itself be sufficient to ensure its author a place of first importance in the history of the advancement of women not only in China but in the world. She was just as convinced that girls needed education in order to fulfill their duties in the home as she was that boys needed it in order to perform the tasks of their own sphere of life. She wished to apply to girls as well as to boys the ancient rule that children should be occupied from the age of eight to fifteen in what may be termed primary studies as distinguished from the higher or cultural instruction after that age. For this later period Pan Chao proposed no changes in the customary procedure of her time regarding young women. Some idea of this procedure may be obtained from passages in the *Li Chi*,[6] which may be taken as a fair indication of the ideals if not the practices of the Han age. It is there stated that a girl at fifteen years of age "assumed the hair-pin; at twenty she was married, or, if there were occasion (for the delay) at twenty-three." "Three months before the marriage of a young lady, . . . she was taught in . . . the public hall (of the members of her surname) . . . the virtue, the speech, the carriage, and the work of a wife."

It is significant that Pan Chao's stand for equal education up to fifteen was taken at a time when boys were already receiving a classical education with a view to official employment. There was no question in the minds of the cultured men of the period that boys ought to be taught, but about girls they had no such conviction. To

Pan Chao this neglect to instruct girls meant a disregard of an essential requirement for the proper relationship between men and women. Her appeal for the education of girls in the primary studies was based on the argument that it was necessary for the correct relationship between the married woman and the family into which she married. Had her appeal been listened to by her own generation, it is possible that later moralists might have incorporated this reform in their teachings, and Chinese women might have been spared the eighteen centuries of illiteracy and the long ages of footbinding to which they have been subjected.

But the doctrine that the early education of boys and girls should be the same was too radical not only for Pan Chao's contemporaries but for all the moralists who succeeded her. It was not until the eighteenth century that the appeal was renewed. In 1738 a work entitled "Women's Culture" [7] by a Fukienese, Lan Lu-chou, was published in two volumes. Its author accepted the principle that education is fundamentally necessary for training girls in morals. "Their dispositions incline contrary ways," he wrote in his preface, "and if it is wished to form them alike, there is nothing like education." [8] "A Chinese Declaration of Rights of Women" was made in no uncertain terms by Li Ju-chên in his novel, "Flowers in the Mirror," [9] which was published about 1825. This man spoke out frankly not only for the moral training of girls according to the four womanly qualifications of Pan Chao's ideal, but also for political as well as educational rights for women as members of society. He advocated the opening of the then prevailing system of examinations for political office to women, which would of course have necessitated the classical education prerequisite to such examinations. This bold advocate of women's education and political rights is a worthy forerunner of the hundreds of young men and women in China who to-day are striving for the equality of the sexes in education and politics as well as in the home.

The relationship of wife to husband is easily the most important of those with which Pan Chao dealt, and she devoted to it three out of the seven chapters of her "Lessons." Her belief in the superiority of man over woman involves no idea of any degradation of womanhood. Rather she took for granted a differentiation of functions in two entirely distinct spheres of life. In their relation to others the husband and wife had but one purpose; in their relation to one another the man controlled the woman, the wife served her husband.

The two constituted a single link in the chain of the life of the family, but the functions of that link were divided; the man's share was without, the woman's within the home. For the man remarriage was authorized by the "Rites," but for the woman no such canonical sanction existed. Her will must be the will of her husband, whether he were alive or dead, and throughout her life her endeavor must be to learn the lessons of respect and obedience, of devotion and tenderness, and of contentment with her lot.

The "Lessons" were addressed to women only, and they portray the model woman as one who by her attitude of respect and acquiescence has succeeded in accomplishing the adaptability necessary for wedded life. Yet throughout the delineation of the model woman's conduct there surely runs the thought that respect and caution were also necessary on the part of the husband towards the wife; that the need in fact was mutual. The method inculcated for the practical application of the moral principles involved is that of constant self-examination and self-restraint. Since for the woman the marriage agreement was final, and the power of the husband over his wife absolute, she affirmed the need of a lasting devotion by wife to husband, and of correct behavior on the part of the woman in order to gain and to hold the affection of the man.

Further, the daughter-in-law must obey the parents-in-law.[10] Although the man had authority over the woman, the old, whether man or woman, was superior to the young. Thus there should always be supreme respect for old age. In all the affairs of the home the mother-in-law was supreme; the daughter-in-law was bound to obey the parents-in-law. "If a daughter-in-law," quoted Pan Chao, "is like an echo and a shadow, how could she not be praised?" If her views differed, the daughter-in-law must sacrifice her personal opinions. There could be no question of right and wrong; it was hers only to obey.

Pan Chao maintained that the wife could live in cordial relationship with her husband's brothers and sisters. This was best assured by the young woman's yielding to the wishes of her husband's family instead of exalting her own. It is true, said Pan Chao, that a young girl going into a strange home will inevitably make mistakes, but if like Yen Tzû she never repeat an error, then she will win the love of her husband's family and they will stand by her. The concrete picture of the model young woman which Pan Chao drew in this connection is certainly applicable only to the family system of the Orient, but the underlying principle upon which it is based is true in East and West alike.

Pan Chao did not, unfortunately, formulate any general principle to summarize the detailed precepts which she laid down. Her treatise is severely practical, and follows a definite plan. Having accepted the two beliefs of her age that man was superior to woman and that the old were superior to the young, she set out to present the picture of a model young bride in three relationships, namely, in relation (1) to her husband, (2) to her parents-in-law, and (3) to her brothers- and sisters-in-law. The humility required in all three of these relationships must be taught to her from birth. For the maintenance of the right relationship with the husband, Pan Chao pleaded that the girl should be educated in the same subjects as the boy up to the period of cultural training. After that, the special cultural training of the girl along the lines of the four "womanly qualifications" of "virtue, suitable language, good bearing, and industry" would fit her to win and hold her husband's affection by "whole-hearted devotion" and correct manners. At the same time the entire educational process —the lessons in humility, the primary studies of childhood, the cultural training—should, when aided by lasting attachment for her husband, in no wise hinder the young bride from rendering the proper obedience to her parents-in-law, and should likewise make her more able to adapt herself in her new home to the wishes of her brothers- and sisters-in-law. Thus she would become an example to the world, the model young bride in her husband's home.

It is regrettable that the form of Pan Chao's instructions gives to permanent truths so impermanent an application. The feminine virtues are immutable, and what is required by modern conditions is a restatement rather than a rejection of Pan Chao's instructions. Twentieth century China can more easily repudiate the rules of the *Li Chi* for the "Inner Apartments,"[11] or the pious platitudes of Pan Chao's successors in the field of morality, than the profound psychological truths which underly the "Lessons." Perhaps it is because Pan Chao understood and valued the position of women in an age of culture and refinement such as the Han period, that her interpretation of the ideals of the ancients has so much value even for the present time. Modern Chinese womanhood needs a leader who, like Pan Chao, can interpret anew for a new age the permanent truths of the functions and relations of the sexes in human society.

NOTES

[1] III, 367: *Chinese Recorder*, XI (1880), 50.

[2] 諸女方當適人；各寫一通庶有補益.

[3] 知免耳.

[4] The *Nü Hsien* or "Pattern for Women" is twice quoted by Pan Chao, but no further information concerning the contents of this lost book has been discovered. See pp. 87, 88.

It may be that the manners and customs in the homes of the women of the Eastern Han period, as well as the responsibilities for the duties involved in them, will be revealed from further study of the Han relics discovered in Han tombs in Korea, see Harada: *Lo-Lang*.

[5] The Chinese marriage agreement is still generally made for the couple by their families. It is customary for the bride and groom not to meet before the wedding ceremony. Any such courting as may take place in these circumstances is done as man and wife.

[6] Legge: *Li Ki, SBE*, XXVII, 479, XXVIII, 432. Cf. pp. 84-87.

[7] *Nü Hsüeh*, 藍鹿洲：女學.

[8] Trans. from *Chinese Repository*, IX (1840), 542. The object of education he thus conceived to be uniformity. Lan Ting-yüan, 藍鼎元 (1680-1733), district magistrate of P'u-ning, 普寧 The *Nü Hsüeh* in six *chüan* consists of extracts from classical and historical writings. It is divided into four parts devoted respectively to the illustration of the virtues, sayings, conduct, and works of renowned women of past times, see Wylie: *Notes*, pp. 37 and 88; Giles: *Biog.*, no. 1083. Without following Pan Chao's order, it quotes her entire treatise.

[9] For "Flowers in the Mirror," see Hu Shih, "A Chinese Declaration of Rights of Women," *Chinese Soc. and Polit. Review* (1924), VIII, no. 1, 100-109; Hu Shih's edition of 李汝珍 (c. 1760-1830); 鏡花緣 (c. 1825), Preface by Hu Shih.

[10] For the reaction in contemporary China against the frequently intolerable despotism of the mother-in-law, see an article by Ku Chieh-kang, 對於舊家庭的感想. *The Renaissance*, 新潮, *chüan* 2, vol. 4, May, 1920.

[11] 禮記，內則, Legge: *Li Ki, SBE*, XXVII, 449-479.

CHAPTER XI

Her Philosophy of Life

The evidence for Pan Chao's historical attainments is to be found in the respect accorded her by Chinese scholars during and after her lifetime, and in her surviving work, indistinguishable as yet from that of her father and her elder brother, in the history of the Western Han dynasty. For her political influence there is the evidence of her two memorials. Her originality as a moralist in the field of feminine ethics is amply shown by her "Lessons for Women." But it is her narrative poems—three short pieces and one long one—that preserve most clearly her delightful personality and her almost enviable philosophy of life.

The reader of these poems, and particularly of the longer narrative, while not likely to find in them any definite religious ideals, can hardly resist the conclusion that she was a woman of faith. In "Travelling Eastward" she blamed herself for being afraid of the journey which lay before her and which would bring her to a new life in a strange place. She pictured herself as strengthening her resolution to persevere to the end of her undertaking by three different means in three different departments of human personality. For the strengthening of the body she sought the stimulus and comfort to be found in a cup of wine; for that of the mind, the reassurance provided by a calm and intellectual survey of the physical conditions which she would have to meet; and to these she added a reminder of her spiritual reliance upon the Will of Heaven in which she had a profound confidence. She would not, she told herself, ever have to "climb into a tree" for shelter, nor yet to gather "worms from dead trees" for food. Moreover she was a human being like other human beings, and like them she would receive guidance from Heaven, and must follow that guidance. Later in the same poem she reminded herself: "I know that man's nature and destiny rest with Heaven." But she did not mean that destiny is preordained; she rather conceived of it as being the Will of Heaven. Like Wang Ch'ung, the Han critic of her own generation, while she believed in Fate or Destiny, holding that every one had his or her own place in the group life of the nation, she also attached just as much importance to the principle of effort [1]—the active, purposeful, pressing forward within the bounds of Destiny.

The whole poem is centered around the thought of keeping to the Great Highway. Regret for things left behind, longing for home, must not be permitted to hinder one from pushing on to the goal which is ahead. Nor must the fear of the unknown future be allowed to perturb one in the course of the forward march. Where the Will of Heaven points, there man must go. It is uncertain to what extent her conception of Heaven may have approximated to that of a personal God. The monism of the Mohists had certainly had its influence on Confucianism as reinterpreted in the early part of the Han period. Yet she cannot have had an anthropomorphic conception of deity. Her thought may have been animistic: a thought of Spirits helping the traveller along the Great Highway of life as he struggles on towards the vision ahead. But if so it was an animism closely allied to the worship of Heaven (at the Altar of Heaven) as perfect unity. For to Pan Chao there was a vision.

To her the Classics were Holy Scriptures, and Confucius and the earlier model kings and wise ones were Holy Men. In them she found her guides in her Way of Life. This Way of Life was her own particular and personal way, though not essentially different from that of other people. She herself was indeed an illustration of the saying credited to Confucius: "a man can enlarge the principles (which he follows); those principles do not enlarge the man." [2] Though she conceived of individuals as having a Destiny for their own lives, they were not mere puppets. "With heads uplifted they trod their way"—their own particular way, not that of anybody else—"to the vision." The worthy, the loyal, the forgiving, the true, the good, the faithful, had always the help and the protection of Spirits in their way of life. As Tzû-lu faced and bravely met his death, so should every individual, with manners correct and body erect, keep his face turned forward in the path. Her admiration for Yen Tzû's characteristic of never repeating a fault is closely allied to the moral philosophy of her delightful verse, "The Needle and Thread." The Holy Men alone were to her without fault; but the wise and worthy hastened to patch mistakes as the needle and thread darned the rent in the garment.

Notwithstanding her confidence in a Golden Past, she was ready to accept the contributions made by her own period. Her father's writings were her ideal, her model; the kind of work that he had done was worthy of her emulation. She seemed to have accepted, too, the social distinctions [3] of her generation. But having herself received instruction at the hands of her own father and mother, she became dissatisfied with the custom of reserving education for boys alone. Her philosophizing in this field is certainly, so far as existing records show, an original contribution to the thought of the Chinese people. She held that education had become necessary for the girls as well as the boys of her period; her whole ethical system was based on this belief. But since she clearly accepted the prevalent opinion of the time that woman's place was confined to the home, she cannot have intended to prescribe for girls a course of cultural or higher training identical with that of boys. Just what her theory of education was there is no material now available to tell, nor even what was the prevalent theory to which she opposed herself. The one-sided emphasis of the period upon the education of boys may have been the result of no definite principle, but have been merely a consequence of the tendency already begun, under the influence of the Han Confucianists, to demand classical education as a prerequisite for the holding of official posts—which as a rule would be open only to men. Yet Pan Chao herself was chosen over other scholars of her day to study, teach, and write in the library wherein was concentrated practically all the historical research of the age.

Her extant works reveal a profound comprehension of the Classical Writings of the Confucian school of thought, and she seems to have desired to carry the teachings of this school into the sphere of woman as well as of man. Her plea for the education of girls was based largely upon the Mencian teachings [4] that "a distinction of right and wrong is the root of knowledge," and that "the feeling of courtesy in speech and manner is the root of what is proper in the treatment of others." These sayings imply that real courtesy to others, and genuine righteousness in one's person and work,[5] are preserved from generation to generation only with the aid of education. Pan Chao seems to have believed (although it is difficult to cite specific passages to this effect) that human nature contains potentialities of goodness which need training for their realization; and if this is the case, her views on the education of girls, radical as they appear, can like her moral precepts and ethical principles be traced back to Classical sources as well as to her own experience of life.

The Confucianists believed in the aristocracy of the wise, and adopted a Way of Life for that class or group rather than for mankind in general. Pan Chao claimed for women a share in the possibility of becoming a "Superior Person" (*Chün Tzŭ*). Her whole interest was directed towards this Confucian ideal personality, and she entirely disregarded the "Inferior People" (*Hsiao Jên*) [6] of her time. She made no mention of, gave no precepts for, the women of the unlettered world. She used no term for those of the so-called lower ranks of life. She made no reference to slavery, which is known to have been one of the social evils of the Han dynasty, nor to concubinage. Just as she accepted the ideas of her generation concerning the superiority of age over youth, and of man over woman, so perhaps she saw in these less fortunate ones of her time no call for an attitude of mind different from that which prevailed around her.

Han Confucianism had assimilated much not only from the Mohists but also from the Lao-Chuang school of thought. Pan Chao had certainly had exceptional opportunities for acquainting herself with Han Taoism. Her uncle "reverenced the learning" of Lao-Chuang, and it is probably because of his influence that all four of her poems, as well as her memorials and "Lessons for Women," exhibit pronounced philosophical eclecticism. Of her poems, "The Bird from the Far West" shows clearly the influence of the Han Confucian school, while "The Cicada" is a song of the Lao-Chuang school of Nature. In the longer poem, "Travelling Eastward," the assimilation of the thought of the two schools is complete, and the whole poem leaves an impression of the influence of the monism and the "effort" of the Mohists. The moral qualities recommended in the "Lessons for Women," especially in connection with the "womanly qualifications" of "virtue," exhibit a Taoist influence, which may also be seen in the closing lines of the long poem. She does not seem to advocate negative inactivity but rather a positive harmony, a conscious adaptation of the self to man and Nature and the Will of Heaven.

To sum up, it may be said that Pan Chao's philosophy as revealed in her writings was the outcome of her own reaction to the circumstances and events of her life. She had undoubtedly formed a definite theory of the cosmos as a result of the exhaustive scientific studies which enabled her not only to continue the "Eight Tables" but to compose the "Treatise on Astronomy," and to instruct the empress in astronomy and mathematics. She had religious concepts concerning

Heaven, the Spirits, and Ancestors. She regarded Destiny as only partially limiting man's freedom of activity, and in no way interfering with the active effort to attain a goal. Her vision of an Ideal inspired her to press forward in her Way of Life. The potential goodness of human nature seems to have been a large factor in her conception of life. Woman, like man, was a moral being, born with the germ of goodness which needed to be cultivated through education. Trained in the school of Han Confucianism she accepted the social order and the system of justice taught by its philosophers, but her own special philosophy of life found forcible expression in her protest against the exclusion of girls from education.

NOTES

[1] Cf. Chapter IX, note 57—the "effort" of Mohism.

[2] Analects 15:28, Legge: *Classics,* I, 302: 人能弘道，非道弘人.

[3] See Fung Yu-lan: *A Comparative Study of Life Ideals* (Shanghai, 1924), p. 173.

[4] 是非之心，智之端也, Mencius, II, I, 6:5, Legge translated (*Classics,* II, 203): "The feeling of approving and disapproving is the principle of knowledge."

辭讓之心，禮之端也, same: "The feeling of modesty and complaisance is the principle of propriety."

[5] 禮義.

[6] 君子，小人.

CHAPTER XII

THE WOMAN OF LETTERS

Pan Chao was a writer of varied literary talent. The descriptive terms applied to her works in the *Hou Han Shu* indicate a wide range of subject-matter; and since the mode of expression necessarily changed with the change of subject, this versatility of knowledge is itself a proof of versatility of style. Modern literary criticism must necessarily confine itself to those of her works which have survived through the intervening eighteen centuries. That these are but a few out of the many accredited to her is not surprising in view of the risks and difficulties of transmission; indeed there is room for congratulation that so much has been preserved. They afford ample ground for the belief that a pleasing diction must at all times have been a conspicuous characteristic of her style.

The preservation of these specimens of her literary composition, other than her share in the *Han Shu,* may be attributed largely to the successive adoption at different periods of three different classifications or divisions of Chinese literature, each resulting in the compilation of monumental collections, based on the efforts of scholars to resystematize the literary heritage of the nation. These were the "Individual Collection," the "General Collection," and the "Cyclopedia."

In Pan Chao's own generation the practice was established of gathering all the various writings of one individual, usually after death, into a single collection, a division which became known in literature as a *Pieh Chi* or Individual Collection.[1] In this manner the works of Pan Chao were posthumously assembled by her daughter-in-law under the title of "Ts'ao Ta-ku's Collection."[2] It is stated in an annotation[3] in the Sui dynastic history that a collection of Pan Chao's writings existed during the Liang period (502–556). This history was written in the reign of T'ang T'ai Tsung (627–649), and the compilers of the three chapters on "Bibliography," where the reference occurs, themselves wrote annotations. These chapters are a priceless record of the history and content of Chinese literature, compiled apparently in imitation of the even more valuable chapter on "Literature," with annotations by its compiler or compilers, which was added to the *Han Shu* five centuries earlier. Originally the histories of the Liang, Ch'ên, Northern Ch'i, and Chou dynasties (502–589) were incorporated in one edition with that of the Sui (590–617), and accordingly the bibliographical chapters now attached to the Sui history were designed to cover the period of all five of these short dynasties.[4] No collection of Pan Chao's work is listed in either of the T'ang dynastic histories, old or new, but in spite of this silence it is possible that one was extant[5] during T'ang times. About 658 Li Shan[6] in a commentary on the *Wên Hsüan* quoted a line apiece from two poems of Pan Chao, a fact which points to the existence at that time, in some collection now lost or unknown, of more works than are at present extant. Certainly a collection of her works did exist, having survived without the aid of printing, four hundred years after her death, when the country had experienced three centuries of turmoil and barbarian invasions.

In the midst of the political disorder and social confusion of these centuries following the dissolution of the Eastern Han dynasty, there was inaugurated that ever-growing division of Chinese literature, the "General Collection." The first specimen, and the model, of this class is the almost venerated *Wên Hsüan,* still extant, which was compiled by a prince[7] of the House of Liang, and completed about 530 A. D. In all likelihood this compiler drew directly from the collection of Pan Chao's literary work the long narrative poem "Travelling Eastward," which has been credited, in all editions since the T'ang dynasty and probably also before that time, to the original source, *"Ts'ao Ta-ku Chi."*

A century later than the *Wên Hsüan,* in the earlier half of the seventh century, when Ch'ang-sun Wu-chi[8] (d. 659) and others were working on the "Bibliography" of the Sui dynastic history, and Yen Shih-ku (581–645) was probably annotating the *Han Shu,* an imperial mandate of T'ang T'ai Tsung (627–645) caused the creation of another division in the department of letters, the "Cyclopedia." This combines to some extent the characteristics of the western encyclopedia and concordance, "embracing the whole field of literature, methodically arranged according to subjects, and each heading giving extracts from former works on the subject in question."[9] The first great representative of this type is the celebrated *I-wên Lei-chü,* compiled by Ou-yang Hsün (557–645) and others.

Since the chief compiler of this work was born in the first year after the fall of the Liang dynasty, and did not die until the nineteenth year of T'ang T'ai Tsung, it is possible that he too had access to the original source for the reproduction of both "The Bird from the Far West" and "The Needle and Thread," as well as certain sections of "Travelling Eastward" and the first fragment of "The Cicada." In modern editions of this cyclopedia each of these excerpts is credited to the individual poem, with no mention of the collected writings. As fully nine-tenths of the works quoted in *I-wên Lei-chü* are no longer extant,[10] it is indeed fortunate that these three poems from Pan Chao's brush were thus preserved for future generations.

Three and a half centuries after T'ang T'ai Tsung's imperial mandate for the compilation of the *I-wên Lei-chü,* Sung T'ai Tsung (976–997) summoned the scholars of his generation to work on a more complete cyclopedia. Li Fang[11] (925–996) and his collaborators completed the thesaurus of one thousand chapters[12] in 983 A. D., and about a year later it was issued under the title of *T'ai-p'ing Yü-lan.* Undoubtedly the compiler was able to consult both the *Wên Hsüan* and the *I-wên Lei-chü,* but he omitted "Travelling Eastward" entirely, and included only the preface to "The Bird from the Far West" and the first part of "The Needle and Thread." But he also quoted a different fragment of "The Cicada,"[13] so that he must have drawn upon a third collection now lost or unknown which may or may not have been the source of the two quotations used by Li Shan in his commentary on the *Wên Hsüan.*

This unknown source for two fragments of one poem by Pan Chao and one line of another may possibly have been some such literary collection as the valuable *Ku Wên Yüan* in twenty-one chapters by an unknown author, of which Wylie wrote in his *Notes on Chinese Literature.*[14] This work as originally found comprised a selection of more than two hundred and sixty pieces of poetry and various other classes of literature, composed between the beginning of the Chou dynasty and the fifth century A. D. According to current tradition it was discovered about 1050–1080 A. D. "in a bookcase of a Buddhist temple where it had been deposited during the T'ang dynasty." Having undergone two rearrangements previous to a reprint in 1482, it now differs considerably from the manuscript found in the temple. In its present form it contains nothing from Pan Chao's brush except "The Needle and Thread." [15]

The most complete collection of her writings subsequent to that made by her daughter-in-law was not brought together until the nineteenth century, when Yen K'o-chün, after more than twenty years of literary effort, finished his "Complete Collection of Ancient Literature" from earliest historic times to the close of the sixth century A. D.: a work which was not published until 1879, thirty-five years after his death.[16] In this collection he placed Pan Chao's writings first among the works of eminent women of the Eastern Han. Besides the reproduction of "Lessons for Women" and the two memorials from the *Hou Han Shu,* he included "Travelling Eastward" from the *Wên Hsüan,* "The Bird from the Far West" and "The Needle and Thread" from the *I-wên Lei-chü,* and assembled three fragments of a fourth poem, "The Cicada," from three different sources. His assembly of the fragments of this poem is an example of a characteristic activity of modern Chinese scholarship. The first and longest part he quoted from the *I-wên Lei-chü;* the second he took from the *T'ai-p'ing Yü-lan;* and the third he found in an annotation in the Li Shan *Wên Hsüan.* Although these excerpts are clearly fragments, as is shown not only by the matter itself but by the uncompleted rime scheme, and the poem in its original form was probably much longer, they do nevertheless, when brought together, make up a logical whole, a satisfactory lyric, "The Cicada."

The four poems of Pan Chao thus made accessible to modern students by Yen K'o-chün all belong to that class of Chinese poetry which is called *fu,* and together they exhibit all four of the characteristics associated with this peculiar style of composition,[17] which reached its climax and indeed almost ran its entire course during the Han period. "The Bird from the Far West" and "Travelling Eastward" both exhibit the first of the four characteristics, a preface describing briefly the circumstances under which the work was composed. According to the *T'ai-p'ing Yü-lan* in the case of the first, and to the *Wên Hsüan* in that of the second, these prefaces were quoted from the "Collected Works of Pan Chao," *Ts'ao Ta-ku Chi.* If the other two poems originally had prefaces, they have been lost in transmission. In "Travelling Eastward" is found a second characteristic, the use of *hsi,*[18] an emphatic particle peculiar to poetry, which by onomatopœia suggests a sigh. In the edition (1894 A. D.) of Yen K'o-chün this character is omitted in only three [19] of the double phrases of the poem. All these poems likewise conform to *fu* canons in that rime is present but of secondary stress.

As in English blank verse, rhythm in *fu* is fundamental, and in all four of these poems it is that of five-beat six-character phrases. In every line there is a cæsura marked in practically every case by the use of a lightly stressed conjunction, preposition, or enclitic as the fourth in the six-character phrase. In the three short poems this rhythm is very regular, there being only one exception [20] in a phrase of "The Bird from the Far West." The long narrative poem, "Travelling Eastward," also employs, with only three exceptions,[21] the five-beat rhythm, until the latter part where it changes entirely to four beats. These few lines of four beats go in couplets, the last character in each of which is the enclitic *hsi,* indicating a pause and taking of breath.

Of the three short poems the least pleasing is "The Bird from the Far West." Its subject was prescribed by the emperor, so that it may not inappropriately be compared to certain labored compositions by poets laureate of the west. To gratify the imperial fancy, and probably also to fulfill the requirements of Han idealism, there is a fulsome use of such terms as [22] "Virtue," "Righteous One," "Spirit of Harmony," and "Unity and Love" at court. The poem is an excellent concrete example of the influence in literature of the theory of the virtue or holiness of the emperor as the Son of Heaven. In extravagant eulogy of the Court of Han it is no worse than many other *fu* of the Han dynasty, perhaps the most famous of which is "The Two Capitals" of Pan Chao's brother Ku, in which the city of Lo-yang is praised as the capital for the Eastern Han.[23] Nevertheless "The Bird from the Far West" may be given a place in the poetry of Chinese classical literature as a rather good example of a *fu,* even though its charm of phrase and delicate choice of word suffer almost as much in literal translation as its rime and its rhythm. The modern reader is not likely to feel much sympathy with the idealism of the Han period, and will value the poem only as a representative of the era which produced it.

The fragments of the lyric, "The Cicada," are more congenial to modern thinking than "The Bird from the Far West." It is true that reminiscences of the cicada may not appeal greatly to the western reader; but the Chinese of all classes and of all sections are so extremely fond of the sounds made both by this insect and by the cricket [24] that they commonly keep at hand a tiny bamboo or reed cage containing one of these little creatures so that the owner may enjoy the sound which it sends forth, and this is done not only at home or at a place of business but even when travelling on the road. "The Cicada" contains its share of praises of the Court of Han, but it is free from the historical allusions which are to be found in "The Bird from the Far West," and its permanent value is certainly not impaired by the fact that it contains only two lines devoted wholly to the idealism of Han Confucianism.

In strong contrast to "The Bird from the Far West," "The Cicada" is Taoist in atmosphere. Notwithstanding the two lines devoted to the Confucian theory of the sacred virtue of the imperial dynasty, the poem as a whole is an example of a Taoist conception of harmony with Nature. It is an illustration of the unmistakably eclectic attitude towards Confucian and Taoist influences which characterize the age in which Pan Chao lived. But apart from its philosophical background "The Cicada" is a simple song of a lover of Nature, and holds its place in literature as a poem which is sure of a sympathetic reception from readers of any period and of any nationality.

Of the three short works, however, it is the delightful moral poem, "The Needle and Thread," which is most attractive to the modern reader. Its metaphorical use of the "pure wool of the lamb" may evoke misleading associations in minds accustomed to the symbolism connected with the word "lamb" in Christian literature. In China the lamb is quite frequently associated with the moral concept of filial piety. But in this poem the reference is simply to the original material of the garment patched or darned by the needle and thread. The use of other terms [25] pregnant with philosophical significance, and of certain allusions in the last two, if not the last four, lines of the poem, makes it fairly sure that there is a double meaning throughout. If so, the real point of the poem is that it is impossible to count (because they are too numerous) the worthy persons, those who obtain commemoration in stone inscriptions and "ascend the hall" (or are promoted). But in spite of such inner meanings, the poem is not confined within the conventions of any single culture or period; its appeal is universal.

It is fitting that Pan Chao should thus have sought to glorify the humble instruments of woman's work. The song probably came straight from her heart, at some leisure moment, and without the compelling necessity of imperial order. The moral meaning, if it be assumed that there is one, is so cleverly handled that it adds to rather than detracts from the charm of the whole. The three short poems together would suffice to give to Pan Chao a place, though a modest one, among Chinese poets.

She is raised, however, to much higher rank than this by her authorship of the long essay in rime, "Travelling Eastward." In the phraseology and structure of this work can be traced the undoubted influence of the type of poetry first exemplified in the *Ch'u Tz'û,*[26] and popularized in the succeeding century by the great poet Ssû-ma Hsiang-ju (d. 117 B. C.). "Travelling Eastward," though less well known than the *fu* written by her brother, is of greater value to the modern reader whether in translation or in the original. It is divided into two parts, of which the first is the more interesting to the twentieth century. Along with the philosophy of life revealed by successive reactions to the changing scenes and situations of a journey, there is an attractive picture of the traveller's love for her country, its history, and its heroes. When once the names and historical settings of the persons and places alluded to have become familiar, the reader of the Chinese text is fascinated by the rime, the rhythm, and the movement of the lines, and by the philosophy of the thought. Much of the picturesqueness of phrase and word is necessarily lost in translation, but there remain such an alluring series of scenes and incidents that even the reader of a version in a western language is likely to return to it more than once as to a delightful example of the travel essay.

The construction of the poem in two sections must have been, in part at least, the result of the influence of her avowed model, her father's poem "Travelling Northward," in which the longer portion similarly observes the rhythm of five-beat six-character phrases but with a less regular use of the emphatic particle *hsi,* while the second and shorter portion, also introduced with the term *luan yüeh,* changes into four-character phrases with *hsi* as the last character of the second phrase. In "Travelling Eastward" this second portion contains an explanation of the reasons for the composition of the work, followed by a moral exhortation. It is of lower literary value than the first part, and belongs rather in the field of moral writings than among poetic works; but the poem as a whole sets Pan Chao in a high place among the *fu* writers of the Han period.

Turning to her historical compositions, criticism is confronted with the impossibility, in the present state of knowledge, of separating her share in the *Han Shu* from that of her father and brother. Her proper individual place in literature as a historical writer must in the meantime remain uncertain. The suggestion of Hsieh Wu-liang [27] that the succinct phraseology of the chapters on Wang Mang are an indication of the style of Pan Chao rather than that of her brother may become a starting-point for a discriminative investigation of the whole. So far as present knowledge goes, the largest part of her work on the *Han Shu* was the continuation of the "Eight Tables." Inasmuch as the form of these was established by Pan Ku on the model of the "Historical Record," and their contents, except for short prefaces, hardly exceed a bare list of names and dates, they afford little basis for adjudgment of her historical style. The "Treatise on Astronomy" furnishes more material for stylistic study, but the intricacy of the subject-matter—the views on cosmogony current during the Han period imposes serious difficulties on the modern student who is not a specialist in astronomy. It is noteworthy, however, that this treatise has as yet received no adverse criticism at the hands of Chinese scholars, but has always been considered an integral and important part of the whole history. It may have been his favorable opinion of this treatise and of the prefaces to the "Eight Tables" which led Liu Chih-chi, in his study of the *Han Shu,* to suggest that a revision of the entire work was made by Pan Chao after her brother's death. Certainly the style of the history as a whole has always been admired by Chinese critics.

To pass to another kind of composition, the two memorials preserved in the *Hou Han Shu* provide ample material for the study of Pan Chao's abilities in persuasive exposition. There seems to be no doubt that these memorials in their present form are substantially accurate versions of the product of her own brush, despite their transmission in a history which received its final form [28] more than three hundred years after her death in a period of internal disorder and barbarian invasion. At the time when she composed her memorial in behalf of her brother Ch'ao she probably, though not necessarily, had in her possession the petition which he had himself sent up to the throne.[29] The relationship between the two in phraseology and development of ideas is sufficiently close to suggest that his petition, to which she referred, had actually been in her hands. This similarity, however, may also be accounted for by her having just received a personal letter from him (mentioned in her memorial), which explains too her accurate information regarding his physical condition and his urgent need of relief from heavy responsibility. The use by both memorialists of a few corresponding terms and of the same illustration—of the old dog and the old horse—may be mere coincidence. Pan Chao's scholarly training provided the historical allusions which invested with authority her presentation of her brother's case. Her style is vigorous and straightforward; exceedingly clear in exposition, moving in expostulation, and vivid in entreaty. It is not surprising that the emperor acceded to her appeal and ordered the immediate return of Pan Ch'ao.

In contrast to the energetic and emotional style of the memorial in behalf of her brother stands the ornate embellishment of phraseology in the memorial to the empress Têng. Its exaggerated obsequiousness was perhaps a natural result of the imposing personality of the empress, but it is more probable that it was due to nothing more than conventional usage. It certainly does not arise from anything in the personality of the writer. Within the brief space of this memorial are crowded at least seven of the more prominent teachings [30] of Han Confucianism: the exaltation of Imperial Power; the existence of the Golden Age of Yao and Shun; the theory of the Will of Heaven as being manifested by the will of the people; the greatness of humility; the magnification of ancient worthies; the authority of Confucius; and the value of the spirit of sincerity in courtesy. Yet embedded between the outer covers of formality and idealism is a brief but straightforward recommendation to the empress, a recommendation that, in matters of grave import for the future, she should adhere to principles rather than violate a good custom on account of an immediate need.

The "Lessons for Women" exhibit her abilities in another and radically different style. There is a marked absence of the hollow verbiage required in the memorials. That she opened the treatise with an introduction deploring her own unfitness for the task is no more than natural, for such terms of depreciation are merely marks of the courtesy required in all formal writings by the ancient Chinese. Her arrangement of matter is logical and clear, her style succinct and direct. Of all her extant works this treatise is best adapted for the communication to western readers, by means of translation, of the flavor of the original. The Chinese, who for eighteen centuries have loved and admired it for its moral teachings, have long regarded it as a model for classical composition.

Pan Chao's literary reputation does not depend on any single type of composition. Her extant writings are a mere fraction of her total work, and cannot fail to make the reader wish that more had been preserved. Yet there is enough to show her excellence in clear historical exposition, in flowery rhetoric, in refined homily, and in rhythmic poetry; in verse designed to flatter an autocratic court, to narrate the musings of a nature lover, to point a moral or adorn a tale. They amply substantiate the traditional view of her countrymen [31] that Pan Chao was a scholar of the first rank in her own generation, and the current opinion that she should still be awarded the foremost place among Chinese women of letters.

NOTES

[1] 別集. The classification *chi* is not found in the bibliographical section of the *Han Shu* (*chüan* 30), but is found in that of the *Sui Shu* (*chüan* 35). Cf. Wylie: *Notes*, p. 227.

[2] *Ts'ao Ta-ku Chi*, 曹大家集.

[3] To the entry of a collection of Pan Chieh-yü's writings, *Sui Shu, chüan* 35, 梁有班昭集三卷, 隋書, 經籍志, 四集.

[4] See Wylie: *Notes*, p. 20.

[5] Her "Lessons for Women," known to have been preserved, is listed in the Sui history and not in either T'ang history.

[6] 文選李善註: (I) A fragment of "The Cicada," citing 曹大家蟬賦, *chüan* 38, 表下, 庾元規讓中書令表注; (II) a title and one line of another poem, 曹大家欹器頌: 侍帝王之密坐, 曹植與吳季重書注 *chüan* 42, 書中 (明嘉靖本, 1529 A. D.).

[7] Generally known as *Chao-ming T'ai-tzû*, 昭明太子, but by name Hsiao T'ung, 蕭統 (501-531 A. D.), see Wylie: same, p. 238; Giles: *Biog.*, no. 717.

[8] Same, no. 142, 長孫無忌.

[9] Wylie: same, p. 182.

[10] 歐陽詢, 藝文類聚. Giles: *Biog.*, no. 1594.

[11] 李昉: 太平御覽. Wylie, p. 183; Giles: same, no. 1122.

[12] *I-wên Lei-chü* has 100 *chüan* or chapters.

[13] Some editions of the *Ch'u Hsüeh Chi*, 初學記 (725 A. D.), *chüan* 30, are said to quote this fragment (but the edition of 1534 A. D., 明嘉靖甲午歲秦金, Chinese Biog., p. 828, 晉府重刻本 does not include it), cf. Yen K'o-chün "Complete collection" . . ., *Hou Han, chüan* 96, 列女傳.

[14] Wylie: same, pp. 239-240, 古文苑.

[15] *Ku Wên Yüan, chüan* 3, 賦.

[16] He was seventy-two by western reckoning in 1834 (1762-1843). 嚴可均: 全上古三代秦漢三國六朝文. (See Appendix, pp. 156 ff.)

[17] Waley: *The Temple*, Intro., pp. 14-18; Margouliès: *Le Fou*, pp. 1-20.

[18] 兮. This character is found in a most remarkable specimen of ancient poetry credited to Han Kao Tsu, who after a victory returned to his native village and had a carouse with the local rustics; see *Han Shu, chüan* 1, twelfth year, 高帝紀; *Shih Chi, chüan* 8, twelfth year, 高祖本紀. For translations,

see E. H. Parker, Notes, *New China Review,* I (1919), 630; Chavannes: *Mémoires,* I, p. CLXI.

[19] We find food and rest enough at Yüan-wu. 食原武一足. We arrive at the borders of Ch'ang-yüan, 至長垣一界. I know that man's nature and destiny rest with Heaven. 知性命一天.

[20] 故翔萬里而來遊.

[21] 諒不登巢而椓蠡兮.
得不陳力而相追.
蘧氏在城之東南兮.

[22] 德, 義, 和氣, 協而相親.

[23] See p. 33.

[24] See B. Laufer: Insect-Musicians and Cricket Champions of China (*Anthropology Leaflet,* no. 22, Field Museum of Natural History, Chicago, 1927).

[25] Such as: 剛, 精, 微妙, 通達.

[26] 楚辭, 司馬相如. Cf. Maspero: same, pp. 597-606; Waley: *The Temple,* pp. 9-47; Margouliès: *Le Fou;* and *L'Évolution de la prose artistique chinoise* (München, 1929), pp. 58-65 ff.

[27] Pp. 47-48.

[28] See the discussion of this question in the Appendix, pp. 158-161.

[29] For the texts, see *Hou Han Shu, chüan* 47.

[30] 盛德, 唐虞之政, 采一慮, 謙讓, 夷齊太伯, 孔子稱, 論語曰, 推讓之誠.

[31] In a personal interview with the writer Liang Ch'i-ch'ao (d. January, 1929) accepted this view of Pan Chao; and, in spite of his wish to repudiate her moral teachings for modern woman, Ku Chieh-kang likewise holds the same opinion of her as a woman of letters. These two men are among the best known spokesmen for the scholars of contemporary China.

LIST OF TRANSLATIONS AND THEIR CHINESE SOURCES

I-IV. BIOGRAPHIES[1] of Pan Chao, her father, and two brothers. *Hou Han Shu,* 後漢書 (*chüan* 84, 40, 47), by Fan Yeh, 范曄 (398-445 A. D.), of the Chin, 晉, and Sung, 宋, dynasties; edition annotated by the T'ang Crown Prince Li Hsien, 唐太子李賢 (651-684 A. D.); accepted when the work was printed by an imperial order given in 990-994 A. D.; and again annotated by the late Ch'ing, 淸, scholar Wang Hsien-ch'ien, 王先謙 (1842-1918). Ch'ang-sha, 長沙, 1915.

V-VI. GENEALOGY[1] of the Pan family, and BIOGRAPHY of Pan Chieh-yü. *Han Shu,* 漢書 (*chüan* 100, 97), by the Pan family, father, son and daughter; edition annotated in the T'ang period by Yen Shih-ku, 顏師古 (581-645 A. D.); accepted for printing under imperial order of 990-994 A. D.; and likewise annotated by Wang Hsien-ch'ien. Ch'ang-sha, 1900.

VII. TREATISE: "Lessons for Women." (A) *Hou Han Shu*: complete citation in biography of Pan Chao. (B) Complete quotation from above also found in: (1) Yen K'o-chün, 嚴可均 (1762-1843): "Complete Collection of Ancient Literature of the San-tai Period, the Ch'in and Han Dynasties, the Three Kingdoms and the Six Dynasties," *chüan* 96, 全上古三代秦漢三國六朝文, 後漢列女傳, Wu-ch'ang, 武昌, 1894. (2) *Kung-kuei Wên Hsüan,* 宮閨文選, *chüan* 9, 誡. A collection, 集, 6 vols. (1846). (3) Hsieh Wu-liang, 謝无量:

"History of the Literature of Chinese Women," pp. 19-28, 中國婦女文學史, 後漢班昭 (3 editions. Peking, 1916-1918).

VIII-IX. MEMORIALS to Emperor Ho and Empress Têng. (A) *Hou Han Shu*: complete citation in biographies of Pan Ch'ao and Pan Chao. (B) Complete quotation from the above also found in: (1) Yen K'o-chün: "Complete Collection." (2) Hsieh Wu-liang: "History of Literature." (3) *Kung-kuei Wên Hsüan, chüan* 5 and 6, 疏.

X. POEM: "Travelling Eastward." (A) *Wên Hsüan,* 文選 (c. 530), *chüan* 9, 賦, editions Li Shan Chu, 李善註, and Liu Ch'ên Chu, 六臣註: complete. (B) *I-wên Lei-chü* 藝文類聚 (early 7th century), *chüan* 27, 行旅: portions only.[3] Complete quotation from *Wên Hsüan* in collections of Yen K'o-chün and Hsieh Wu-liang, and in *Kung-kuei Wên Hsüan, chüan* 1, 賦.

XI. POEM: "The Bird from the Far West." (A) *I-wên Lei-chü, chüan* 92, 雀: complete. (B) *T'ai-p'ing Yü-lan,* 太平御覽 (983 A.D.), *chüan* 922, 大雀: preface only. Cites "Collected Works of Pan Chao," 曹大家集, as source. (C) Complete quotation from *I-wên Lei-chü* in collections of Yen K'o-chün and Hsieh Wu-liang, and in *Kung-kuei Wên Hsüan, chüan* 1, 賦.

XII. POEM: "The Needle and Thread." (A) *I-wên Lei-chü, chüan* 65, 鍼: complete. (B) *Ku Wên Yüan,* 古文苑, *chüan* 3, 賦: complete. (C) *T'ai-p'ing Yü-lan, chüan* 830, 鍼: first part, 鍼一貫. (D) Complete quotation from *I-wên Lei-chü* in collections of Yen K'o-chün and Hsieh Wu-liang, and in *Kung-kuei Wên Hsüan, chüan* 1, 賦.

XIII. POEM: "The Cicada." (A) *I-wên Lei-chü, chüan* 97, 蟬: first fragment, 伊一往. Cites 後漢曹大家蟬賦. Quoted in *Kung-kuei Wên Hsüan, chüan* 1, 賦. (B) *T'ai-p'ing Yü-lan, chüan* 944, 蟬: second fragment, 吸一灼. (C) *Wên Hsüan, chüan* 38; 表下[2]: third fragment, 復一際, note on 丹款. Cites 曹大家蟬賦. (D) Yen K'o-chün: "Complete Collection," fragments from three above sources gathered together, early nineteenth century. (E) Hsieh Wu-liang: "History of Literature," first fragment only, oblivious of the work of Yen K'o-chün.

The sources for a study of the life and writings of Pan Chao are preserved in trustworthy records. Aside from her share in the *Han Shu*, or "History of the Earlier Han Dynasty," the few but varied specimens of her composition may be found in the *Hou Han Shu*, or "History of the Later Han Dynasty," and in later collections of literary works. These collections are listed above and are dealt with in more detail below and in Chapter XII. The compilation of the *Han Shu* is discussed in Chapter V, and that of the *Hou Han Shu* is related quite fully in a foreword to the edition by Wang Hsien-ch'ien (1915). Appended to the edition which was prepared by order of the emperor Ch'ien-lung in 1739 there is a report[3] to the throne by Yü Ching, 余靖, and Wang Chu, 王洙, which lists less completely, but characterizes in part, the historical works on the Eastern Han dynasty down to 1035 A. D.

According to these accounts the *Hou Han Shu* by Fan Yeh who died in 445 A. D. was based upon compositions whose sources were originally contemporary records. In the reign of the emperor Ming (58-75 A. D.) of the Eastern Han dynasty an imperial decree ordered Pan Chao's brother Ku the historian with three others, Ch'ên Tsung, 陳宗, Yin Min,[4] 尹敏, and Mêng Chi, 孟冀, to compile the annals of the founder of the dynasty,[5] and to compose the biographies of the notable men of the reign period Chien-wu (25-55 A. D.). Much later, Liu Chên,[6] 劉珍, and Li Ch'ung,[7] 李充, without following a systematic plan, wrote the annals and the biographies for the succeeding periods through that of Yung-ch'u (107-113 A. D.). There is no mention of annals and biographies for the remaining years (114-125 A. D.)[8] of the reign of the emperor An, but the composition of the biographies of illustrious men of the reign of the emperor

Shun, 順帝 (126-144 A.D.), was a work called the *Han Chi*,[9] 漢紀, in 114 chapters.

In the next two and a half centuries there were prepared eight historical works which are listed in the report of Yü Ching and Wang Chu. In the period Hsi-p'ing, 熹[10] 平 (172-177 A.D.), a group of four scholars composed the *Tung Kuan Han Chi*, 東觀漢紀(記), a work which under the Ch'ing dynasty was reconstructed from extracts[11] cited in the *Yung-lo Ta Tien*, 永樂大典 (1403-1408 A.D.). In the time of the Three Kingdoms, in the state of Wu, 吳 (222-277 A.D.), the governor of Wu-ling, 武陵, Hsieh Ch'êng, 謝承, wrote the *Han Shu*, 漢書, in 130 *chüan;* and during the Chin, 晉, period (265-419 A.D.) Hsieh Jung,[12] 薛瑩 (d. 282 A.D.), the *Hou Han Chi*, 後漢紀, in 100 *chüan*. Then in the period T'ai-shih, 泰始 (265-274 A.D.), the assistant director of the secret archives, Ssû-ma Piao,[13] 司馬彪 (240-305 A.D.), under the title *Hsü Han Shu*,[14] 續漢書, reassembled all the former recitals and, commencing with the emperor Kuang-wu (25-57 A.D.), wrote anew the history of the Eastern Han dynasty. Sometime in the Chin[15] period Hua Chiao, 華嶠, amended and rectified the *Tung Kuan Han Chi*[16] under the title *Hou Han Shu*, 後漢書, in ninety-seven *chüan;* Hsieh Shên,[17] 謝沈, wrote also a *Hou Han Shu* in 122 *chüan;* and the director of the secret archives Yüan Shan-sung, 袁山松, composed one of 100 *chüan*.

To the list of source books in the report of 1035 A.D., the foreword of the Wang Hsien-ch'ien edition of the *Hou Han Shu* (1915) adds twelve. The names of these historical compositions have been preserved in the dynastic histories of Sui, 隋志, and T'ang, 新舊唐志. Some of them, like the *Hou Han Chi*,[18] 後漢紀, in thirty *chüan* by Yüan Hung, 袁宏 (328-376 A.D)., did not follow the form of the *Han Shu*, but were concise narratives year by year of events of importance on the model of the *Ch'un-ch'iu*, 春秋, which may account for their omission by Yü Ching and Wang Chu. Chavannes[19] thought it strange that Yüan Hung's history was not included in the report of 1035 A.D.

Then came the work of Fan Yeh (398-445 A.D.), the governor of Hsüan Ch'êng, 宣城, who added to and collected from all the former histories. He divided his compilation into three sections: (I) Annals of the emperors and empresses, 帝后紀, in ten *chüan;* (II) Special Treatises, 志, in ten *chüan;* and (III) Biographies of notables in eighty *chüan*—a total of 100 *chüan.* Before he had completed the treatises he was put to death for a state offence, so it is probably only the first and third sections[20] that are from his brush. These sections, however, furnish the material for the study of the life and writings of Pan Chao.

In following centuries other scholars worked on Fan's history. Under the Liang, 梁, dynasty (502-556 A.D.) Liu Chao, 劉昭, assembled and annotated, if he did not amend and enlarge the text; and at the call of the T'ang Crown Prince Li Hsien, 唐太子李賢, a group of the most celebrated scholars of the day were summoned to prepare a commentary on the *Hou Han Shu.* This commentary with assembled text was presented to the emperor at the beginning of the period I-fêng, 儀鳳 (676-678 A.D.), and placed in the archives of the imperial palace; and has been preserved as the commentary of Li Hsien, 李賢注, in modern editions.

The T'ang text and commentary were used when the *Hou Han Shu* was first printed in accordance with an imperial decree issued in the period Shun-hua, 淳化 (990-994 A.D.). In 1034 A.D. the assistant director of archives, Yü Ching, reported to the throne that upon examination of the *Hou Han Shu* printed by the *Kuo-tzŭ-chien,* 國子監, he had found so many errors in the text that he feared students in the future would be led astray. He had compared this edition with other texts and had made a research in other books in the hope of having a text more nearly correct.[21] Thereupon by imperial decree two *Han-lin,* 翰林, scholars and others made a minute revision of the text, and after their report Yü Ching and Wang Chu, by order of the emperor, collated the texts and their conclusions after their investigations. A formal statement was made to the throne in 1035 A.D., and this report has been preserved in the Ch'ien-lung edition of the dynastic histories in 1739 A.D.

According to a discussion of the *Hou Han Shu,* its sources and its authorship, by Wang Hsien-ch'ien (1915), there were six official printed editions[22] of the *Hou Han Shu* under the Sung dynasty. In the Ming period the work was included in the official publication of the twenty-one dynastic histories, both in the period of the Southern Ming, 1532 A.D., and in that of the Northern Ming, 1596-1606, although in both issues old blocks which were in good condition were used.[23] There were private editions, the most celebrated of which was that of the famous bibliophile, Mao Chin (1598-1659)[24]. The province of Fukien issued an edition of the two Han histories,[25] and there were private editions in small type for the use of scholars of the Yüan and probably of the Ming periods.

The results of the investigations by scholars of earlier centuries, as well as those of the Ch'ing period, in the problems connected with the *Hou Han Shu* may be found in the edition of Wang Hsien-ch'ien (1842-1918) which was published at Ch'ang-sha, 1915. It is arranged with the supplementary eight treatises (30 *chüan,* see note 20) as the third section of the work, instead of as the second one which is the arrangement found in the Ch'ien-lung (1739 A.D.) edition.

Of the collections listed above, pp. 156-158, and dealt with in some detail in Chapter XII, that by Yen K'o-chün has been of most practical use for this study, chiefly because it is the most complete. The collection probably most easily secured, however, is found in Hsieh Wu-liang's "History of the Literature of Chinese Women." This so-called history is printed in an inexpensive western format, yet in small type which makes it difficult to read. Unfortunately, neither collection contains explanatory notes, but Yen K'o-chün gave references to his sources for the individual selections.

The collection by Yen K'o-chün (1762-1843) was not published until thirty-five years after his death. A fellow-townsman issued the original edition in 1879, which is listed in the catalogues (see *Hui K'o Shu Mu,* 彙刻書目, 15th 册) under the title 全上古三代秦漢三國晉南北朝文. In 1894 in Wu-ch'ang, 武昌, Hunan Province, Wang Yü-tsao 王毓藻 (preface dated 1894) reprinted it, wherein instead of *Chin Nan-pei Ch'ao* the title contains *"Liu Ch'ao,"* 六朝. It is the latter edition which has been used in this study. In the *Bulletin of the National Library of Peiping* (January-February, 1931) may be found a Supplementary List of Essays to Yen's Collection, but the list includes no additional material for the collected works of Pan Chao.

Although neither the work of Wang Hsien-ch'ien on the text and the authorship of the two Han histories, nor the compilation of the extant writings of Pan Chao by Yen K'o-chün in his "Complete Collection" satisfies the desire of the author of this study for information concerning this remarkable woman, they do furnish much more material for research than has been included in this study of her life and writings.

NOTES

[1] Although translations of the genealogy and the five biographies were made by the author of this study, with the exception of the biography of Pan Chao (see Chapter IV, pp. 40-41), only selected passages have been included in the present study.

[2] See Chapter XII, note 6.

[3] Translated by Chavannes, *T'oung Pao,* VII (1906), 211-215.

[4] Biography of Yin Min may be found in *Hou Han Shu, chüan* 79.

Mêng Chi is called Mêng I, 孟異, in the biography of the Pan Ku; same, *chüan* 40.

[5] See also the biography of Pan Ku, cf. Chapter V, note 23.

[6] See *Chinese Biog.,* p. 1456. For his appointment see *Hou Han Shu, chüan* 10, biography of the empress Têng (鄧太后), where the date is within the period of two years, 109-110 A.D.; *chûan* 5, in the annals for 110 A.D., second moon; and *chüan* 78, biography of Ts'ai Lun, 蔡倫, where the statement of his appointment is dated 117 A.D. (in the period 元初 instead of 永初).

[7] See *Chinese Biog.,* p. 384; *Hou Han Shu, chüan* 81.

[8] The years in which occurred the death of Pan Chao.

[9] This work must not be confused with one of like title composed by Hsün Yüeh, 荀悅, under order of the emperor Hsien, 獻帝 (190-220 A.D.), which is a history of the Western or Earlier Han period. Cf. Wylie: *Notes,* p. 24.

[10] Text has *chia,* 嘉, see Chavannes' note, *T'oung Pao,* VII (1906), 213.

[11] Pelliot reported (*BEFEO,* II, 1902, 334; cf. same, III, 315-340) the preservation of additional citations in the *Ying Sung Pên Shih Lüeh,* 影宋本史略. The *Shih Lüeh* (preface dated 1225 A.D.) was lost in China, but found in Japan and reprinted.

[12] Biography may be found in *San-kuo Chih,* 三國志, section *Wu,* 吳 *chüan* 8.

[13] Biography in *Chin Shu,* 晉書, *chüan* 82; Giles: *Biog.,* no. 1759.

[14] According to *Chin Shu, chüan* 82, Biog. of Ssû-ma Piao: sixty *chüan;* Foreword, *Hou Han Shu,* Wang Hsien-ch'ien edition: eighty-three *chüan.*

[15] In the *Shih Lüeh,* 史略, *chüan* 2, may be found a short notice of Hua Chiao, but it gives no exact dates of his life.

[16] Text reads *Tung Kuan Chi,* 東觀記.

[17] At the time when the *Shih Lüeh* was written (preface dated 1225) the

works of Hsieh Ch'êng, Hsieh Jung, Ssû-ma Piao, and Hsieh Shên were already lost, cf. Chavannes, *T'oung Pao,* VII (1906), 214, note 3.

[18] See Wylie: *Notes,* p. 24.

[19] *T'oung Pao,* VII (1906), 214, note 4.

[20] In the first two printed editions of the *Hou Han Shu* there were included no treatises (see below); in the later Sung and Yüan editions they were the third section; and in the *chien-pên,* 監本, of the Ming period they were made, apparently for the first time, the second section. For a study of the authorship of these treatises, see *Hou Han Shu* (Wang Hsien-ch'ien edition), vol. 1, 後漢書集解述略, and the foreword, vol. 25, to the first treatise. (Cf. Wylie: *Notes,* p. 17; Chavannes, *T'oung Pao,* VII, 1906, 214-215; *Ssû-k'u Ch'üan Shu Tsung-mu, chüan* 45, pp. 23-25.)

[21] Chavannes suggested that his studies were included in a work called, "Errors in the Printed Edition of the Han Histories," 漢書刊誤, in thirty *chüan* (same, p. 211, note 3); cf. Wang Hsien-ch'ien: same.

[22] Shun-hua, fifth year, 淳化本, 994 A.D.; Ching-tê second year, 景德本, 1005 A.D. (both without the treatises, 續志); Ch'ien-hsing, first year, 乾興本, 1022 A.D. (the first edition to contain the treatises); Ching-yu, 景祐本, 1034-1038; Hsi-ning, 熙寧本, 1068-1077; Shao-hsing, 紹興本, 1131-1162 (the earliest edition which was extant at the end of the sixteenth century). Chavannes (same, p. 211, note 4) was of the opinion that the first printed edition is identical with that completed in 1022 A.D., but Wang Hsien-ch'ien stated that both earlier editions, *i.e.,* those of 994 A.D. and 1005 A.D., were printed (初刻本 and 校定本, 板本).

[23] 明南北雍本, see *Tz'û Yüan,* 子, p. 389, 酉, p. 167, 午, p. 120.

[24] 毛晋. 汲古閣本.

[25] 明閩本; 元小字本.

INDEX

The Index is compiled with the primary purpose of guiding the reader to subjects discussed in the text of the book. Wherever it seems that additional material would be helpful, references are also made to the Notes and Bibliographies, and in a few instances, to the Introduction and Appendix. Other material in these sections of the study, not included by direct references, especially the names of some authors and titles of some books and articles, can be found by use of such references as are made.

The first occasion on which Chinese text is given for a transliteration or a translation is indicated in the Index by printing the number of the page in italics. Cross references may be found under headings in parentheses.